The Boys of D

The Boys of Diamond Hill

The Lives and Civil War Letters of the Boyd Family of Abbeville County, South Carolina

edited by J. KEITH JONES

foreword by Richard B. McCaslin

McFarland & Company, Inc., Publishers
Jefferson, North Carolina, and London

LIBRARY OF CONGRESS CATALOGUING-IN-PUBLICATION DATA

The boys of Diamond Hill : the lives and Civil War letters of
the Boyd family of Abbeville County, South Carolina / edited
by J. Keith Jones ; foreword by Richard B. McCaslin.
    p.   cm.
Includes bibliographical references and index.

ISBN 978-0-7864-6333-6
softcover : 50# alkaline paper ∞

1. Boyd family — Correspondence.   2. Soldiers— South
Carolina — Abbeville County — Correspondence.
3. Confederate States of America. Army. South Carolina
Infantry Regiment, 7th. Company D.   4. South Carolina —
History — Civil War, 1861–1865 — Personal narratives.
5. United States— History — Civil War, 1861–1865 — Personal
narratives, Confederate.   6. South Carolina — History — Civil
War, 1861–1865 — Regimental histories.   7. United States—
History — Civil War, 1861–1865 — Regimental histories.
8. Abbeville County (S.C.) — Biography.   I. Jones, J. Keith,
1964–
E605.B78   2011
975.7'35 — dc22   2011003922

BRITISH LIBRARY CATALOGUING DATA ARE AVAILABLE

Front cover: Color lithograph entitled "Confederate camp"
by Louis Zimmer, 1871. After a painting by C. W. Chapman,
Ordnance Sergeant, 59th Virginia Regiment, Wise's Brigade
(Library of Congress).

Manufactured in the United States of America

McFarland & Company, Inc., Publishers
  Box 611, Jefferson, North Carolina 28640
  www.mcfarlandpub.com

To the memory of my father,
William S. Jones,
a true Southern gentleman to the end.

Acknowledgments

This book would not have been possible without the help of a few people and institutions. First the Duke University Special Collections Library for preservation and use of these letters; next the following libraries: the Abbeville County, South Carolina, public library, the Greenville County, South Carolina, public library, the Furman University library, the South Caroliniana Library at the University of South Carolina, the Davis and Wilson libraries at the University of North Carolina, and the May Memorial Library in Burlington, North Carolina. Karen Ulsperger at the Pope County public library in Arkansas was especially helpful in furthering my research, along with Camp #39, the Olde Abbeville Camp of the Sons of Confederate Veterans, the Old City Cemetery of Lynchburg, Virginia, and the Confederate Relic Room in Columbia, South Carolina. Thanks to Gloria Harris, Nita Jones and Sybil Sanders for your help with your ancestor, Fenton Hall.

Special thanks go to Lynn Salsi and Dr. Richard B. McCaslin for their advice and guidance. Very special thanks go to Sharon Strout, who transcribed a large portion of these letters and cross-checked the others. Her efforts in bringing these letters to a publishable form speeded up this effort immeasurably. Finally thanks to my wife and daughter for putting up with the time I have invested in this effort and listening to my ramblings on the subject.

Table of Contents

Foreword
by Richard B. McCaslin

Daniel Boyd lost four brothers and his brother-in-law in the Civil War. The second son of Robert Boyd of Abbeville County, South Carolina, Daniel enlisted with his younger brother Pressley in the Seventh South Carolina Infantry in 1861. Within a year, their younger brother Thomas joined the Nineteenth South Carolina Infantry, while their oldest brother William enlisted in the First South Carolina Rifles, all before the Confederacy enacted the first military draft in American history. Perhaps concerned that he might be posted far from South Carolina, Fenton Hall, who had married Mary Jane Boyd, joined the Sixth South Carolina Cavalry at Charleston. And when Daniel returned to his regiment after recuperating from the wounds he suffered at Gettysburg, he took his youngest brother, Andrew, with him as a recruit. In less than four months, Andrew was wounded during the fighting in the Wilderness and died in a Virginia hospital. By that time, the others had all died in service, too, and Daniel was the sole surviving sibling.

Historians are always looking for new, accessible primary material on the Civil War. For that reason, presses produce thousands of published pages every year. Little of that is as compelling as the story contained in this volume. The Boyd family committed its entire future, as represented by five sons and a son-in-law, to the Confederate war effort, and they paid an almost unbearable price. Only one of the sons, Daniel, came home from the war, and neither he nor his father, Robert, long survived the end of the conflict, as the material contained in this work explains.

The United States government has taken steps to ensure that modern families do not suffer such losses, but there were no such laws to shield the Boyd family. The story of their commitment, as told in the letters reproduced, reveals not only rich details about life and combat in three Confederate armies, but also the human impact of the war.

1

Civil War scholars, professional and lay alike, are especially pleased to have primary sources that provide broad perspectives, covering many battles and other topics of interest through long periods of the conflict. Daniel and Pressley endured months of camp life and illness, and both were hospitalized, before their first battles with the Seventh South Carolina during the Seven Days. Neither of them suffered serious wounds, but their brother William, who had joined the First South Carolina Rifles in March, was mortally wounded at Frazier's Farm on June 30, 1862.

Pressley died when the Seventh South Carolina stormed Maryland Heights at Harpers Ferry in September 1862, closing the trap on thousands of Federal troops who surrendered just days before the "Bloody Seventh," as Daniel and his comrades were becoming known, fought again at Antietam. The regiment punished the Federals who charged Marye's Heights at Fredericksburg, but then endured only light fighting at Chancellorsville.

Daniel's luck ran thin at Gettysburg, where he was wounded and captured, then exchanged to recover at home. He rejoined the Seventh South Carolina with his brother Andrew, only to lose him in the Wilderness. After more costly victories and crushing defeats near Richmond and in the Shenandoah Valley, Daniel returned home with his regiment to the Carolinas, where he endured his last discouraging battles at Averasboro and Bentonville.

While four of the Boyd siblings fought, and three died, with the Army of Northern Virginia, another brother, Thomas, endured repeated bouts of sickness only to fall in the battle of Murfreesboro on New Year's Eve, 1862, while serving with the Army of Tennessee. Fenton Hall, their brother-in-law, was killed in a skirmish at Willtown Bluff with Federals raiding the South Carolina coast in July 1863, just seven months later.

Of course, illness, wounds, and death are not the only topics of these letters. The Boyds also write about everything from money troubles to lice and even spelunking. Military scholars can find material on desertion, friendly fire, furloughs, paroles, hot air balloons, and the practice of hiring a substitute. Politics, of course, is an occasional subject, as is religion. This collection includes letters from family friends and military associates of the Boyds, further expanding the perspective to include more events in the eastern and western theaters, at the front lines and on the home front. There are even flashes of humor as the Boyd siblings and their friends and relatives struggled to retain their humanity in an increasing inhumane conflict.

Finally, the editor adds comments that enrich our understanding of the people and places mentioned in these letters. In sum, this is a useful as well as compelling volume, and scholars and buffs alike will find much to study and enjoy in these pages.

Richard B. McCaslin is the chair of the Department of History at the University of North Texas.

Prologue

The Diamond Hill section of Abbeville County, South Carolina, lies close to Lake Secession along the Rocky River near the Anderson County line. It is so named for the "diamond mine" situated in the area, which actually bears quartz rather than diamonds. It was in this section that the Boyd family peacefully farmed the land. The 1860 census shows Robert Boyd as a 60-year-old farmer with four of his seven children living with him. The Boyds were simple people of meager means. His grave marker indicates that he was born October 16, 1804, in Ireland. His wife, Catherin Phropet (or perhaps Prophet), was born March 14, 1813, and had died July 3, 1846.[1] That year was a hard one for him. Later in 1846, on November 4, Robert Boyd was listed as being in jail in Abbeville and that he petitioned for relief under the Insolvent Debtors Act.[2]

The eldest of Robert Boyd's children, Mary Jane, was 28 and lived nearby with her husband, Fenton Hall, and their 2-year-old daughter, Essa. William was 25 and Daniel was 22. William had his own household and Daniel was not listed in the census for that year so it is uncertain which household he occupied. William was married to Mary Ann Crowther and was the father of two children with her.[3] Robert Presley Boyd, 20; Sarah Boyd, 18; John Thomas Boyd, 16; and Andrew Boyd, 14, remained in their father's home.[4]

South Carolina adopted articles of secession on December 24, 1860. The winds of war had been blowing for months, and a number of militia units had formed by this time. The Boyd family's home county of Abbeville has the distinction of being considered both the birth place and death place of the Confederacy. A month before the state seceded, the first meeting to consider the issue was held on a spot now called Secession Hill just east of modern-day Secession Street in Abbeville. There, local citizens selected delegates for the state convention that would meet the following month. It was also in Abbeville at the home of Armistead Burt that the last official meeting of the Confederate cabinet was held on May 2, 1865.[5] Abbeville is also notable as the birthplace of former

Vice President John C. Calhoun around whom centered the "nullification crisis" that many historians feel kicked off the states' rights drama over unreasonable tariffs that would eventually lead to secession.

These events would rip the lives of these peaceful farmers asunder over the next several years. On April 13, 1861, General P. G. T. Beauregard fired on Fort Sumter.[6] Two days later on April 15, the Seventh South Carolina Volunteer Infantry Regiment organized at Camp Butler near Aiken. Among their number on this date were 23-year-old Daniel Boyd and his 21-year-old brother R. Pressley Boyd along with their best friend James Hyley Alewine.

The Alewine and Crowther families were closely related to the Boyd family. Daniel and Pressley's older brother William's wife — Mary Ann — was the sister of James Alewine's mother Sarah. At some point, probably during the war, widower Robert Boyd, would marry Hannah, the sister of Mary Ann and Sarah.

1861

Company D of the Seventh South Carolina Volunteer Infantry was raised from Abbeville County at McCaw's about January 18, 1861. Robert Anderson Fair was elected as the original captain and Samuel J. Hester as their first lieutenant. Captain Thomas G. Bacon of Company H was elected as the colonel of the Seventh on Feb. 23.[1] Bacon was 48 years old and had served as a major in the pre-war state militia. He accidentally shot himself in the left thigh with his navy revolver in March 1861 and had recovered enough to reenter the service as the colonel of the 7th on April 15. Robert Anderson Fair of Abbeville — the original captain of Company D — was elected the first Lieutenant Colonel of the regiment and Hester replaced him as captain of Company D.[2] The Seventh had moved to Camp Pickens near Barnwell, South Carolina, by May 3.[3]

There was no time to waste for South Carolina and the young Confederacy. They had no standing army and thousands of young farmers and shopkeepers to turn into soldiers. Trouble was coming, and the Boyd brothers and their cousins and childhood friends would have to be ready. To accomplish this, the state called upon the cadets from the Citadel, a private military college in Charleston, to whip their initial seven regiments of infantry and the Hampton's Legion into shape. The cadets drilled the green troops six hours a day.[4] The monotony and drudgery of camp life and drill was not what most of the men had expected.

It was from Barnwell that Pressley wrote the first surviving letter home to his sister Mary Jane Hall. He tells her that Daniel had been sick but is getting better. He mentions fellow member of Company D Michael Taylor as having been home. Concern is expressed that most of the information he is hearing inside the camp is false and he asks that she and her husband, Fenton, write him with any news they hear at home.

Camp Pickens
May the 3, 1861
To Mary Jane Hall

Deir sister,

I take my pen in hand to let you no that I am well and harty. Daniel had been sick. He is gitting well. We hav moved to Camp Pickens, Barn-well district about 5 miles off Akin. It is a much better place than where we was we hav good watter here but we didn't hav iney til we got here. Well Mary, I herd that you was all well when Mikle Talor went hom. He saw James brother and sad that he had herd from all of you. I was glad to here from you. We hav not got nary letter yet. I herd that ther wer another call for volenteers in Abbeville. I want you to tel me wher it is so or not. Thay hav been several company went from here. Old Govner Pickens trys to mak us belev that he can mak us go Virgina, but we ain't goin. I herd that you was all looking for us home in three or four weaks but you need not for us til nigh April. I am tolerable well satisfied. We git planty to eat sech as it is. We had the best diner today that we have had sens we left home. Mikle Talor fetch it from home. We all was that we saw hard times but we dint no what hard times was til now. We dont her no talk off fiting. We cant her no news here. You can her mor then we can. We sumtimes her one thing then we her it aint so. We dont know when we her the truth. We hav been clening off a camp grond today. We hav got a pirty plase to stay at now. I want you and Fenton to rit to me and tell me how you ar gitting along with yor crop and how it looks and tell me how Daddy is gitting along. I want you an Fenton to rit to me as soon as you get this letter and tell all the rest to rit. I am in a hury now and I can't rit.

Barnwell District Woodward postoffice
Back yor letters
Capt. D 7 Ridg Woodward barnwell Dist., S. C.
To Mary Jane Hall,
    R. P. Boyd

    A few days later, Presley and Daniel received a letter from their father. In it he expresses his concerns for their welfare and contentment. It is note-worthy from his words that many members of Company D had been home on furlough. He refers to their Aunt Sally, the wife of his brother William, as having been sick. William Boyd was born ca. 1810 in Ireland and was twenty years older than his wife, Sarah Hall, who was born ca. 1830. Sarah — Aunt Sally — was also the older sister of Fenton Hall; Mary Jane's husband.

Diamond Hill Sta.
7th May, 1861
Daniel & Presly Boyd,

Dear sons,

I avail myself of the present opportunity to write you a few lines to let you know that we are all in the enjoyment of usual health. I have received one letter from you and also a letter by last mail to William. The friends are all well. Tell James Alewine his folks are all well. I want you to be certain and write to me as soon as you get this & let me know how you are satisfied, who is in your mess, how you are pleased with your officers, whether your location looks like a healthy one, the waters, etc. Also let me know if provisions will be allowed to be sent or if you would like to have a box of provisions sent, if so write in what way it would be best to send it.

Your Aunt Sally was sick last week but is better. She was at my house on yesterday. I am getting on tollerably well with my crops. Corn is generally small for this time of year. The wheat crops generally are promising.

I have nothing more that is interesting to write, as you will hear the general news from those of your Company who are now up on furlough. When you write let me know where to direct my letters to you.
I remain your father,
    Robert Boyd

On May 14, Presley sends a letter from Camp Butler to his brother Thomas. He talks about camp life there and around Columbia. There is mention of discontent among the volunteers camped in Columbia, that they have fallen out and "shot one another and stuck [bayonets]." He also goes on a bit about the South Carolina soldiers' unwillingness to go to Virginia. Many South Carolina men enlisted with the intention of defending their coast from Yankee invasion.

May the 14th, 1861
Barnwell District Camp Buttler

Deer Brother.

I take my pen in hand to let you no that we are all well and in hop that thes few lins will find you all well. I resievd your letter and we got the clothe and provisions. We wer the gladest set that you ever saw when the provisions com. We eat the hartiest diner that we hav eaten sens we left home. We ar well satisfied now ther is going to be another call for volenteers this weak. But I don't think tha will be meny volenteers in our compnee. Tha all says tha will die in this camp beefor tha will go to Virginia . Old Govner Pickens saiyd if we don't volunteer he will send us back to Charleston to bilt forts. We her that ther hav been sum ships com to Charleston and tha wer shooting at them but we don't know it to bee so. The volenteers at Columba has fel out and shot one another and stuck Benets. It was too company fell out. We hurt thudding in our camp yet our mess hurt but nary a cross word. We git along fin. Samuel M Collins was telling us that you had herd that Daniell had got killed. We wil bee glad to her hes told such lys as that. I don't think iney of our Companny wod tel sech a tale as that. You need not beleave one half you her. Tha ar bilding hous lik tha was going to keep ous her all yer. We hav built our camp off in a field.

We hav built arbors over our tents. It looks lik a town. Broks ar torable good her. I saw corn at Charleston knee high. Tha ar hoing cotton in places. If you ples tell William rit to me and tell me hoo that was wish the cars wold run off and kill all the volunteers. I want to no hoo he is. He is a great raike. I don't know hoo he is. I wod bee glad to see you all now but I don't expect to com hom till the first off Augst when peaches git rip. Bee glad to see sum off you com to see ous when you git don work. Tell Mr Frasier that I hav not forgot him yet. Tell him I wod lik rit wel to sum off his wiskey whil now I want to rit all the news. Tell me what the gals is dooing. Tell Mary and Fenton to rit and all the rest. I will hav to com to a close I am botherd so I can't rit. Rit to me as soon as you git this letter. So far you well.

RP Boyd to John T Boyd
back yor letters RP Boyd Barnwell Dis Woodward post offis car of Cathern an Jeffers
Companey D 7 Regement SC Volenteers

On May 21, Daniel wrote to their father from Camp Butler reporting more speculation about their impending departure for Virginia.

To R Boyd
S C Barnwell District

Camp Butler May the 21 1861

Dear father.

I seat myself to wright you a few lines to you for now that I and Pressly ar well and hoping thes few lines may find you all well. I received your leter that A. Gaby brot . I was to her that you ar all well and geting along well. You wanted to know how we ar satisfied, as for my part I am very well satisfied her. I have gained 3 lbs in five days. We hav a beutiful place here. We hav abundance of rain. It is very nice. Ther is very little sickness in the camp now. The ar all full of fun and joks.

We ar ecspecting a call for call for volunteers to go to Virginena. I do not know whether our company will go or not. They do not talk much like it. They are willing [to go] to Virginna if they wer shure they wold get to stay there but when ever they volunteer they will be sent any wher they see proper to send them. The most of the companey says that they would rather go to Virgina than to go to the isleands but when ever they go to Virgina they will go to a wors place. If our company gos I will go too. We hav different opinions about it. Some thinks that we will be disbanded and set home if they do not volunteer and throun back in to the [illegible word] companys and drafted. President Davis has ordered eight thousand volunteers for the Confederate Army. When ever the 7th Regiment gos I think old Abe will back out. They ar improving in drilling very fast. I think in few weeks we will be equal to Jacksons Army. Thos that has ben in war says that we beat any thing they ever saw for length of time. If we hav to serv our twelve months out I wold rather do it her. We wil stay her too weks longer and then I do not now wher we will go. It may be that we may be disbanded and sent home.

We ar feeling fine now. We get plenty to eat. We drew flour and bake our bread. I want to her what you haft to say about volunteering again. I want you to wright to me as soon recev this and tel me how the folks ar getting along. I not got but one leter from home yet. Tel the folks to wright me giv all the news. James Alewine is well. If we go to Virgina we will come home before we go. Nothing say more.

Direct your leter to Daniel Boyd Company D 7 Regment SC Volunteers in car of Captain S. J. Hester.

Daniel Boyd to Chester Robert Boyd and family

Woodward Post

Off to Virginia

On June 15, 1861, Pressley writes his father from Camp Twigs, as he describes it, 130 miles from Richmond and 80 miles from Washington, D.C. The South Carolina boys had finally moved to Virginia. Pressley tells his father they are nine miles from the enemy but they have not been engaged. He talks about their trip from South Carolina to Virginia.

There is a description of the recent Battle of Big Bethel, where the First North Carolina, thereafter known as the Bethel Regiment, along with the Third Virginia was attacked by 3,500 men sent out by federal General Benjamin Butler.[5] On June 10 the 1,200 Confederates inflicted 79 casualties on the federal forces while suffering only one death among their ranks. Henry L. Wyatt was killed and Charles Williams was severely wounded in the first major battle of the southern nation's struggle for independence.[6]

Virgina Camp Twigs, Saturday, June the 15 1861
Mr Robert Boyd

Deer father,

I seat my self to wrigt you a few lines to let you no that wee ar bouth well and wher wee ar. Wee hav moved about one hundred and thirty mils from Richmond. Wee are in about 80 mils from the Citey off Washinton. Wee hav campt her but wee don't know how long wee will sta her but it is thot that we will sta her sum time for we hav put up arbers over our tents today. But we dint know that we was going to moov till about too hours bee for we had to start. We ar now in about nine mils off the enemy. We had not had many battle yet but we don't know how soon we ma hav one. Tha was a battle fot the outher day in about nine mils of ous at Bethel church. Tha was three hundred yankeys kild and one off the Virgin and three or for woendt. Tha ar killing som off the yankeys ever day and taking sum off them prisoner. Tha hav got sum of them in jale and sum building baterys. I expect will bee building batery in a few days. Ther but too Rigemet betwin ous and the enemy but tha ar coming in every day. Tha ar a rigement jest now land and is going to camp her with ous. Tha was thirty thousand soldiers at Ritcmond bee four we left and tha ar coming in every day. Virginia has got one hundred thousand soldiers in survis. It is a grat sit to see so miney folks together. We thot we saw a heap when we was at Charleston but we dint see iney thing til we got to Virginia. But we ar not nie no town now. We ar in about too mils off the nuse Junking. We ar torable well satisfied now. Watter is not very plenty wher we ar now. We hav to go a long way to git it. Vergina is a beautiful cutry. It is not as hot her as it is in South Carolina. I like North Carolina a lot better. It is a pritty plase then it is her and the folks is so much better. The ladys giv ous supper twist as we com thru North Carolina and tha meet ous at avery time the cars stopt and brot ous watter and sum thing to eat. And all the men women and children waving thar hats and hancerchiefs and halorring hooraw for the South Carolina boys. We her that all the volunteers that we left at Camp Buttler is gon home. I want you to writ and tell me wher it is so or not and tell me how you ar gitting along with yor crop. I wod like rit well to bee at hom to help you but I nine hundred mils from hom . But I hop when thes few rech you tha will find you are all well and gitting along well. Daniel rote you a letter about a week ago. Tell Saml Alewine folks that hee well. Hee is standing gard to day and mee and Daniel wil stand tomoro. Tha ar but four of ous in a mess. Me Daniel Saml Alewine Hierm Barton. Rit to me as soon as you git this letter. Back yor letters R P Boyd Compney T 7 Reg SCVS Richmond Virgina car of G W Montegue

R P Boyd to Robert Boyd

Manassas

In a letter dated July 23, 1861, that appears to be incomplete and is unsigned, the author — probably Daniel Boyd — opens "Dear Father and Mother." On July 18 at 11 A.M., a Union reconnaissance force near Mitchell's Ford and Blackburn's Ford under Brigadier General Daniel Tyler encountered the brigade of Confederate Brigadier General James Longstreet while attempting to locate the left flank of the Confederate army. Longstreet was soon reinforced by the brigade under Colonel Jubal Early. The combined forces of Longstreet and Early forced a federal retreat depriving Union commander Brigadier General Irvin McDowell of the intelligence he sought in planning his attack against the Southern army.

The Seventh South Carolina was a part of the action at Mitchell's Ford under the brigade of Brig. General Milledge Luke Bonham. They first came in sight of the enemy near Fairfax Court House and the men fully expected to do battle there. Only the officers knew that Brigadier General P. G. T. Beauregard had no intention of engaging the enemy on that ground, so when the federals approached, Bonham gave the order to retire. The sense was that Union General Irvin McDowell was trying to cut them off from Manassas. They began withdrawing toward Centreville. After a hot grueling march, they reached Centreville and formed in line of battle to meet the enemy, but found that the federals were not pressing the pursuit. The South Carolinians waited there, sleeping with their arms until midnight, at which point flares signaled Bonham to continue the retreat to Mitchell's Ford.[7]

Major Emmet Seibels of the Seventh had this to say: "Who in that retreat can forget the dark & chilly night at Centreville, where we remained wearied & unrefreshed by even a draught of water, in battle array until One o'clock at night?" Soon General Bonham rode up to the men in person and gave the retreat order. They moved slowly and quietly to avoid alerting the enemy of their movements. It took four hours to move the four miles along the road to Mitchell's Ford on Bull Run, arriving at nearly daylight. The men were unhappy about retreating from the federals, but Beauregard accomplished his goal of instilling a false confidence in his enemy.[8]

On July 21, McDowell launched a full frontal assault against Confederate forces under Beauregard and Brigadier General Joseph Johnston located across Bull Run Creek near Manassas Junction; thus initiating the Battle of First Manassas also known as First Bull Run. The battle resulted in the first major Confederate victory and signaled the north that putting down the rebellion would not be the simple matter that they had expected.[9]

The letter details the information available to the common soldier in the Seventh South Carolina Infantry at this time. The four-page letter ends abruptly, leading one to believe that perhaps there was another page which did not survive. It also denies history the certainty of the identity of the author. The author first mentions the welfare of Pressley Boyd and James Alewine, so it appears most likely that the letter was written by Daniel Boyd, but the salutation of "Father and Mother" is a mystery as Daniel's mother was deceased at this point and the 1860 census does not list Hannah as living in Robert's household. This may indicate that Robert and Hannah were already married prior to 1860 if the Boyd sons were referring to her as "Mother." The fact that Daniel's name does not appear in the 1860 census might indicate that the census taker was less than thorough while at the Boyd home that year.

Vienna, near Washington, July 23 1861

Dear Father and Mother,

Through the mercy of a kind Providence as I am again permitted to drop you another letter which will inform you that I am well as is Pressly, also James Alewine and we have enjoyed tolerable good health since I last wrote you. And since that time events have transpired that will gladden the hearts of thousands whilst there is many who will be found to mourn the loss of some friend, brother, sons or husbands. We have had two battles since I last wrote. One was Thursday the 18th and the other Sunday 21th. The first was fought on our right and in sight of wher we were stationed at Bulls Run, a creek 2 miles from Manassas Junction. The enemy opened upon us directly in front where we were situated with there cannons. The first shot a shell fell and burst over us and did not harm. They kept up the fire from there artillery for one hour all to no effect, when it was soon discovered that they was in motion and marching to our right and soon a sharp engagement ensued between our men and the enemy with musketry which is kept up from 11½ to 3½ o'clock. Canonading kept up all the time, our men drove the enemy from the field to the point where they first opened on us. Canonading still going on and at 4 or 4½ our canon drives them out of sight. Our loss is variously set down at fro up to 25 killed and up to 75 wounded while the loss on the enemies line is set down at 750 to 1000 killed and a great many wounded. The enemy did not even return to bury there dead only what they stole off at night or buried at night. Our party found and buried 20 or more and when we left that place there were still some of there dead bodies unburied which will remain ther to rot. The smell was getting very bad when we left. I heard Col. Bacon say just now that the northern papers acknowledge a loss of 2500 to 3000 in that days battle. The enemy remain in the woods about 2 miles from us and recount there forces up to Sunday morning when they make there appearance as they did the first day and commence firing as they did with about the same success and is kept up all day from that point doing none but little damage. At 8½ they began a heavy canonade on our right and is soon followed by a heavy volley of musketry volley after volley from that time to 4 o'clock P.M. The cannonading is awful and to describe the roar of musketry I can not unless it would be to say that it was more like the approach of storm of wind and thunder than any thing else. Our men suffered severely from the fire of the enemy tho nothing to compare with the enemy. Our men was at one time whipped but for the timely aid of 18000 men and Genl Beauregards presence when all rallies and the enemy falls back, our men moves forward and the victory is soon won. The enemy has 57000 men all at one point hoping to effect a passage by force of numbers but as the battle is not to the strong our 18000 held them at bay and the timely aid of 18000 more soon puts them to flight. Our loss is set down at from 500 to 800 killed and 3700 wounded while the enemies loss in killed is set down at 4000 to 5000 and probably thousands wounded. The Baltimore papers set down there loss in killed wounded and missing in both engagements at 25000 to 30000, awful if this figures be true. This is one of the grandest victories of modern times. We have probably 1500 to 2000 prisoners and last night put a stop to the pursuit. We might now have had 23000 prisoners but night and the next days rain appears as a chance for there escape. I will now tel you of the prizes taken from this battle. We captured 48 pieces of cannon fuse and report is that there is 600 with most if not quite that amount of casons (artillery ammunition wagons), 3000 to 3500 stand of arms, waggon loads of ammunition and provisions blankets and camp accoutrements enough to acquip an army, 130 to 200 of the finest horses and the numbers of wagons not set down. The whole line of retreat is marked with awful distruction. The dead and wounded have been picked up for miles and I have no doubt that there will be hundreds all in retreat that will never be saw. I have not been to the battlefield. Some of our men have and they discribe the line as awful, the dead being in every consevable position, some sitting with both hands clenched to trees or bushes and hundreds on an acre of ground, whilst there lay the poor wounded all amongst the dead and these spent the night amongst the dead and the groans of dying, many unable to move whilst others scramble and crall until they find some other poor wounded companion and there they lie trying to comfort each other by each others presence. No friend to care for them, no one to give them a drink, no one to dress their wounds, all there friends have died and gone. Oh civil war where will your lessons stop or have an end, the enemy have again left there dead unburied and there wounded uncared for. Where is civilization and religion. Where is all that philanthropy that they claim. This act alone is enough to bring down Heavens judgements upon them if nothing else. As soon as our men get all our wounded cared for they have set about the holy work, taking care of the enemies wounded who hope they will treat kindly and winning the good will of them, if no more. That done and then there is dead to bury which will be done by our men and they will have a bad time of it as the smell will be intolerable before they get through. There is supposed to be 100 to 130 dead horses on the field. I wish I could have gone to the battlefield but could not. On Monday morning our Regt. was sent out in persuit of the enemy and as guard to our position and the prisoners that might be taken. The day is rainy and we have a bad time of it marching out 2½ miles and remain in the rain all day and back through the mud and rain at night. When we arrive we have no tents and one fire only for our company and nothing to eat. Still it rains and this is our night to be remembered. The poor wounded; just think of them one whole day and night in the rain. On Tuesday morning we get orders to march and at 11 o'c we start for Centerville where we arrive at 3 o'c and remain until 11, cooking supper in the meantime and provisions for two days. At 11 o'c we start for the place and are all night in the march. Poor men are all nearly worn out for want of sleep and traveling so much as we had not slept for two nights. How long we will remain here I have no idea tho not long. We are after the enemy to arise them out of the state which will take some more hard fighting. The enemy is at Alexandria and the Virginians fight at both places. They are strongly positioned. There is a great many of the enemy who are not disposed to fight and would rather now be our prisoner as Lincolns soldier. Such are to be expected.

[Unsigned and possibly incomplete, probably written by Daniel Boyd]

In a letter dated August 4, 1861, Pressley writes to his eldest sister, Mary Jane and her husband, Fenton Hall, about his experiences the day of the battle. He also mentions a smaller fight at Falls Church that the Seventh South Carolina was not involved in. The strains of army life are beginning to tell on Pressley. He speaks of those sick with the measles and of not having enough to eat or a bed to sleep in.

Viana Virgina, Augest the 4th 1861

Deer Brother and Sister,

I wonst more tak the oppertuny off writing you a few lins to let you know that we ar as well as [illegible word] all tho I hav not been well for the last three or for days. Hoping when this few lins coms to hand this ma find you all injoying the same good blessing. Well I hav not got iney news to rit to you now as I reckon you hav hurd all about the fight. We send father a letter that told all about it. We hav a grat deal off sickness her. Saml Alewine is sick. Hee has got the measles and so has Saml Simpson and Henry Hamtom and a grat miney others. I expect to tak them for I sleep with them every knight. It is anuf to put iney boddy out of hart to bee sick in camp for they cant git iney thing tha want. Tha are not tend too. Tha ar about half off Hester's Compnee sick. Well Mary we hav not had nary nother fight sens the Sunday fight. Onley I lurn that tha was a battle at Falls Church, a few mils from ous. I did not lurn

much about it onley we ganed the victory. It was a grat excitement her
the day off the fight when canon balls and bom shells was falling all
around ous. Tha was one shel bused about fifteen steps from meet tha
cut the lims off athe trees over our heds and the balls fell all around ous
and never tuch a man. Tha commenst firing at ous about 9 oclock in the
morning and hel on til 4 in the evening.

Then tha bee gon to retreat. Then we all took after them but cood
not over tak them. Tha throw down their guns blankets knapsacks and
every thing tha had and we folered them til 9 oclock in the night. Then
we went back to our brest work tierd down with out iney thing to eat
all that day or nit and it was raning very hard and we had to li down on
the wet grond and the next morning we got up and stared in the dubble
quick for about for mils. Then we stopt and got sum thing to eat. Then
we stared agan and march about 15 or so mils. The men was all brok
down. Tha la down all along the rod and when we stopt we all la down
and rested. I never was as ni brok down in my life. We ar still at the
same plas where we stopt at a plase cald Viania. I do not no how long
we wil stay her. I wod be glad if tha wod mak pease for I tell you we hav
seen a hard tim of it. Well Fenton and Mary you think you see a hard
time. But I tell you you se a plasier to what I doo for I no you git anuf
to eat and a bed to sleep on. That is what I never hav saw sens I left
home. Well Mary we have send father a news paper. He will git it all
year. I want you to tell him to writ to ous as soon as he can and tel ous
when he has got it yet or not. I will hav to com to a close for the want
of sumthing to rit. So rit to me as soon as you can for I wod lik to her
from home avery weak. Giv my best respects to all the friends.

R P Boyd to Fenton and Mary Hall

---

*The next letter is unsigned, but like the other unsigned letter, it appears
to have been written by Daniel Boyd. He mentions that Pressley and their
friend James Alewine both have the measles like 50 other members of Company D. The greatest enemy of the Confederate soldier — disease — is beginning to take a toll. He notes that roughly half of the Seventh South Carolina
is sick with the measles. The inflationary effects of war are beginning to take
effect, and the author notes the prices being demanded for goods.*

Viana Virgina, August the 8th 1861

Dear father brothers and sisters

I seat my self to rite you a few lines to let you no how we ar getting along. I am well my self. Pressly is sick. He is takeing the measles. James Alewine has got the mesels. I hav not got much to rit at this time. Ther is a grate deal of sickness her. Ther is fifty of our company got the mesels. I have not taken them yet but I do not no how soon I may take them. Ther is five of my mess sick. Hiram Burton has got the fever. J Simson and Henry Hapton they are both sick. My friend Lienius Clinkscale has got the mesels. Ther but very excitement here. Lincons troops hav gon over Petomic or the most of them. I do not think that we will half to fight eny soon. We are moving this evening about a half mile from where we are to se if we wil get batel. Ther is more than half of the Redjment sick now. All that is sick will go to Shacket tomorrow and then I wil be lonsom . All my best friends ar sick. Sam Bowen has been sick but he is got well and com bac to the camp. Ther is a grat many deaths her. We are fifteen miles from Washington and about ten miles from Alexandrea and five miles from Farfacks. I wil not say anything about the battles that has been fought.

We hav clamed our money. We got 27 dolars and a half for our surves and 21 for to bie our cloths with. We hav send to South Carolina for a uniform. It wil be cut at Abeville C H at Farelingtons shop. I want to go to the cort house and get it and hav it made and Pressly all so and tell James Alewines folks to get his and make it at his request and I want you make me a good par of shoos and send them to me and a par of breaches wool made and too pair of socks and send to Pressly the same and a par of drawers a peace. If James Cromer and Calvin Alewine coms to Virginia send it with them. We see a hard time her. We half to pay from 20 to 50 cents for envellops and 40 cents for paper. Every thin is so high. We cant bie it for we half to pay 25 cents for butter and 25 cents a peace for chickens and 25 cents a pound for honey and caint to be got at that. Pervisions is scarce her and likely to be scarcer for Virgina is fool of traps. It is reported that Lincons men took six of our cavalry the other day. They was led by a man the name of Means. He has run away. He had beter sta away. Nerley all the citasens has run away and left her property behind. We are all in about seven miles from the enemy. We ar the advance forces of the Petomic and ar in a dangerous place for ther is fourty four Redgments her. The rest is about 4 miles.

[Unsigned, probably written by Daniel Boyd]

Twelve days later, he was, still very sick, Pressley wrote his father from Richmond. He said that he did not have the measles like reported in the earlier unsigned letter. Instead he claims he had an unnamed illness he had suffered from many years before. He notes that many have died from measles and specifically names Henry Hampton as one who had. Their good friend James Alewine was still sick, but apparently was recovering quicker than Pressley was.

Richmond Virgina, August the 20th 1861

Deer Father,

I seat myself this morning to drop you a few lines to let you know that I am gitting sum better. I was taking sick on the 4th off August. I stad in camp too weaks and then I was sent to Richmond to the hosptil and I hav been her aver sens. I have been very sick and I am very weak yet. But I think that I am gitting better now. Tha was ten days that I never got out off the hous. I hav not taking the measles yet. I don't think I will. I hav got the same complant that I la sick with at home so long ago. The Dr tends on mee very well. He coms to see me twist a day. My far is tarable ruff. All the rest off the boys that com with me is gon out in the country. I have not saw iney off them sens tha left but I got a letter from James Alewine and he said that hee will com after mee as soon as I get well anuff to go. He is about six mils from mee. Hee says that he is treated as well as if hee was at home. Tha wod have taking mee but the dockter wod not let me go till I got better. I wod bee glad if tha wod com after me for I am tyerd off this plase. Tha are sum dying avery day and nit. Henry Hapton died on the cars as we com her. He had the measles. The rest of the boys is all gitting better. I wod hav got a furlo to go home but tha wont let iney more go home. I wod have went when W. R. Mar [probably Morrow], W. B. Harkness, Zekle Nares all went but I was so weak that I cood not go. So I don't expect to go at all now. I have never herd from Daniel sens I left camp. He was not very well the day I left. Well I hav not got iney thing to writ as times is very dul her. I recon you git all the news if you git the news paper that we sent you. I wod lik to her from home very much. I have not herd from home three or four weaks the last I herd. I got a letter from William. I will hav to com to a close for the want off sumthing to writ. I can not tell you wher to writ to me or not for I don't how long I will stay her. But I think it will bee a good while bee for I go back to the camp. I will rit in a few days. So no more at present.

Robert Pressly Boyd to Robert Boyd

Six days later on August 26, Daniel was also sick as he reported in a letter to their father written on his behalf by his friend L. C. Clinkscales from the hospital in Culpeper, Virginia. He reports having no word from Pressley or their friend James Alewine. In this letter he details the current prices of various foods in the area.

Culpeper C H Va, Aug 26, 1861

Dear Father.

I again embrace the opportunity of sending another letter to inform you that I am still at the hospital where I was when I wrote to Brother William. I feel as well this morning as usual and will return to camp this evening if our physician does not object. I have not heard from R P Boyd since he left camp nor from James Alewine. They are both together and I suppose are at Richmond. I see in one of the Richmond papers the death of W H Hampton announced. I suppose it was our Henry Hampton as he was from the 7 Regt S C V. If so his friends from Richmond have wrote long before this. There is several deaths here every day, one in the lower room of our hospital yesterday afternoon. I do not find this a place for sick men to improve fast. The diet is rather poor consisting of bakers bread, coffee and beef about half cooked and half salted. It is stewed or boiled somehow so that it is not fit to eat. I am glad that I am able to get away from here. I prefer the camp to this place. I see a good many returning back to camp and not so many sick coming down. I hope the health of the camp is improving. I have no direct news from camp and can not tel you anything of the army movements tho we have reports here every day that there has been a battle at some point, by waiting it all turns out to be a hoax. There is something astir as troops are passing up the road daily towards Manassas and are sent on to the vicinity of Fairfax where we were stationed before the battle. Some anticipate an early battle, others think that there is no danger unless our forces cross the Potomac. Others again are talking of peace as peace meetings are being held in the Northern states and the newspapers are beginning to speak out against the war and in favor of peace. Peace would be a great blessing at this time as it is at all times but to see the sufferings and privations of death of poor men and soldiers away from home together with the devastations spread abroad the country shows but faintly the horrors of this unholy war. I have saw the suffering of the sick and the poor wounded and this alone is horror enough for me. My friends McCurry, Taylor and Clinkscales are improving tho none of them are able to return to camp yet. I am anxious to hear from home and hope I will get letters when I get back to camp. The most of the deaths here are from relapse and relapse being brought on by exposier or eating fruit, watermellons, etc. Peaches are scarce and sell at form 20 to 37½ per dozen. I do not think they are as good as in S C. Apples 10 to 15 cents apiece. Pears 5 to 10 cents. Watermellon is 15 to 50 cents apiece. Irish potatoes $1 per bushel. Chickens 25 to 50 cents. Everything high and a good place to spend money. I will close to mail as the opportunity soon closes. Write soon and direct to Manassas Junction as before. My love to you all and inquiring friends farwill..

By L C Clinkscales for Daniel Boyd

In another unsigned letter of August 30, 1861, from Culpeper, Virginia, the author is again apparently Daniel Boyd. He is writing to one of his brothers at home and says that Pressley and James Alewine are improving and are expected back with the regiment soon. Reference is made to a skirmish their pickets engaged in with the Yankees in the recent days. He says that the enemy suffered 20 killed and 19 prisoners taken. He makes reference to other friends who are sick at the time and laments an unfairness in which soldiers are discharged and sent home and which soldiers are forced to stay with the army.

Headquarters Advanced Forces of the Petomic, VA, August 30 1861

Dear brother

I take the opportunity to drop you a few lines to let you no how I am getting along. I am tolerable well at this time. I hav got bac to the camp. I was glad to get back to her from the rest of the boys. I herd from Pressly and James Alewine this morning. Tha ar getting better. They will be able to com back to the Redgment next weak if they hav no bad luck. Pressly had the typhoid pneumony. I hope he will soon get well and return to the camp again. I hav been very uneasy for him. He has suffered a grate deal. The health of the camp is getting som better than it was but ther is a grate meny sick yet. I left L. C. Clinkscale and Ned McCurry and Ben Talor at Culpeper. Tha was not well enough to com bac to the camp. Clinkscale is going to try to get discharge. I do not think he will be able to stand camp life. Ther is a great many getting discharged and go home. Them that aught to discharge cant get them and them aught not to hav them get them. We hav rite smart excitement her. We hav orders every day or too pack up and be reddy to march. We ar exspecting a fight every day. I think we wll hav battle before long. Our pickets had a fight the other day. We had too kild five or six wounded. Our men killed twenty Yankees and took nineteen prisoners. They say they ar advancing. Let them come. We hav whipt them several times and we can do it again as often as they come. Genneral Baureguard has one hundred and twelve thousand in his command. We her reports that Genneral Lee has taken about ten thousand prisoners in western Virgina but I do not no whether it is so or not. We hav a heap of rain. It is very disagreeable an wet weather for the mud is like soap and ashes. It stick glue when it gets on our cloths. We cant get it off of ous.. We hav got the box of cloths and pervision. It com while I was gon to Culpeper. The jug of brandy broke and it was lost. The honey com safe. Was very sory that the brandy got lost. But I had a bottle of 3 year apple and mee and Will Bowen took a harty drink of honey and brandy.

[Unsigned — probably written by Daniel Boyd]

Pressley recovered and returned to camp on September 3, 1861, as he states in a letter to his father written in Fairfax County, Virginia, on September 10. There was not much action during this time, but he refers to minor skirmishing between various Confederate and Union pickets. He says that the Northern artillery regularly fires across the Potomac at them, but to little affect.

To Robert Boyd 1861
September the 10th 1861 Virgina Far Fax Conty

Deer father,

I take the opportunity this morning to drop you a few lins to let you know that I hav got well and got back to camp. Daniel has got well. He was in camp when I got back. I got back the 3 of this month. I was glad to git back for our Rigement is in better spirits now then I have saw them sense the battle. Well the person Saml Alewine [sent] did not com after mee. He was takking down with a sever pane in his hed and ear and it was too weaks befor he cod com. He send after mee 3 tims but tha had moved me to another rume and the one that com after me cold not find me. It is sech a large hous that you wil hunt half the day then not find me. When James went off they wod not let mee go. Tha sad if I went out it mak me wors. Tha told me to wat til I got better. Saml

Alwwine com to Richmond on the 2 and he stad all nit with me and we went back together and J Alewine has taking the pane in his hed and has suffered a great del. He is sum better to day. Well I reseved yor letter yesterday and I was glad to her from hom. But I wod be a heep glader to see you all onst more but it will be miney day befor we see each other agane. But I hop we will meet agane.

Well you waned to no wher we recevid the clothing and pervision. We got avery thing safe but the brandy. The jug brok and lost all the brandy. I was sory to see it lost but cold not help it. It all over the things that was in the box. We had brandy beeskit to eat. It dint hurt iney thing but the flour. I am mush ableig to you for sending up the clos and pervision. You spok in yor letter off sending ous sum mor clothing but if you git this letter befor you do it don't send iney mor onley our uniform for we don't ned them. We wil hav mor than we can care if we hav to march and that is what we wil have to do. We got the letter that you sent to Richmond when we got back.

Well thar is not mush talk of a fight her now but our pickets and the yanks has a little fight avery day or too. But it don't amount to mush. We can her them shooting thar canon. Tha shoot across the Petomic and you ma no that tha don't doo mush harm. I hav nothing mush to writ. Tell L Murdock I will writ to him in a few days. I wod hav wrot now but have nothing to writ. I have not saw Sam Newel yet but I think he will bee her to day or to morrow. I will have to bring my letter to a close for the want off sum thing to writ. I am looking for a letter from William this weak. So not mor at present. So writ to me as soon as you git this.

R P Boyd to Robert Boyd

Pressley wrote his father again on September 22. The Seventh South Carolina was at Falls Church, Virginia, but Pressley was sick again and had been sent back to camp at Flint Hill, Virginia. He had spent four days at Falls Church and speaks of going up on Munson Hill from which he could see the city of Washington.

September the 22th 1861
Flint Hill Virgina, Far Fax C H
Deer father,

I seat my self this morning to drop you a few lins to let you no that we ar well. Hoping when this few lins com to hand ma find you all in good helth. Our [regiment] is at Falls Church. Tha hav been gon a weak today. I went with them and stad four days and took sick. Tha sent me back to the camp but I am gitting better. I don't know when tha Rigment will com back to the camp. Tha are expecton a fight that bee for long. I was on Munson Hill when I was at Falls Church. I saw the sitty of Washanton. Tha had not been iney fighting lately onley the picket shot at one another. Tha ar in sight off one another all the time. Well I hav nothing worth writing. It is very cool her this morning. It is cold anuf for frost. Mr R Morow and Hatness got her on the 19. We recived all the clothing and socks that you sent ous. We got the shoes and all so we got the clothing that you sent in James Alewines box. Don't send iney mor for we hav got mor now then we can car if we hav to march. Our uniform has not com yet. Tha will bee her in a few days. Mr R Morow and Hatness tell me that tha went to see you when tha was at home. Tha said that you was all well. I was glad to her from you. Tha said that tha drunk sum good peach brandy with you. I tell you I wod like to be thar to drink sum with you. But sav me a dram till I com. Morow and Hartness tell me that you will mak mor corn this year then you have don in severls years. I am glad off you making such good crops for it will be neaded if this war gos on. I will hav to bring my letter to a close for the want of sumthing to writ. Giv my best respects to Aunt Sally and Nancy and all the rest. I have wrot severls letters to all off you that I don't think you aver got. If you did I never got no ancer. So nothing more at present. onley remember until deth.

R P Boyd to Robert Boyd

The next existing letter was written a month later on October 24. Pressley addressed this one to his three brothers who were still at home and their sister Sarah as well as their father Robert.

Rock Run Camp near Centerville
October the 24th 1861

Deer brothers and sister.

I take the oppertunty this evening to drop you a few lins to let you no that I am well and harty at this time. Hoping when this few lins coms to hand ma find you all well. Daniel is well. Daniel reseived a letter from you last Sunday wich I was glad to her that you was all well. Thar is a good deal off sickness in camp. A man died yesterday. He was cut to peces with a knife. It was one off Capt Codys men. We hav cold wether her. It snowed last nit but not much. We hav had a big day today. Jenerl Boreegard and sum of the outher big ofisers was her revewing ous.

Well tha ar talk off figting her. I don't think tha will be iney mor figting her this winter for the rods is giting so bad that old Abe can't com. The rods is the worst I ever saw. It rains ever weak. I have jest herd today that tha was figting at Fort Pickens in yesterday. Tha wernt no boddy hurt on our hill. I hav not herd iney lat news from port Royal. We her that all the men is gon from Abbeville to Chalstown but I don't think tha are for I no that tha ar sum that ant gon nor want go. We ar throwing up brest works. When we ant standing gard we ar at work. Tha hav not took up winter qurters yet. Tha ar som talk off ous been sent back to South Carolina but we don't belev it.

Well Father mee and Daniel has sent twenty dollar apeas wich mad fourty and be sids we sent you a check on bank check for the muney that was left off our uniform. You can git it iney time if you will go after it. I want you to writ soon and let us no wher you hav got it or not. We sent it with Waren Belcher. He sad that he wod put it in the po offes at Cason. I reckon you hav got it be for now if you aver git it. Well Tomas you waned to no wher I had ever saw D C Little and how he was. He was her last Sunday. He look the best that I ever saw him. S S Newel staret hom Tuesday. He can tell you how we look.

I will have to bring my letter to a close for the want of sumthing to writ. Excuse my bad writing for I am in a hury. So writ to me offen and me all the news. So nothing more at prest. So remember until deth.

R P Boyd to J T and Andrew and S C Boyd and Father
November the 11 1861
R P Boyd
Rock Run County

The next letter, of November 11, was written to Robert Boyd and signed jointly by Pressley and Daniel Boyd. It first states that both are well at that time. As was common early in the war many of the farm boys like Daniel and Pressley were coming in contact with common childhood diseases for the first time. Most city dwellers had suffered from these illnesses in their early years and were now immune.[10] The fact that so many of the young Southerners in the Confederate army were farmers was an advantage early in the war. The rugged self-reliance and hunting skills accompanying life in the country made them natural soldiers. The isolation that accompanies such a life also meant that many of them had not encountered these diseases at a tender age when such maladies were trivial. The very thing that made them strong also made them weak. Despite this, Daniel and Pressley had managed to survive the early rounds of epidemic that had claimed so many Southern lives.

They note that Port Royal had fallen on the South Carolina coast and express concern that so many of South Carolina's troops were in Virginia. Like many South Carolina soldiers they felt that they should be defending their home state instead of Northern Virginia.

Rocky Run November 11th 1861

Dear father.

I seat myself this morning to drop you a few lines to let you no how we ar. I am tolerable at this time. Pressly is well. The health of the camp is not as good as it has been. I have not got much news to writ at this time. I her that the enemy has taken port royal in South Carolina. If it is so stir up thes fellows that has hel back to defend our State and not by back at home eney longer. I her that som of them wants com and and join our company but they had bettered defend our own State and let Virginia defend herself. I think that ther was a battle ninth som whers in the neighborhood of viana but I hav not herd where it was. I herd cannonading and musketry from nine oclock til dark that evening but we hav not herd whether it was a battle or not. We do not no but seam very much like it was.

Well we hav draud our money and I and Pressly wil send twenty dollars apeace home with Warren Belcher. He sed he wold take it to diamond hill post office and leav it ther. I cold hav sent 20 dollars more but I did not like to trust too much with a stranger. I wil send you check for you to draw the money over what baugtt our uniforms. It is in the Charleston bank at Abbeville C. H. and James Alewine wil send 20 dollars and a check for his part of the uniform is nine dollars 84 cts which is the amount dew us. I want you to tak it and use it as you need it and I pay William what I ow him and use the rest as you please. Tell James Crowther to get what is coming to James Alewine and giv it to his mother and for her to use it as she pleases by the request of J H Alewine. Rite to me as soon as you get this and let me no if get it rit soon. I hav not got tim to rite eney more for Belcher is going to start son. Nothing more at present.

Daniel and R P Boyd to Robert Boyd

1862

Pressley Boyd wrote next to his father and sister Sarah on January 9, 1862. In this letter, addressed from Rock Run Camp in Fairfax County, Virginia, he noted the enlistment of their brother Thomas. John Thomas Boyd, then 18, enlisted in Company G of the Nineteenth South Carolina Volunteer Infantry Regiment on December 19, 1861,[1] a new company that had just been mustered into state service that same day and would be inducted into Confederate service on January 3, 1862. Joseph H. Cunningham was their first captain.[2]

He mentions several friends, including William Bowen and P. Murdoch. He laments the lack of information in the camps and notes that there seems to be no indication of any fighting to come. He says, "I don't think the Yankees wil ever com back to Bull Run as long as the war lasts."

Far Fax Conty Va Rock Run Camp
January the 9 1862

Deer father.

I seat my self this morning to drop you a few lines to let you no that we are bouth well at this time. Hoping when this coms to hand ma find you all well. I recived yor letter yesterday. I was glad to her from you all. Wm Bowen said he was at yor house and saw you all. He said you all look well. I am sory to her that Tomas had to leave you. But I glory in his spunk. Well I hav no news to writ for I am never out of camp to her ineything. If you her as much about the war as we do ther ar no talk of figting her. I don't think the Yankees wil ever com back to Bull Run as long as the war lasts. But it better for them to not com for tha wod git the worst whipping that tha have ever got be fore. We her tha ar figting at port Royal. Wm Bowen said tha was figting thar as he com back. Well tha are trying every wa tha can to git ous all to voleteer for too years. Tha ar a grat miney has re volunteer but my notion is to go home befor I volunteer agan. Then if I hav to go I am going to go and fight for South Carolina. Tha hav past a law in Virgina to keep all the volunteers in the feald and not let them go home when thar time is out and tha are talking off doing ous the same wa but I don't know what tha wil do. Well that is all I no about that. Well tell Fenton and Mary Jane Hall that I wish them to have good luck with that fine boy. I hop to liv to see him next April and all the rest. Tell Sarah I will now drop you a few lines to let you no that we recived the gloves socks and cunbfert. Tha was very excepable for we hav sum of the coldest wether I ever saw. It has been snowing and sleeting for the last three or 4 days but is cler today. Well Sarah give my best respects to the girls that send me the Cristmas gift. I thank them very kindly for being so kind. I want you to writ to me and let me no wher Tomas is and what the name of the post offes. Well I have nothing more to writ at this time. Tell P Murdock I will writ to him befor long. Tell him I ancered his letter but I reckon he has not got it. Giv my best respects to ant Salley and Nancey. I wil hav to bring my letter to a close for the want of sumthing to writ. So nothing mor at present. I remain yor brother til deth.

R P Boyd to Sarah C Boyd and Father Robert Boyd

Three days later, Pressley wrote a letter to Thomas. He notes that the weather had been bad with two big snows. Boredom seems to be a theme in this letter like his last. He notes having received two recent letters from Thomas in camp (they have not survived). Pressley also speaks of dissatisfaction with their officers, stating that the only officer that is in camp with them is their third lieutenant.

He reports seeing three men from another state being punished at Manassas Junction for some transgression by being bound "with ther hands tied up to a pole so they had to stand on ther tip toes and ther feet in stocks for too or three" hours.

Rock Run January the 12th 1862

Dear Brother.

I seat my self to drop you a few lines to let you no how we are getting along. We are all tolerably at present hoping when thes lines comes to hand they may find you all well. Well Tom I have not much news to wright at this time. We do not here eney thing from the Yankees now. We are living her doing nothing. The weather has been so bad that we cant do eney thing. We hav had too big snows. The ground is coverd with snow now. It is about 3 inches deep. Our regment is out on picket now. They hav bin out in all the snow. I did not go out with them this time. I staid with James Alewine. He was sick when they went out. W M Bowen got back on the 8th. I received the letter that you sent with him and all the rest of the things they sent. I also received a letter from you yesterday. I was glad to here from you and to here that you are well and satisfied with your officers for that is more than I can say. We hav not got but one officer in camp. That is our third loutenent.

I want you to wright to me and giv me all the news and giv me the names of all your mess and giv what company and full directions how to direct my letters and all about it. I was at Manassas Junction yesterday and I saw three men with ther hands tied up to a pole so they had to stand on ther tip toes and ther feet in stocks for too or three [hours]. That is the way they punish even her for develment. Don't never let it be said that a South Carolinaan be don that way. You wanted to no what sort of Chrissmas. Well I will tell you we did not have eney. It looked more like Sunday than eney day that I hav seen since I hav bin in the army every [thing] was still. I must bring letter to a close for the want of something wright. So wright soon. Nothing more at present but remains brother till death.

Daniel Boyd to J T Boyd

The next letter was written on February 18, 1862, from Johns Island, South Carolina, to Robert Boyd by his nephew William B. Tucker of what was to become Company F of the Second South Carolina Rifles. As with the others at various times, he was suffering from disease. In his case it was the mumps.

Tucker gives a great amount of detail of the military maneuvering that had gone on between the Confederate and the Federal armies on the island. He asks after his cousins, Daniel and Pressley, among others.

Johns Isleand Feb. the 18th 1862

Dear Uncle and cosins.

I seat myself this morning to inform you all that I am well only I have had the mumps. I think that I will be able to drill this weak. I hope this may find you all well when recd. I have nothing much to write to you at this time. More than theare is a good deal of talk of pease at this time, thear is some talk of all the troops being sent home on both sides and then England is going to try to make pease then between the north and south. It is thought that it will be don. The report is that it will be don in a short time. I hear that we have had another fight in Tennessee and that our men whiped the Yankees out. We see a hard time hear now. We have marched about 80 miles in three days on this isleand. The yankees come up in one mile of us last weak. We was at Bars Bluff of Wadmalaw Island. We could see the men and guns on thear vessels very plain. This place is called Camp Ivers. I don't think we will stay hear long. We are in a very daingerous place yet. We have only one place to get out and that is if we had to run. The Yankees only has one way to come to us now and that road is well guarded. They could taken us all last weak if they had new our position. They had three chances to surround us. We was in gun shot distance. They could of shell us to death with thear guns. We had no canon at tall. I don't think that thear will be any fighting to do on this isleand now for they have had every chance to fight us and now the spring time of year is com and they will have to leave. The wether is very warm for the time. It has rained a good deal on us for three or four days. Thear is a good deal of sickness in camps at this time. I want you to write to me and let me no when you heard from Daniel and Pressly. I written to William some time ago and I haint heard from him yet and I written also to David Murdock and Fenton Hall and I haint got no answer yet. I would be glad to hear from you all. I want to hear from ant Salley and all of my friends for I don't know when I will get to see any of you if ever or not but I hope I will get to see you all again. So nothing more at present. Give my respects to all of the correction. So nothing more but remain your friend till death.

W B Tucker to R Boyd

Direct your letters to Johns Ferry, Col. Moors Battlion, Capt D L Donald, Co F

The next letter was written by Thomas Boyd on March 26, 1862, who by that time was in the Nineteenth South Carolina Infantry in camp near Charleston, South Carolina.[3] He reports having heard that his father Robert Boyd had been sick. He writes of the lack of war activity and the routines of camp life. The enlistment of their brother William that took place on March 19 is noted and it is stated that he hears that William is coming to his regiment, but this would turn out to be false. William Boyd would be a member of the First South Carolina Rifles Regiment, also known as Orr's Rifles after their founding colonel, former Speaker of the U.S. House of

Representatives James Orr, who was a native of neighboring Anderson County.[4]

Camp Wason
March the 26th 1862

Dear Father, sister and brother

I seat myself tonight to write you all a few lines to let you no how I am. I am tolerable well at present hopeing they may find you all well when received and let you no that I got the letter that you rote on the 16th. I was glad to hear from home but was sory to hear that father was sick but I hope you all be better before this reaches you. I have no war news to wright at this time. Everything is still down here and we hear nothing from the yankeys at all. The weather has been cold ever since I came back at night but it is very warm in the day time. The health of the Regt is tolerable good. There are [some] of our company is in the hospital. They are Wm Philips and John Tucker. They are very bad. I was at the city today and saw Philips. He is low down. I don't know what ails him. We have to drill six times a day about five hours. We one company dril at 7 oclock one at 9 1/2 and one at 11 and battalion drill at half past too and company drill at 4 1/2 and dress parade. The artillery was trying one of their canon this evening. I could hear the balls and shell plain and heard the shell burst about two mile off. I have heard that William has volinteerd in our Regt and that David Murdock and fifteen more was coming to join our company. I would have been glad if they could all have staid at home but it looks like they will take all before they stop. I thought Wm was going to come and join our company. I sent him a pass port to come. Tell him if he goes to come by here and see me. I rote him a letter to him soon after I come back and I have not got any anser yet and I writin to Fenton and Mary also March the 27th. Ther is no news in camp. This morning it is very cold and cloudy. There are fifteen of our Regt took off to cut boat timber. Marion Carlile went out of company G. They have been gone eight days. They are at mount pleasant five miles from Charleston. We plenty of beef to eat but little bacon. We get some corn meal and some flour, sugar and lard.

I want you to write to me and tell me all the news and how you all are gitting along with your farms and if you have planted any corn yet. Sarah I want you to send me some stocking yarn to mend my socks witch you can send with Wickliffe when he comes back or you can send it in a letter. I will have to come to a close for the want of something to write.

Write as soon as you can and let me no if you have got any letter from Daniel and Presley yet. So nothing more at present but remain your son and brother till death.

John T Boyd, Robt, Sarah Boyd

In the next letter dated April 16, 1862, Thomas wrote that the Nineteenth South Carolina had left Charleston on April 10. They had been ordered to Corinth, Mississippi, on the heels of the Battle of Shiloh to reinforce General P. G. T. Beauregard, who had taken command after the death of General Albert Sidney Johnston during the first days fight on April 6.[5] The letter is unsigned, but the movements of the regiment and the members of the company referenced leave little doubt as to the author's identity.

The letter extensively details the movements of the Nineteenth from the time they departed camp at Charleston to their current location at West Point, Georgia. They were destined for Corinth after travelling through Atlanta but were turned back at Chattanooga by news that the federal army had taken Huntsville, Alabama, and burned bridges they needed to complete their journey. They camped in Dalton, Georgia, on their way back to Atlanta, where Thomas appealed upon the kindness of a local woman for a meal and "got the best meal that I had eat since I left home and did not have to pay a cent." He noted that the lady of the house was also from South Carolina.

Their route was changed several times, and upon reaching Marietta, Georgia, they were ordered to turn back and "fight our way through to Beaureguard." Upon reaching Dalton, their course changed once more. They camped for the night before proceeding and Thomas took several of his friends to the same house of the South Carolina lady to enjoy another fine meal. The men had to convince her to accept any pay for the food. The following morning they returned to Atlanta by rail then continued on a southwesterly course to West Point, where this letter was written.

Along the route to West Point, Thomas describes being stopped by the derailment of a train traveling ahead of theirs at Newnan in Coweta County, Georgia. The letter is resumed the next day, April 17, and states that they are to depart later in the day by steamboat for Mobile.

West Point Georgia
April the 16th 1862

Dear Father

I seat myself to write you a few lines to let you that I am well hopeing they may find you all well when received. I recon you have heard before now that we have left Charleston. We left there on Friday the 10th and have been traveling ever since. We went from Charleston to Atlanta and from there to Chattanooga Tennessee. We started to Corinth Miss but when we got to Chattanooga we heard that we could not go that way for the yankeys have got Huntsville and burnt the bridge. We got there Sunday morning and staid there all day. When we started back to Atlanta we came back 40 miles to Dalton and staid there till morning. We had nothing to eat but crackers and some ham. Some tried to cook and some went to the hotel and paid 50 ct but I started out and went to a house and called for something to eat. The woman said if I would stay till sunup she would have breakfast which I done and got the best meal that I had eat since I left home and did not have to pay a cent. She was a South Carolinian and a better woman never lived. We left that place at 8 oclock and got to Marietta at 6 in the evening when we met more troops and General Donalson from S C and he turned us back to fight our way through to Beaureguard and we went back as far as Dalton when the Gen got a dispatch from Corinth by the Montgomery Ala. That was in night time. We staid at Dalton till morning and me and five more went to the same place to git breakfast.

We got another grand meal and she did not want to take pay but we paid her 50 ct apiece. She gave me the finest tin bread and meat to do me all day. We left there at 8 and got to Atlanta at sundown and left there for West Point but we had went 60 miles when we were stopped. One of the trains that was before us ran off the track at a place called Nunnin Coweater [Newnan Coweata] county Georgia at a place 60 feet high and killed one man and crippled a good many more and killed six horses. It was a Tennessee Regt. We left Nunnin the next morning and got here at 12 oclock and is here yet Aprile the 17th. We will leave here some time today and go to Montgomery and take a steam boat to Mobile. We have been on the road 5 days and nights and it will take us 7 or 8 more. We have not had but one night sleep on the ground and that was last [unclear, appears to be Tuesday]. There are 5 or 6 Regts here now. The 10th S C Regt is here. The hole militia is called out in Mississippi. Ther are agoing to be one of the hardest fights at Corrinth that has been fought yet. There are or will be one hundred thousand men there. We are now about 3 or 4 hundred miles from home and have got more to go. I am tired down riding on the cars for we have to ride in box cars without seats but planks. The folks in [indistinct, probably Senoia] in

Georgia very friendly. They gave us some thing to eat when we stoped. Some even git to us at Marietta. I got the letter that Mary and Fenton sent me. I did not git the provisions that you sent me. It was left at Charleston S C. I would like to git it.

[Unsigned apparently written by John Thomas Boyd]

Thomas next writes his father from Mobile, Alabama, on May 1, 1862. He had been sidelined by pneumonia there after arriving on April 20. He and another ill comrade, W. H. Cochran, had remained behind while the regiment had proceeded on to Corinth. By being sick they were spared involvement in a serious accident. The regiment's train derailed after leaving Mobile, killing six members. At the end of the letter he asks after the wife of his brother William, Mary Ann, and their daughter Cornelia. He wants to know where they are staying now that William is in the army.

Mobile Alabama
May the 1st 1862

Dear father,

I seat myself this evning to let you know how I am gitting along. I have been very sick. I have had the pneumonia but I am gitting better. I can walk all over the house but I am very weak. I came here on the 20th of Aprile when the Regt came and I lay in bed most all the time till yesterday I got up an walked about. W H Cochran is here with me. I have been treated well. I git more than I can eat and can git any thing that I want but I have no appetite to eat. The Regiment left here on Wednesday and the cars ran of the track and killed six of them and hurt several more. I have not heard frome them since. I recon they are at Corinth. It is 375 miles a north east course from here. I would like to be able to go to them or to go home till I go stout again but that is what I cant git to do at this time. I am tired staying here. I think if I hav no bad luck I will be able to go in 7 or 8 days. I want to git good well before I go so I wont have to go to the hospital any more. I don't hear much news her. The yankeys is about to take New Orleans. The men kep going on to Corinth. They are looking for one of the biggest fights that has ever been fought yet. They say if we whip them there the war will be ended. I wish it would for I am tired of it. If I could keep well I could do better. I was here three days before I knew that there was any of our men here and I felt like I would give my years wages to have been at home but the Alabamians was very kind to me and waited on me, them that was able.

I am most out of something to write. I feel very weak. I would like to be at home the worst sort but it looks like I will not git home soon again. They have made a law for to keep all twelve months men in for the war and have no 12 month now. I have nothing more to write at this time. I think I will be able to go out in town in two or 3 days. I want to hear from home. It has been a good while since I got a letter. I want you to write as soon as you git this and back it to Corrinth Miss and I will be there by the time it gits there. So nothing more at present but remain your son till death.

John T Boyd to Robert Boyd and family

Excuxe bad writing. Give my respects to Mary and Fenton and Daved an all the rest. Tell them all to write and not wait for me to rite. Rite to me and tell me how Mary and Cornelia is gitting along and where they are staying.

John T Boyd

Next Thomas wrote his father on May 11, 1862, from Tishamingo County, Mississippi. The letter is unsigned but based on the discussion of his health status; there is little doubt as to the letter writer's identity. He said he had reported to camp after two weeks in Mobile, but had quickly relapsed and reports in this letter having had pneumonia for three weeks. He was better and writes of his expectation to report to camp the following day. He further states that the overall health of the entire regiment is poor. Water shortage in the camp is noted and he mentions minor skirmishing as well as a battle the previous Thursday — which would have been May 8.

The regiment had just reorganized for the war and Thomas details the company and regimental election of new officers. He expresses the desire that if his brother-in-law, Fenton Hall, has to join that he enlist in his company. The Lewis Hall that Thomas refers to as getting a fine rifle left behind by the enemy is a nephew of Fenton Hall.

Army of the Mississippi
Tishamingo County Mississippi
May the 11th 1862

Dear father

I seat myself to write you a few lines to let you know how I am git-

ting along. I am tolerable at this time. I have been sick three weeks with
the pneumonia. I staid in Mobile two weeks and came to camp. This day
was a week ago and have not been able to do any thing since but I will
report for duty in the morning. The health of the Regt is not very good.
Several of our company is sick. The watter is very scarce here, so much
so that we can hardly git any. We have been moveing. Today we have
moved one mile from where we was. We are in two miles of the yankeys.
They had 3 or 4 little fights this week and our men run them every time.
On Thursday Price took 800 prisoners and on Friday nearly the whole
army was ordered out and our Regt went. They marched six miles and
attacked the yankeys, supposed to be some six or eight thousand strong
in a field where they was camped and commenced firing on them. They
fired one time and run and left every thing they had. We did not loss
many. They lost a good many. Our Regiment did not git there in time to
take a part but they got blankets, over coats, knapsacks, haversacks, oil
cloths and a great many more things. Lewis Hall got a fine rifle gun. I
think we will have it in ernest before long but I think they will find it a
hard road to travel if they [do] it for there are so many men here. There
are some 200 thousand round Corrinth and we have breast works 20
miles long. There are one hundred of our Regt went out on picket yesterday and is out yet. James Jones went. We don't drill any here or stand
gard either.

 We had to reorganize for the war yesterday. Lt Edward Noble was
elected Captain. Cap Guning got four votes. R M Chatam 1st Lt Serg
Mulikin 2nd and Marion Carlile 3rd. Lithgoe is Col, Maj Shaw Lt Col
and I don't know yet who is Major. I think we have got the best officers
we ever had yet. The wether has been very cool here at knight but it has
turned very warm now. I think it would be a healthy place here if we
could have watter. We are in the woods where the land is very rich about
two miles north from Corinth. I don't think we will stay here long for
the watter will give out in three days. I wish they would take us back to
South Carlolina for the roads is so bad here when it is not a shoe mark
left in dust, it is in mud when it rains. It is the messiest place I ever saw.
They say that it is worse than it is in Virginia. We had to travel 1800
miles to git here. We are 320 from Mobile and I don't know how far
from home. I want you to write to me as soon as you git this and let me
know how you are gitting along and when you got a letter from Daniel
and Presley and when you heard from William. I heard that they have
gone to Virginia. If I could git off I would go to him but there are no

chance to git off. All of the men that is over 35 years old will git off before long and then the company will have to be filled up from home with them that is between 18 and 35. Tell Fenton that if he comes in I would like for him to come to our company. Tell him I will write to them as soon as I can. I will not pay for this letter for they will go surer than they will to pay for them. You can pay for them out of the money I sent you and use the balance as you like.

While Thomas was recovering from pneumonia in Mississippi Daniel was also sick in Virginia. The next letter to Mr. Boyd was written by Daniel from Manchester Hospital in Manchester, Virginia. He talks of the sickness in the Seventh and of the lack of provisions. He mentions "R. P."— brother Pressley — seeing their brother William as he passed through Petersburg with the First South Carolina Rifles.

There was apparently much dissent in the Seventh at the time as Daniel expressed his wish to transfer to "Mashels Redgment," meaning the First S.C. (Orr's) Rifles commanded by Col. J. Foster Marshall.[6] He went on to say he wanted out of the Seventh and expressed a preference for Mississippi service. He also asks after William's wife and children.

He mentions the Battle of Williamsburg, which kicked off the Peninsula Campaign from a few days prior and makes mention of other South Carolina regiments involved. Daniel especially notes the actions of the Fourth South Carolina Infantry.

Manchester Va
May the 13th 1862

Dear father,

I take the present opportunity to drop you a few lines to let you no how I am. I am in tolerable health now. I have bin sick. I have got up to go about. I am at Mancester Hospital. B F is hear with me. He has bin sick but he has got well. W M Bowen is hear sick. He has bin very sick. He is gitting better. S M Bowen is hear too. We hav a graet deal of sickness in our Regment. Our company is nearly all at the hospital. We hav see the hardest time now that we hav ever saw since we hav bin in the army. We hav not had eny tents sense the first of March. We hav lost all our cloths. I hav not changed cloths but onst sense the first of March. We hav to take the weather as it com. We hav to sometimes sleep on piles of brush to keep out of the water. We half to march through mud

and water up to our knees. We half to march day and knight. We half
to march 3 days on one days pervision. Our men has suffered for som
thing to eat. Our troops fell back from Yorktown to Chickahominy River
wher they intends to fight till they die. We has gained another victory
at Williamsburg. The 7th Redgment was in the fight on Sunday. We did
not loss eney men. They was released by General Andersons Bregaid.
They was on picket when the enemy attack on Monday morning at 6
oclock. The fourth South Carolina Redgment was the first one fired
again. They was in the fight all day. They fought like heroes. James Milford was kiled on Monday. Ther was eight or ten kiled in the fourth
Redgment. Our loss is about 500 kiled and wounded. All of our dead
and wounded fell into the hands of the enemy. We are expecting another
hard battle at Chickahominy River every day. It is about fifteen miles
from Richmond. It will be a harder battle than ever was fought with the
Southerners as determined to whip them wher ever they fight on land.
I hear tell Jackson is still persuing them. It is reported that he is on his
way to Washington. G T Beauryguard has whipped them at Corrinth
and is thought he will have possession of Tennasee. I think too or three
more such whippings wil satisfy them. We are getting troops every day.
We half to fight three to one of us. Col Mashels Redgment and McGovern
is at Fredericksburg. They ar about sixty miles from Richmond. Ther is
som of the boys hear. I met up with som of my aold acquaintances. I
was glad to see them. I and them enjoys our selves time together telling
a few stories. R P saw the boys as they past through Petersburg. He saw
William and D. Cleland. They was both well then. They appeared to be
well satisfied with their trip to Va., but I think they will soon git tired
of it sense they travel the road the aold 7 has traveled. They wil no what
war is. Well I recon you wold like to no the reason I did not come home.
The reason is they will not let us go. The men is very much dissatisfied
and when the big battle com off will get to go home. I wold like to come
away with them if I can get to, but I do not no weather I will ever hav
the pleasure to return back to aold Carolina or not. I am a going to try
to get transferred to Mashels Redgment for I wont stay in the 7 if I can
get out of it, for our colonels have left us. We half to reorganize our
Redgment this week. We will lay aside some of our officers when the
election comes off. Our company is broke up now. Some of the officers
is in Richmond now. I intend to try to get to som other Redgment if
ther ar eny chance. I wold like to go to Mississippi if I cold get it. I want
you to wright to me as soon as you get this leter and give me all the news

and let me no if you hav herd from Thomas and wher he is and the post office and I want to no Mary Boyd and the children is gitting along and how Mary Jane and Fenton is and all the [unintelligible] boys is. Tell James Alewines folks that he was tolerable well when he lef camp. It hav bin aleven days. I do not no when I wil go to the Redgment. When you wright direct your letter to Richmond. I must bring my letter to a close so rite soon and tell the rest of my friends to wright. Tell James Crautter to rite to J Alewine for we hav not herd from him sense the first of March. So nothing more at present but remains your affectionate son till death.

Daniel Boyd to R Boyd, May the 13th 1862

It didn't take William long to begin to feel the depredations of camp life. On May 18, 1862 — just two months after enlisting — he wrote to brother-in-law Fenton Hall, listing his location jokingly as "Camp ner starvation." The First South Carolina Rifles were in camp in Spotsylvania County, Virginia, near Fredricksburg.

William mentions the Battle of Yorktown, where the Confederates took 900 prisoners. He also details the marching the regiment has done and tells of the friends in the First Rifles who are sick. The farmer in the Boyds shows through as William discusses crop conditions in the area as his brothers often do in their letters.

Camp ner starvation
Spotsilvany County Virginnia
May 18 1862

Dear frend,

I seat myself for the first time to let you no that I am well and hopeing when thes few lines come to hand they may find you all well. I hant mutch news of importance to rite. We are in six miles of Fredericksburg and in fore miles from the yankeys. We ar camp in the woods and old feilds all round as the picket brot in six prisners yesterday evening. They took them about fore miles abov her. We are a looking for a battle every day but I don't think we will ever hav one at this plase. They had a fight at Yorktown this weak. We took nine hundred prisoners. I [haven't] herd our loss. I cant say whether the 7 Regiment was in the fight or not. The yanks took three of our men the other day. Wednesday we got our ordors to march that the enemy was advancing in larg forces. We then had to pick up and start to meet them. We marched to Massapony Church then we stoped. Then we got ordors to march down the telegraph rode, then started and marched about five miles, then stoped for the knight. We lay down with out eny thing to eat. We remain at the same plase yet. It is a mean plase. Ther is no water niy. I don't think we will stay her miny days. It is very warm her. It don't rain mutch her. Wheat looks torable well. The farmers has just commencts planting corn. This is a woren out part of the country. The best plase I hav seen is at Guineas Station. The land ther fifty achors, is worth as much as $150, such like as A C Bowen. It all bottom and the best water I ever saw. Ther is a heap of sickness in camp. Ther is about three hundred sick in this regiment. J W Milford is very sick with the diarear. D Cleland aint well. B Bowen has the measles. Morrison has pains.

I don't like camp at all nor I don't think I ever will. I had rather bee on the island as her this way. Walking and toting all on our back is anof to kill eny man. Ther is a huge trooped camp around her. It looks like ther is men anof in the field to bring starvation on tho we git plenty when we aint moving about. We git bacon, flower, coffee, sugar. We will draw money in a few days. Cap Miller is making out the payroll now. I wold lik to bee at home with Mary and my little chrildren. I miss them a great deel. I hope the time will come when we will all meet again.

I hant had to stand gard but yonct senc I hav been in camp. They don't drill ous mutch. Our officers is easy on us. I want you to rite to me and tell all the news and if the draft has com off or not. Hand this to Mary and let her read it. I will bring my leter to close for the want of news to rite, so nothing more at present, only remain your frend till death.

Will Boyd to Fenton Hall and family. Direct to Richmond as before.

William also wrote to his father on May 18, 1862. He talks of boredom and illness in the camp. He details the costs of food and goods at the time.

Camp Ledbetter Virginnia
May the 18 1862

Dear father,

I seat myself this morning to drop you a few lines to let you no how I am. I am well except a bad cold and hopeing when thes few lines com to hand they find you all well. I hant got much to rite. I don't her much war news now. I think they are lying still on both sides now. I her they will do no more for sixty days. They say ther will be peace before long but I don't know. It looks like it can last much longer. We are in six miles Fredericksburg and about sixty or 70 from Richmond. We are lying about doing nothing at all. We drill too or three times a week. There is a heap of sickness in camp. J.W. Milford an D Cleland is gon to the horsepital. I herd from them yesterday. Cleland was beter. Milford was no better. He has diareer. Our doct is no count. They don't tend to the sick lik they ar. The pay is all they count. They cant get medisons. This is a pore part of the world. Ther is nothing her.

I receiv your letter. I was sorry to her that Thomas was sick. He is long ways from home an no friend to wait on him. You want to no how fur I was from Daniel and R.P. I don't know how fur it is. I recon we are about 75 miles apart or more. I never her from them at all. I her the Regiment is 25 or 30 miles below Richmond. They hav reorganize for the war and elect new officers. Gant Milford was killed in the Battle twenty five miles below Richmond and eight more in that Regiment but I did not her ther names. The times is hard her. We don't git anof to eat. We can eat all we git for too days in one. I never node what it was to do with breakfast til dinner time befor I half to do it now. Sometimes we go to the mill and buy meal at one dollar per bushel. Some buys sheep at four dollars apeace and beef that a man can shoulder for eight dollars. Chickens from 85 to $1 apeace. Eggs 40 cts per dozen. Butter 75 cts per round. We draw flower, bacon plus sugar. Nothing for coffee.

The weather is vey warm her now. It has been raining for a day or too. It has been very windy but has cleard of now. I hant saw a stalk of corn senc I hav been in Verginniy nor much wheat and what wheat is is very sory. It don't look like ther will bee eney thing made in Va. I her they are 7000 sick at Richmond. They are from 50 to 100 dying every day there. I will haf to bring my letter to a close for the want of news to rite, so nothing more at present, only remains your son till death. Rite soon. Direct your letter to Wm Boyd, Company G, Orr Rifle Regiment, Richmond Va, in car of Cap Miller.

Will Boyd to Robert Boyd and D Murdock.

The next letter was written by Pressley to his father from Manchester, Virginia, on May 25, 1862. He and Daniel were both sick in the hospital at the time. He gives news of and asks after other friends. He notes that Daniel had sent money home with their captain, Warren Allen. He said that Allen would visit and give Mr. Boyd all the news of the war. It is mentioned that Andrew was planning to enlist and Pressley expressed the wish that he stay home, saying that the family had already contributed four members and that was enough.

May the 25th 1862
Manchester Va

Deer Father.

I shall now tak this opportunity off writing you a few lines to let you no how we ar gitting along. I am gitting along well. Hoping when thes few lines coms hom tha will find you all well. Daniel is not as well to day as he has been. We ar bouth at the hospital yet. We recevd yor letter dated the 11 of May. I am glad to her from you. The rest of the friends is all well except Burriss died. About the first of the month he died from a risen in his throat. Also Gant Milford was kiled in the fight at williamburg. I saw William Robertson James more and Levi Gamble and Ben Gamble, Jess Moura and several others. I was with them all day yesterday. Tha said that tha saw you a day or so befor tha started. Tha said that you was all well and gitting along very well with yor crop. Well we ar still looking for the big fight to com off. The artillery blasted our regiment yesterday morning but it did not last long. Our regiment is in too miles of Richmond but tha ar under marching orders. Tha don't git to stay at one place long at a time. I went out yesterday to see them. Tha was all well and getting along tolerable well but tha ar but few in the regiment now.

Well we hav receivd our money at last and I herd Daniel had sent one hundred dollars home, 50 dolars apiece. He send it with Waren Alan our Captan. He lives in Abbeville Court House you can go and git it. He said that he can rit you a letter when he is home. He can tell you all about ous and the war. So when you git the money writ to ous and let us no. But am no ways uneasy about it for it is sent with a man that will doo the things I wish. You will see Sam Bowen for he is gon home. I wod lik the best in the world to go home for about thirty days furlough but tha ar no chances to go now. But I hop it will all so work out writ sum day. I hav not herd from William sens I saw him but I herd that tha was at Fredricksburg. I want you to tell the others to tack my letter for when I writ to Thomas Boyd I was sorry to her that he was sick. I hav never

got a letter from him sens he left hom. Geoff McCurdy told me that
Andrew was talking about enlistment. I want him to stay at home for I
think four is anuff to go out of our family. You must not send iney thing
to ous until we git camped for we can not git it. Tell Mary and Fenton
Hall to rit to me and let me no how tha ar gitting along. I will bring my
letter to a close so nothing more.

R P Boyd
Robert Boyd

*The next letter to Robert Boyd was written on June 4, 1862, by Capt.
T. W. Allen, Daniel and Pressley's commanding officer. He says that he
expects to be in Abbeville soon on a recruiting trip. He notes that they "had
a hard time in the peninsula."*

Bennettsville Marlboro District SC
June 4 1862
Robert Boyd, Esq.
Sir:

I left Richmond last week. Saw your sons Dan and Pres., members
of my company. They were in the hospital at Richmond. Had been unwell
but when I left were quite well and expected to return to the Regiment
in a few days. The Regiment was some two miles from Richmond. The
boys needed rest more than any thing else. We have had a hard time in
the peninsula. My own health is feeble. I am home on a short furlough
to recruit both my health and company. I expect to go up to Abbeville
as soon as I receive my papers from the Regiment giving me instructions
for recruiting. I think I will be up by the last of next week. Your sons
gave me each fifty (50) dollars for you. I would enclose it by mail but
don't like to risk it. Should I be disappointed in getting up next week I
will send the money by mail. I hope the delay will not discommode you.
I will write you as soon as I reach Abbeville. The boys were all doing
well when I last heard from them.

Yours truly,
T W Allen

*William Boyd also wrote Andrew and Sarah a letter the same day —
June 4, 1862. He said that the First South Carolina Rifles were within two
miles of Richmond and spoke of the Battle of Seven Pines which had taken
place the Saturday and Sunday before. He noted that the Yankees were*

*within a mile of them and that they could see the enemy moving around.
Also interesting is that he wrote about seeing the hot air balloons used by
the Union army to spy on the Confederates.*

Camp ner Richmond Va

June the 4th 1862

Dear brother and sister,

I seat myself for the purpose of droping you a few lines to let you
no how I am gitting along. I am torable well tho I don't feel so well as I
did when I was at home. I hope when thes few lines com to hand they
find you all well. I hant got much news to rite at this time. We ar in too
and a half miles from Richmond. We are moving from plase to plase.
We can see the yanks. We are in a mile of them. They ar looking for a
battle evry day but I don't think we ever will hav one at this plase. They
throed bombshells at ous the other day. They burst before they hit the
ground. We can see air balloon when ever we look for it. It is up all day
viewing the camps. They had a hard fight on the Chickahominey River
last Saturday and Sunday tho I recon you hav herd about it before now.
We lost about 400 men. Charley Anderson was wounded in three places.
It is supposed he will git well but is all that I herd of. Ther is hevey firing
on the river to day. The day of the fight I cold her the guns all the time.
We started to go som wher but I don't know wher. Then we was ordered
back to camp. Then we remained till morning. Then we moved close to
the enemy. We have marched about 75 miles last week. There was a heap
of our men giv out. I toufed it out. I was very tired. There is a heap of
sickness in camp. We hav lost three men out of our company sence we
com to Va. Lang Pratt died this morning at Richmond. He was the best
fellow we had in our company. It is some more that they exspect will be
called. I havnt herd from Daniel and Pressly sence Wm Robison com
back. He saw them. They was well then but they hadant gon back to
camp then. They was going back in a few days. Well, I say I am very
tired of camp life. My mess is as contrary as the day is long. They ar too
hard to pleas but don't say nothing about it to no body. We don't git
anuf to eat. We flower and bacon we half to by and pay a big price. I
recived a letter from Fenton Hall. I was glad to her from you all. I will
to bring my letter to a close. I send my best respects to you all my friends.

William Boyd to Sarah C and Andrew Boyd

June 4th 1862

William began a second letter on June 4 to his father, noting that Press-
ley and family friend James Alewine came to visit after he sent his previous
letter. In the letter concluded the next day he notes another man from his
company, Thomas Low, had died that day — June 4. Pressley and James had
brought news that Daniel had been promoted to corporal in their unit of
the Seventh South Carolina.

June the 4

Dear father,

    I will drop you a few lines. I am well this evening. Wile I was riting
Pressley and James Alewine com her. They are all well. They ar camp too
miles from her the yankys is throwing bum shells and caning balls at
them all day but they never do eny damage. They return the fier. They
run them from ther Batery. They ar one mile apart. The yankys has brest
works in front of the 7 Reg. Daniel is pointed corporal. I wood like to
go and see them if I cood git, but I can't git to go away from our camp
They hav sent hom one hundred dollars by the Capt. They was out in
the battle Sunday they got just as it was over. Ther was another man died
today in our company, his name was Thomas Low. This is four we have
lost in a week. I will close for the night.

    June the 5, I am tolable well this morning. It is cloudy and cool this
morning. It looks like it wood rain. it is Disagreeable when raining without tents, it rains a heep her. A. C. Bowen is sick, he has the diarear. D.
Cleland an D. Milford is well. Well I have rote all that I can think of at
this time. I will close. Nothing more at present. Only remain your son
till death.

    William Boyd to Mr. Robert Boyd

    Send my respect to Uncle William Boyd family and tell him I will
rite to him before long.

    W. Boyd

The next letter was written July 2, 1862. It was unsigned, but was
almost certainly written by Daniel. He alludes to discontent in the army
and desertions. Some are mentioned who had left and returned to the camp.
He also takes the opportunity to take a jab at those who had gone home,
leaving the war, saying, "I want to know how the petty coats and hoop skirts
fits the boys that went home."

Mentioned is an engagement at Leesburg that involved the Fourth

South Carolina Infantry. The continuing theme of much hoped-for peace talks is discussed as well as an interesting tidbit about an exchange between Colonel Thomas Bacon, commander of the Seventh South Carolina, and General Millege Luke Bonham in which Bacon threatened to take his men back to South Carolina. Colonel Bacon was born in Edgefield, South Carolina, on June 24, 1812. Bacon was a namesake of his uncle, Thomas F. Glascock, who had been a brigadier general in the Georgia militia during the American Revolution. Bacon was a noted rider and breeder of race horses and owned some of the most noteworthy racing horses of the time. The familiar nature of the exchange with Bonham can be explained by the fact that the two were long-time friends. They had served together in the Palmetto Regiment in the Seminole War and held various offices in the state militia prior to the war.[7]

Fairfax C H Va

July 2 1862

Dear father,

I seat myself to wright you a few lines to let you no that I and Pressly ar well at present, hopeing thes few lines may find you all well. I received your letter yesterday. I was glad to her from you and that you wer all well. I herd from hom about too weaks ago. You wanted to no if R F Bell and Anderson Watts had got [back]. They got her on Teusday. They sad that they never let any one no that they wer coming. I want to no what made them leave in the knight. They ar sick of it oredy but they cant help them selves.

You wanted to no if it wer so that me or Pressly had crippled a yankee. It is fals for I never had chance to but once. I hav not much to wright. I was out picket yard yesterday. We was in mile of the enemy. Ther 75 of us. We was commanded by Capton Prescott. If we had met with them we wold had a few shots. We wer close to the enemy. We has not had to fight yet but I look for it every hour. Ther has been several little battles around. I herd that Colonel Slones Regment had a fight at Leesburg. I do not no whether he lost eny men or not but he go ind the field. The Yankees got too of our cavelry men Saturday and four horses. Our cavelry hav taken a grate meny of ther men prisoners and several horses and arms likely kiled too Yankees the other day. It is said that the enemy hav left Falls Church and gon to Alexandreia. We hav ben stand at bay about a week. We can not go much closer without fighting. We hav commenced bilding brest works to day. I think we wil stay her several weaks. President Davis is waiting to see what Congress will do if they do not make peace then. Then war wil commense in ernest. We hav put up a telegraph that gos to all the camps in 5 hours time. We can hav 50 thousand men her. Ther is some sickness her. Ther is several cases of the mesels her. I not got them yet but do not how soon I may hav them. We hav not got eny money yet. We do not fair as well as we did in South Carolina. We can not by eny thing for every thing is dear that we can not by them. We do not get enough of bread but we get enough of every thing els. Colonel Bacon told Jenerel Bonham if he did not treat his men beter he wold march them back to S Carolina. We hav cold weather her. We hav a good rain yesterday. James Alewine is well. I want to know how the petty coats and hoop skirts fits the boys that went home. The girls throd them petty coats and bonnet and they throd us roses and poun cake and wished us good luck. The last time I herd from Hesakiah Hall he was seting close beside of his lady dear. Want to no if W W Burris is coming back or not. I want you to wright me soon as you can and giv all news. I want if you hav got wheat out and how much you maid and how you getting along.

Thomas wrote to Fenton and Mary Jane Hall the next day, July 3, 1862, from Tupelo, Mississippi, where his regiment, the Nineteenth South Carolina, was camped. Fenton was soon to enter the war himself as Thomas alludes to in this letter. There is mention of Fenton getting a "passport" to come down to Mississippi to visit. Thomas said that Fenton would have to apply to the colonel of his regiment. He concludes his letter with a few lines to his other sister, Sarah. He tells her they expect to be ordered to Chattanooga and gives the names of his messmates.

Camp near Tupelo Miss.
July 3rd 1862

Dear brother and sister,

I take this opportunity of writing you a few lines to let you know that I am well at present, hopeing they may find you all well. I recived your letter that was dated June the 3rd. I was glad to hear from you and that you was all well. I have nothing to write today. I have heard that there are orders for us to march before long and go ten miles a day and carry our guns and knapsacks but we do not no where we will go. Some say to Chatanooga Tenn but we have a great deal of sickness yet. Obe McMillan is dead. He died the 25th of June. It looks like they will soon all dye if they have to stay here. The weather is very hot and dry. In some places the corn is so burned up that it will not make seed. Wheat was sory. It was killed with the rust. I got a letter from William. He was well. He said that he was tired of the war and would like to be at home. There are two of in the same notion but we have it to take and it is the best way to take it easy. We have about 125 men able for duty in the Regt. I think we will son have no Regment at all. I heard that they have sent back to South Carolina for men to fill it out. You said that you wanted me to send you a passport but our Captain is not here and I cant git one, but Lt Mullikin said that if you would make aplication to the Colonel of your Regment you can git transportation at Columbia S C from the Quartermaster there. I would like to see you and all the rest of you if I could. I will have to close for the want of something to write. Write to me evry chance you have. So nothing more at present, but remain your brother till death.

John T Boyd to Fenton and Mary J Hall
To Sarah C Boyd, J T Boyd
A few lines to Sarah

Dear Sister,

I drop you a few lines to let you no that I am well, hopeing they may find you all well when received. I have no news to write. We are under marching orders but I don't know where to. I think we will go to Chattanooga. Some say that we will go east. I don't care if we do if they will take us far enough. You wanted to no who I had in my mess. They will be M. D. an Wm Arnold, J C Alewine, and myself. Alewine is at the hospital. I have not heard from him lately. I did not git the socks you sent me but I bought a pair to day. I don't need no other clothing. Write to me as soon as you git this. Nothing more at present.

J T Boyd

The next letter was written by Pressley on July 6, 1862, from their camp on the edge of the Frazier Farm battlefield. He talks of the wounded and dead among their friends and brings the distressing news that their brother William, of the First South Carolina Rifles, had been wounded in the Battle of Frazier's Farm. He states that he has not seen William nor does he know the nature of his wounds. Sadly, they would soon learn that William had died five days earlier on July 1.[8]

William's service record notes that he died of his wounds on the Danville Rail Road in Virginia. He was en route to the Confederate hospital in Farmville, Virginia, where he lies buried in the Confederate Cemetery.[9]

Pressley laments the death and suffering he witnessed all about him during and following the battle. This letter also details a hazard of all wars — friendly fire. Pressley says that the first time he was scared was when "a regiment of our own men fired into us behind."

July the 6th
Hen Rico County Va
Frasier farm ner the battlefield

Dear father,

I onst mor tak the plasier to drop you a few lines to let you no that I am well at this time, hoping when these comes to hand may find you all well. Daniel is well. Well father we hav been fighting her for six or seven days. I hav been in three battles. I hav not got hurt yet nor Daniel is not hurt but how we hav com threw safe I cannot tel for the bulets and canon balls com all around very thick as ever I saw hale fall. Father I am sory to inform you that brother William is wounded. I hav not saw him sens he was wounded. I dont know whether he is bad wounded or not nor I dont know wher he was hit but I hop he is not dangers. And ther ar a grat miney others that I saw but havnt got time to mension. We had seven wounded and one kild in our company. Hiram Burton was kild. I wil giv you names of the wounded. Lieutenant Robert Carlisle, Dick Pressly, James Gibirt, R.H. Brooks, Asbery Hall, O.A. Norwood and Pink Haddon and som outhers that I cant think of. Ther ar about the third of our rigtment kild and wounded but we hav ganed a grat victory. We hav drove the scondrels back to ther gun bots. The battle first commenst in about five miles of Richmond and now we ar about 18 miles from Richmond and the Yanks is still going wher I never wil see them again for I tell you that it's no fun fighting. I am in grat hops that the war wil com to an end befor long. I dont think it wil last much longer for we whip them in ever fight that we hav had. The Yankees left ever thing that tha had. Tha hav all got fin guns, the infield rifle, and we got coffee anuf to do ous several days, knap sacks, blankits, ten wagons and horses, comisary stors and a grat miney outher things. Well father you hav no idy what a sit it is to go on the battle feld. After battle the men so thick that you mit walk them with out ever setting your foot on the grond. O it is a dredful sit to her the moaning of wounded and to see the men shot down all around you. But a man has no time to think nor look at outhers al tho I was not skerd the lest bit until a regiment of our own men fired into ous behind. About the battle of battles. I thot then that my time had com. It was a roaring of muskits and canon and the balls was fling in cordination a thick as hal. It semed like tha hit our tree in the woods. But if I cold see you I cold tell you more about it. We ar camped in the age of the battle feld. It is affel to be close to it now for ther ar so miney ded men and horses lin on the feld yet. I will bring my leter to a close for want time to writ. I want you to writ to me son for I hav not herd from home in sum time and let me no if you hav herd from William or if he has got home and all. So if you have ever herd from Thomas Boyd and wher he is I will writ to sum of your sons. I wold lik the best in the world see you all now but ther ar no chance. Rit soon. So nothing mor at this time.

R P Boyd to Robert Boyd
July the 6th 1862

The next letter was written by Pressley in Richmond to Mary Jane and Fenton Hall. He notes that he had finally heard about the death of his brother William, but had not seen anyone from William's company (1st South Carolina Rifles, Company G) to give him any more information. Daniel was sick and Pressley acknowledged finding out from their earlier letter to him on July 14 that Fenton was going to have to leave home for the defense of Charleston. He once again expressed his wish that the war would soon end.

Camp ner Richmond
Henrico county Va
July the 22 nd 1862

Dear brother and sister,

I seat myself this morning to writ a few lins to let you know how we ar gitting along. I am well at this time hoping when thes few lins coms to hand tha ma find you all well. I recived yor kind letter that was dated the 14th of July. I was glad to her from you all. Daniel is not well. He has been sick for too days. Thar ar a grat miney sick in the Rigtment at this time and Fenton I hav not got iney news to writ at this time for we hav had dul times sens the fight. We ar in reglar camp now and I hop we wil git to sta her and rest. We did not her of William's deth til Mr.

Williams and Mr. Powers coms back and told ous. I was sory to her of his deth. I am sory for Mary and her por little children. But it cant be helpt. I hav not saw iney of his compt. sens the fight that cood giv me iney satisfaction about him. All that I had herd is what you wrot in yor letter but I do hop he is gon to a better world wher war nor trubble wil never trubble him iney mor. I hav never got a letter from Thomas sens the first of March and it was the one that he rot the day befor he started to Missisippi. I recon you hav herd that J E Simpson is ded. He died with the tifored fevor. Ther are but three left in our mess. All of our woned is going home as fast as tha git able to go. But tha no chance for a well man to go til the war ends.

Well Fenton I her that you wil hav to go to Charlston but I hope it is not so for if you all hav to go I dont no what the woman and children wil do but tha wil have to do the best tha can. I wish this war wod com to an end for I am gitting tyard of it and I want to git home to see you all onst more for it wod be a grat plasier to see you and git to stay with you. But we are far apart and God only nos when we ma meet again but I hope and trust to God that we ma meet soon. Well I recon you have herd a grat deel about the fight as ther are several gon hom. But you wil her mor then is so for we cant her the truth one hundred yards her in camp. Well I am gitting about out of sumthing to writ you. Can tel father that I got his letter and was truly glad to her from him. I wil writ to him in a few days. Also I am going to writ Thomas a letter this evning or tomorrow. Writ to me soon and tel me all that is gon and who is left at home. I bring my letter to a close for the want of sumthing to writ. So nothing more but remain your brother til death.

R P Boyd to Mary and Fenton Hall
July the 24th 1862

The next letter was written by Daniel on August 1, 1862 from Richmond. He notes learning of William's death from Ben Williams as Pressley had. Benjamin W. Williams was also a member of Company D, Seventh South Carolina.[10] Daniel signals his acceptance that "a great many more of us wil half to die" if the war does not end soon and indicates that he believes it will never end.

He speaks of the position of the enemy and rumors of their next moves. It also contains the names of the recent dead among the company. He states, "There is from three to four hundred dies every day in Richmond. Richmond is one half turned into hospitals." He also speaks of times being very hard and gives details of prices being charged for goods about Richmond.

He asks for news of his brother Thomas and sends regards to others. He especially wants to know about William's wife, Mary, and their children. Mary Ann Boyd was left with a boy — J. Pressley — and a girl — Cornelia. Daniel pledges to take care of them if he lives to return home.

Camp Reserve, Richmond
August the 1st 1862
Dear father,

I seat myself to wright you a few lines to let you know how we are getting along. We ar well at this time hopeing when thes few lines coms to hand they may find you all well. I received your letter about a weak ago. I was glad to hear from home and to hear that you were all well but I was sorry to hear that brother William was dead. I did not hear it til Ben Williams told me the news. He died the death that a great many more of us wil half to die if this miserable war don't soon stop. It dos not look like it wil ever end. Well I hav not got much news to rite at present. We ar lying about drilling a little. The enemy is 30 miles from us on James river. We cold hear heavy cannonaiding this morning down on James river. They was trying com up with their gun boats. The firing lasted too or three hours. We hav not herd from them yet. There is another big battle expected in Wester Virginia. They have picket fighting every day or too. I think we will half to go their before long for the Yankees is moving their troops their. I dont think that their will be eney more fighting around Richmond for they got soo bad whipt before they wil be afroid to attempt it again. We are tearing down their breast works so if they come they wil half take the open field for it. They not hav time to build new ons the next time they com for they wil half to fight or get whipt wors than they ever got before.

Well the reasom I hav not rote to you sooner I hav been sick. I was sick a weak with diarear. I was very weak but I hav got well again. We hav a great deal of sickness in camp. When we get sick we half to stay in camp for they hav quit sending eney to the hospital. We hav lost several men since the fight. I wil giv you names of som of them that hav died since I last rote. My friend James E Simpson, O.A. Norwood is too that belong to our company, Frank Gasaway is dead. Newton Bowen and a great meny others. There is from three to four hundred dies every day in Richmond. Richmond is one half turned into hospitals. It is a disagreeable place to be at. Times is getting very hard hear. Every thing is high that is to sell. I wil giv you the prices-coffee $2.50 per pound, sugar $1 per pound, pork 50 cts per pound, beef 50 per pound, melasses $1.50 galon, potatoes 50 per quart, onions $1 per dosen, appeals 50 per dosen, chickens $1.40 apece. So you may guess how times is hear. But we hav got plenty of money and we wil bie while it lasts. I want you to rite to me soon and giv me all the news and tel me what sort of a crop you hav got and let me no wheather you hav herd from Thomas or not and whear he is and I want to no how Mary and her children is for they hav a hard road to travel through this world. If I live to get home I take cer of them. Write soon as you get this. Giv my respects to all my friends. Tell unkel Bill and J Murdock to rite to me so four well.

D Boyd to R Boyd

Daniel wrote his father again on August 18, 1862. He says that Pressley had been sick, but was improving. He notes that they have been moving frequently and at that time had been moved to Malvern Hill. This was a week after the battle. He includes a piece of intelligence the Union army would have considered valuable had his letter fallen into the wrong hands. He states the opinion that the army had moved so strongly to reinforce Jackson that if the enemy were to move on Richmond they would not be able to defend it.

He mentions the names of several new conscripts assigned to the company. He also specifically speaks of the death of a soldier named W. A. Kay and pays him the great compliment of saying that he "was a good fellow and as good a soldier as ever trod Suthern soil."

August the 18th 1862

Dear father,

I seat myself to wright you a few lines to let you know that I am well at this time. R P has been sick but he is getting better. He was sick about a weak. James Alewine is well and the rest of the boys is well. The health of our camp is very good at this time. Our Redgment is improving very fast. I will giv my reason for not riting before now. I hav not had time to rite for we hav been amoving about for the last too weaks. We move every other day. We moved yesterday. Our Regtment is gon to day down to Malverns Hill. That is the place wher the great battle was fought on Tuesday. McClelands army has nearly all left James river. They ar gon to reinforce Pope. All of our force is gon but McLaws division to reinforce Jackson. They ar looking for another big battle up in the valley. They hav fight in up ther a few days ago. They bring in prisoners every day or too. I think if Jackson give tem a good whipping in the valley they wil be satisfied of the war. The prisoners says they ar tyard of the war now and wishes it wold end. It is reported that the Yankees is on Malverns Hill this morning. If they ar they will git fits if they do not leav before our men gets there. They come up ther to keep our men from reinforceing Jackson but they are behind times for we hav send all of that we can spare for if they was to make and attact hear they mite take Richmond before we could. Troops enough hear to drive back but they would half to do som hard fighting before they get there for we have got some of the best fighting that is in the army. I wil turn the subject.

Well I tell you we hav got a good supply of con scripts. We got too hundred and thirty of them. We got twenty of them in our company. I will givv you the naimes of som of them. Calaway Willford, Press Fethiston, William Baty, John Sadler, John Scot, L Speer, W L Clinkscales, W H Masters, Ben Fox and a good miney more. Tha was about fifty that wanted to come to our company. If our men keep dying we will need all we can get. I will inform you of the death of W A Kay. He died the eighth of this month. He is Lias Kay son. He was a good fellow and as good a soldier as ever trod Suthern soil. Well I hav not got eney mor news of importance to rite to you at this time. I want you to rite to me. I hav not got a letter from you in a month. I want to no if you hav forgot or is not ok. Wheather you rite or what is the matter rite soon and giv me all the news. I want you to tell me what sort of a crop you hav and how much wheat you made. Tell Unkle William to rite me and tell L Murdock to rite to me soon and let me hear from him. I want to hear from home often for I hav giv up all hops of ever getting home. I will rite as soon as I can. You may think I hav nothing to do but rite but you may mistaken for we more to do than ever had before. James Alewine got a letter a day or so ago from J Crowther and he sed that you had got a letter from J Boyd. I want you to tel him to rite to us. We hav rote severals letters to him but hav not got a letter from him since he left S C. Rite soon so nothing more at present but remaines your son til death

D Boyd to R Boyd

There is a large gap until the next surviving letter which was written by Daniel on October 19, 1862, from Winchester, Virginia. Since the last letter Pressley [R. P.] Boyd had died. He had been killed in battle on Maryland Heights overlooking Harpers Ferry on September 13, 1862, during the run up to the Battle of Sharpsburg or Antietam. As part of the division of Layfayette McLaws and Joseph Kershaw's Brigade, the Seventh South Carolina was temporarily detached from Longstreet's Corps and assigned to Jackson's Corps. They were to cross South Mountain and seize Maryland Heights from which they could command Harpers Ferry below. Maryland Heights is the southernmost promontory of Elk Mountain.[11]

Kershaw's Brigade partnered with General William Barksdale's Brigade of Missisippians crossed South Mountain into Pleasant Valley then scaled Elk Mountain at Solomon's Gap, four miles north of Maryland Heights. From there they advanced along the rocky spine of the ridge. They found Solomon's Gap undefended and had occupied the ridge by nightfall of September 12.[12]

Captain Henry King, the aide de camp to General Layfayette McLaws, was with Kershaw and said that the woods were almost impassable, "rocks — no road — blind path & no path." He said that the enemy was located beyond an abattis about 6 P.M. and that skirmishers attacked them quite late, but that General Kershaw determined to postpone the main attack until morning. The men were suffering from lack of water since the morning and had little to eat with no fires allowed. They slept on the ground, "surrounded by troops & hearing the groans of wounded men." At some point during the night he reports that water finally arrived, being brought from two and a half miles away.[13]

Early the next morning, September 13, Kershaw's and Barksdale's men set out to take Maryland Heights against 1,600 mostly green Yankee troops under the command of Colonel Thomas H. Ford, who formed up in line of battle a quarter mile in the front of the veteran Confederate troops. Captain King reported that the horses were sent to the valley because the terrain was too rough for riding. The "long roll" roused the troops at seven A.M. and Colonel David Wyatt Aiken and the Seventh South Carolina attacked at 7:50. After 15 minutes of rapid firing "he drove the enemy, his men crossing the abattis beyond, near the point of the Mt. which was also protected to entrenchments." Colonel Henagan with the Eighth South Carolina and General Barksdale's Mississippians respectively to the right and left both went against the enemy with little success. Then Aiken and the Seventh were sent in again at about 9:45 A.M. and "Then began a terrible engagement of small arms. Aiken held his position, losing many men, but could not take the entrenchments beyond the abattis."[14]

The federal troops were driven back. This turned into a full rout when

Colonel Eliakim Sherrill of the 126th New York fell with a horrible facial wound. With no reinforcements coming, Colonel Ford was forced to evacuate his forces from the mountain to Harpers Ferry below.[15] _At some time during this action Pressley Boyd was killed. Now Robert Boyd had lost two of his five sons. Daniel advises in his letter that he can draw Pressley's pay and send it home and advises William's wife to draw his final pay as well._

After losing his brother Pressley only days earlier, Daniel marched with the Seventh all night on September 16 from Harpers Ferry to arrive at Sharpsburg just after 7 A.M. on the next day. Around 9 A.M. the Seventh with Kershaw's Brigade accompanied by Colonel George T. Anderson's Brigade of Georgians rushed the southern edge of the West Woods, behind the Dunker Church, with their arms at the right shoulder shift. Anderson's Georgia Brigade in the lead advanced to the stubble field 600 yards south of the Dunker Church before they came under Yankee fire. Anderson's men went prone and Kershaw's South Carolinians passed over them and double quicked to the West Woods. They pushed through the West Woods and attacked the left flank of the 125th Pennsylvania, as they neared the Pennsylvanians Kershaw's men dropped their rifles into their hands and opened fire. The Yankees were also taking heavy fire from General Jubal Early's Brigade from the right. The Confederates continued pounding the unreinforced Pennsylvanians until they collapsed into a full rout. Kershaw drove them through the West Woods and formed up in front of the Dunker Church.[16]

The survivors of the 125th Pennsylvania were caught between Battery D of the 1st Rhode Island Battery and Kershaw's Brigade. The frantic Pennsylvania troops ran into and pushed through Kershaw's moving column, many of whom were wearing blue uniforms, adding to the confusion the Yankees were experiencing. The colonel of the 125th passed beside one of Kershaw's regimental color bearers and later reported considering seizing the banner before scrambling to the safety of his own batteries. Kershaw's men charged across the Hagerstown Pike toward the Federals as Woodruff's Battery to their right rear opened up on them. Despite large gaps in their lines, Kershaw's South Carolinians pressed on. The Pennsylvanians fell back and lay down behind the battery to return fire. Tyndale's Brigade of Ohioans fixed bayonets and took aim at the South Carolinians as they neared the guns. The Ohio brigade fired on Kershaw's men at 25 yards. Kershaw's Brigade managed to hold for a few minutes before retiring to the West Woods. There they were reinforced by Ransom's Brigade and together formed for a second advance.[17]

The federals repositioned their artillery to defend against Kershaw's advance. Kershaw's troops closed in on the Mumma farm for a second time. They charged across the Pike into the mouths of two batteries, their muzzles throwing a wall of flaming lead into their charging line. The survivors *retreated into the West Woods, leaving the ground littered with the dead and dying of the Third and Seventh South Carolina Regiments. The Seventh's colors lay covering the body of the last member of its color guard. Kershaw lost over half of his men in this attack.[18]*

One wounded South Carolinian called out to Private Fred Gerhard — one of the 125th Pennsylvania's men scavaging through the weapons and provisions of the dead. He asked to be moved into the shade. Gerhard attempted to help him, but upon discovering that the Carolinian could not walk because he was partially disemboweled laid him back down and left him in the sun. He reasoned it that it was useless to expend the energy on a dying man. One federal sergeant scraped the brains of a Confederate from the muzzle of Thomas M. Aldrich's cannon and kept them as a souvenir. As Kershaw's and Ransom's men retreated, Confederate sharpshooters were picking off Union artillery men. Kershaw's survivors reformed along the ridge west of the Dunker Church and fired volleys down upon the Yankees with great effect. During about forty minutes of fighting, the Seventh lost 140 of the 268 men engaged. Their own Colonel D. Wyatt Aiken was wounded at the muzzle of the northern cannons.[19]

He was struck in the left chest between the heart and the lung. Aiken lay prostrate behind a fallen tree being peppered by enemy fire. Captain Thomas Hudgins of Company B carried Colonel Aiken to the rear and placed him behind a large log and gave him water. Aiken's wound appeared to be mortal, so Hudgins loosened his colonel's sword and promised that he would return it to Aiken's family back in Abbeville County. Private Augustus M. Aiken of Company C, the colonel's brother, and his servant, Limas, soon reached the place where Aiken laid suffering. Believing he did not have much time, Aiken instructed them to bury him in Virginia until after the war then to move his body home to Rock (Presbyterian) Church in Abbeville District. Aiken, with the help of his brother, rolled himself onto his elbows and knees so that the draining blood could cleanse his wound. As the fighting moved off toward the Sunken Road, Gus Aiken and Limas were able to move his brother to a nearby house. The two men spirited the colonel across the Potomac River after dark in a canoe to Sheperdstown in what is now West Virginia. So severe were his wounds that Colonel Aiken's obituary would appear in the Charleston Daily Courier two weeks later on September 30. To paraphrase Mark Twain, however; the rumors of his death were greatly exaggerated. Colonel Aiken would indeed survive his wounds and recover in time to lead his men at Gettysburg.[20]

Aiken was a native of Winnsboro, South Carolina, and had been a mathematics teacher before moving to Abbeville District.[21] Aiken, South Carolina, was named for his uncle, William Aiken.[22] An educated and well travelled man, Aiken had visited England twice.[23] On one of these trips, he had crossed the English Channel and toured continental Europe with his brother William who was a medical student in Paris at the time.[24] *A widower from his first marriage, Aiken's second marriage to Virginia Carolina Smith of Abbeville District included as one of his groomsmen his friend, the later General States Rights Gist.*[25] *A renowned champion of agriculture and top citizen, Aiken had helped found the Abbeville Agricultural Society.*[26]

Also wounded that day was Daniel's and Pressley's close friend James H. Alewine. On September 26, James was admitted to General Hospital No. 4 in Richmond, Virginia with a "Gunshot Wound." His age was listed as 23 at the time. On September 30 he would be sent home to recover.[27] *Daniel laments missing his old friend and the rest who had been killed or wounded and sent home. The weather had turned bitter and want of winter clothing is foremost in his mind. In this letter he requests several articles be sent to him when Alewine returns. He details a recent election for first lieutenant in his company which was won by Bob Davis. The loss of William and Pressley must have been weighing on Daniel's mind as he expresses concern of not hearing from his brother Thomas of the Nineteenth South Carolina Infantry since the Battle of Munfordville, Kentucky on September 17, which took place while Daniel was fighting in Sharpsburg.*

Camp near Winchester
Berkley County Va
October the 19th 1862
Dear father,

I take my pen in hand to drop a few lines to let you know that I am well at this time hoping when thes few lines come to hand it may find you well. I hav not herd from home in too months. I hav no news of importance to wright to you. We hav been at this place ever since the fight. We got marching order yesterday. I do not think we will stay her much longer. Ther is a great deal talk of us going to South Carolina this winter but I think that talk is all. I think we wil go back to Raperhannock in a weak or too. We cannot stay hear much longer. Ther is but very little to eat about hear. We do not get enough to eat. We get beef and bread without salt. You may no it is poor eating. We cannot bie eneything for we are out of money and hav bin without for som time. We hav not drawed eney money since last April. Every thing sells high here. We are nearly out of cloths but for my part I have got enough to do me til Christmas. We are beginning to get winter cloths and shoos. I got me a par of shoos. I had to pay three dollars and a half for them. That is cheaper to what som sells at. Boots is worth from twenty to fifty dollars. We wil get our uniform in a weak or too. It will cost us eighteen dollars. It is what they call confederate cloth. They are roundabout coats. Our qwartermaster has just com from Richmond with our money. I recon we wil get som money now. Our uniforms wil be hear to knight. They are very much needed for the weather is very cold this morning. We hav had som heavy frost for the last weak. Troops ar moving this morning. I do not no wher they are going. Som ar gon towards Martinsburg. They are scattering the army to prevent sickness.

The smalpalks is laying at Winchester. Ther is too larg hospils of smallpocks ther. We hav had one case in our regtment. They ar getting scattered through the army. If they ar not stopt they will be wors than the Yankees. They send every man of that gets sick now for they ar aferd that they will get scaterd through the army. They are giving the sick furlowes. I herd that James Alewine hav got home. I was glad to hear that he had got home. It was the first time that I hav herd from him since he got wounded. I want him to wright to me and let me no how he is getting and how he enjoys him self since he has got home. I wold like to be ther to spree round with him but I am aferd it wil be a long time before I get the chance to get ther. I hav been verry lonsom since they all got wounded and went away for they was the ones that I staid with the most. Ther is only four of the old prenis creek boys left. We all get along like brothers. We hav had another election for lieutenant. We had four candidates. J T Kenady, J P Black, J P Huckaby and Bob Davis was the candidates. Davis was elected. I think we wil hav another election befor long. We ar going to run S P Haden the next time. I want you to get me a par of boots and hav them maid with pegs and send them with James Alewine and I wold like have a home maid overcoat if I cold get it and I want a wollen shirt and too or three pares of socks and hav me a hat maid and send it with James and send me some brandy, and if you wil get me a power of attorney from the clerk of the cort and send to me. I can draw R. P. Boyds money and send it to you and tell Mary A Boyd to do the sam. I want you to rite to me soon as you get this and let me no if you herd from J T Boyd since grate battle in Kentucky. Rite soon and giv me all the news and tell my friends to rite to me. I wil half to bring my letter to a close for the want of something to rite. Nothing more at present but remains yours til death.

Daniel Boyd to Robert Boyd
Oct the 20 1862

The next letter was written from Culpeper, Virginia, on November 14, 1862. It appears to be incomplete as it ends abruptly and is unsigned. From the subjects discussed and the people mentioned, it was almost certainly written by Daniel Boyd. He notes several letters he has received from others including James Alewine charting his recovery. He tells of deaths in the company and mentions news of several others. He also talks of a recent hard four-day march and general boredom with the war.

He had been paid and states his intention to send some of the money home. He worries of having too much money on hand because of theft within the camps. Daniel also says that he has Pressley's watch and wants to send that to his father as well. He debates the dilemma of not trusting it to the mail, but worrying that he may not be able to get home to deliver it himself anytime soon. There is mention of a debt owed to him by Sam Bowen and hint of a possibly contentious relationship over it. Daniel says they agreed that they would "settle it our selves if we live to get hom."

Camp ner Culpeper
November the 14th 1862

Dear father,

I take the opertunity to wright you a few lines to let you no that I am well at this time and hoping when thes few lines comes to hand they may find you enjoying the same blessing. I received your letter which was dated the 20 of October and I also received one from J Alewine and one from Mary Jane. I was glad to hear from home and to hear that James Alewine is doing so well for it was the first time that I hav got a letter from hom since William Harkness came back. We hav saw som hard times since I wrote last. We hav had som hard marching to do. We marched from winchester to culpeper in four days. We marched 20 miles a day. It was the hardest marching that I ever don since I hav bin in the army and had but little to eat and no time to cook it. We do not fare much better now for we draw too days rashing and eat up in one. We can not bie eney thing about hear. The health of our regment is tolerable good at this time. We hav lost too men out of our company. The names is Ezekle Strickland and John Richerson. Is both dedd. We hav som more that we hav not herd from since the battle of Sharpsburg. Som that was wounded ther has died. James E Stevenson is dead and severals others. Ther has bin som fighting up hear last weak. General Jackson has whipt the yankees again. We hav bin under marching orders for som time. Their is som talk of us going to South Carolina but I do not think we wil go ther but wil go som wher south.

We hav drawed our money. I drawed one hundred and five dollar. I wold be glad if you had part of it at hom for it is mor money than I like to cary at one time fo they hav got to stealing from one another. We hav got our uniform and I like it fine but it looks too much like the yankees. They are blue pant and black coats. We did not get it before we needed it. The weather has bin very cold. We hav had one snow. We stand in need of blankets and shoos. Worse than eney thing else their was an order read yesterday that for the men to keep fires burning all day and rake away ashes and sleep ther at knight and make shoos out of rawhides. It looks like the south will soon whip itself. Well you wanted to no if I wanted eney cloths. I want a shirt and pair of drawers and a jacket and too or three pair socks and a pair boots if you can get them. If not send a pair shoos for ther is no chanel to get eney here and send me som brandy if you please and a hat. You wanted to no if Sam Bowen had paid or not. He has not paid yet. I recon you want to no how we maid our bargin as I hav not told eney body yet. He was to pay me for what time I worked which I consider worth about fifteen or eighteen dollars. The bargin was that we wold settle it our selves if we live to get hom, but if Mr Bowen mind to pay you I am wiling for you and him to settle it. If you need eney money let me no and I wil send you som. I wil send you R P watch to you the first chance I get and his money. I wold like to brig it home but ther chance to get their it looks like they don't intend us to get home. I am agoing come the first chance I get. I getting most miserable board of the war and living on half rashings and sleeping on the ground with one blanket to lie on and one to cover with.

[unsigned — probably written by Daniel Boyd]

The next letter was written on November 26, 1862, by Thomas Boyd from the hospital in Dalton, Georgia, to their sister, Mary Jane Hall. He had been sick for about a month, but said he was on the mend at that point. Pneumonia and diarrhea had resulted in his being sent from Knoxville to Chattanooga then on to Dalton. He talks of current prices there and mentions the last he had heard from his regiment, the Nineteenth South Carolina, was in Tullahoma, Tennessee.

Dalton Whitfield County Georgia
November the 26th 1862

Dear sister,

I seat myself this morning to write you a few lines to let you know how I am getting along. I am just only tolerable well at this time. I am slowly on the mend. I have been sick for a month. I taken sick at Knoxville Tennessee and went to Chattanooga and lay there 16 days so week that I could not git up and down. I staid there until the 21st and I was sent here. I had the pneumonia and I have had the diarah since I came here. I like this place very well. I git plenty to eat and go where I want to. The ladys in the place is very kind to the sick. They have a society to cook for all the sickest ones. I git my ration from them as I cant eat the bread and beef they have. I git good bread and coffee and soop. Every thing sells high here. Pork is 25 cts per pound. Salt is $40. A bushel potatoes is two dollars. I can git milk at 15 cts a quart. With what little nowersshment I can buy and what I draw I can live here finely. I am going to stay here as long as I can git to for I can not stand so much hard marching. I dont no any thing about the Regment. The last time I heard from it, it was at Talahoma. I tried to git a furlough but faild.

I rot a letter to father on the 20th at Chatanoga but I think you will git this as soon as he gits his. The weather is very cold here and cloudy. I have not drawed my money yet but I will draw some to day or to morrow. They are paying off the sick here. Well I am about out off something to write. I want you to writ to me as soon as you git this for it has been a long time since I heard from home and I want to hear from there the worst sort. Tell father to write and all of the connections. I cant write to them all. Paper is so high and hard to git. I would like to come home and see you all if I could but I cant. I would like to be at home now to eat fresh meat and turnips and all such things. I often think of the times that I uset to have when I thought it hard time but I never new what hard times was. I would rather live at home and work for my victuals and clothes as to be in the army and git just $25 a month. I will close. Write soon. Direct your letter to J T Boyd, Dalton, Whitfield Co., Georgia, Dalton Hospital

J T Boyd to Mrs Mary J Hall

November the 26 1862

When this you see, Remember me, Though many a mile apart we be.

The next letter was written by Daniel Boyd two days later on November 28, 1862, from Fredericksburg. They had left Culpeper on November 17

and marched to Fredericksburg. He tells of being set up facing off with the Union army on opposite sides of the river. His delimma about Pressley's watch was solved, as he had sent it home to his father with Lt. James C. Carlisle that morning. He had gotten word that James H. Alewine was expected back from his wound furlough that day.

He closes his letter telling that he is about to go down into the town for picket duty noting that the people had all left town and they had good houses to stay in to keep warm while on duty. Despite his skepticism that there would be no fight, they were only a couple of weeks from one of the largest battles and greatest Confederate victories of the war.

Daniel's doubts are understandable since the Union army under Major General Ambrose Burnside had first arrived opposite Fredericksburg in Falmouth on November 17 and had thus far made no move to cross the river since their pontoon bridges had been delayed. Union Provost General Marsela Patrick had been in negotiations with the mayor of Fredericksburg for the evacuation of the civilians prior to the impending federal bombardment. On the morning of November 22, Mayor Montgomery Slaughter crossed the river with a group including Brigadier General Joseph Kershaw and Lieutenant Colonel Elbert Bland, who was then commanding the Seventh South Carolina. Patrick received them at the mansion of J. Horace Lacey. The meeting would last for nearly an hour in which Patrick assured them that "the town will not be shelled until she fires" first. Despite these assurances, refuges fled into the countryside by the hundreds. As Burnside's army continued to wait on the opposite shore, Robert E. Lee decided to have Lieutenant General James Longstreet's First Corps fortify the town and the heights above. Lee, however, knew that he would need more than the 40,000 troops currently at his disposal to face the 120,000 men of Burnside's and sent for Lieutenant General Stonewall Jackson's Second Corps to come up from the Shenandoah Valley.[28] It was during this period that Daniel wrote the next letter.

[top of page torn obscuring first couple of lines]

opertunity to let you no that I am well and hopeing when thes few lines comes to hand they may find you enjoying the same blessing. I not got much news to rite to you at this time. We left Culpeper about the 17 of this month. We marched to Federicksburg in quick time to meet the enemy. We got ther in time for them. We hav bin looking for a big fight ever since we hav ben hear. Our picket lines is about four hundred yards apart. They ar on one bank of the river and we ar on the other. Their has bin a great talk of the Yankees burning the town but I do not think their wil bee eney fight hear. I think we wil go to Petersburg. I hav herd that all the men from thirty five to fifty has bin called out. Lieutenant James Carin told me that he saw J Murdock as he went to Charleston. He said that you wer all well and he sed that James Alewine wold hear this weak. I am looking for him today. Lieutenant James C Carlisle started home this morning. I sent R P Boyds watch with him. I told him to send it to diamond hill post office so that you cold get it. I did not send eney money for I thought I mite need it my self. I want you to rite to as soon as you get this and let me no if you wil half to go to Charleston or not. I wold like to come home and se you all this winter if I cold get off but it looks like they ar going to keep us amarching all winter.

- Page 2 -

[top of page torn obscuring first couple of lines]

comes we hav not got eney thing. We kneed blankets very bad and shoos. I think we wil all freeze this winter if we don't soon get something to shelter us from the rain and snow. I want you to rite to me and tell me hoo is gon and giv me all the news. I wil half to closs my letter for I half to go on picket this evening. I think we wil hav a fine time. The folks has all left town. We wil hav good houses to stay in. I hope it wil be the last time that wil half to go their. I am about out of something to rite. Rite soon for it gives me great satisfacktion hear from home. Give my best respects to all my friends. Nothing more at present but remaines your son til death.

Daniel Boyd to Robert Boyd
Direct your letter to Richmond Va
November 28 1862

The next letter shifts us to the defense of the coast of South Carolina. It was written on December 13, 1862, near Charleston, South Carolina. It was unsigned and possibly incomplete, but the author was almost certainly Fenton Hall based on location, writing style and references made in the letter. His regiment, the Sixth South Carolina Cavalry, was based in that area at the time.[29]

Fenton had enlisted in the army on June 29, 1862. The Sixth was organized July 21, 1862, with companies A through F. Fenton's Company G had been part of the 16th Battalion and would become a part of the Sixth on August 6.[30] *Its commanding officer was Captain John R. Miot and the men were from Richland, Abbeville and Edgefield Districts.*[31]

It contains details of sickness and death in his regiment. There is also

*an interesting anecdote about a number of their horses running away while
grazing during a church service. Apparently Fenton's horse was one of them
and he tells of catching the horse 18 miles away.*

Desember the 13th 1862
Camp ner Charleston S C
Deir wife,

I take my pen in hand to let you no that I am well at this time hoping
when this com to hand it may find you an the children all well. I reseved
your kind letter yesterday evening. I was glad to heir from you an to heir
that you an the children was well. I glad to heir from J T Boyd. I exspect
he has sean hard times sinc he lef home. I no he wold like to be at home
as so wold I like to be at home. I hop an trust to god the time will sune
com when we will all git to com hom an pese be mad. I am like J T Boyd.
I thought I sed harde times at home but it wold be a plesher for me to
be at hom to see them hard tims now. Well I have not mutch news to
write at this time. I wroat you a leter las tusday. We ar camp on the
savanna rale rode five miles from Charleston. Our company is beter
satisfied heir then tha war at Adams run but I exspect we will have to go
back thir before long but do not no when. we com up heir las Satrday.
Thir was a good paster heir. We all turned our horses out on Sunday
morning an their was twelve or forteen of them run of. I got mine day
before ystrday. I got him about eighteen miles from heir. W N Hall got
his las night. We have to go a good pese to picket. We have to gard three
bridges. Two of the bridges is about twenty miles. We have nothing
mutch to do ondly to provent pepel from driving thir catel an hogs over
in to Charleston an to notis all the wagons so that tha have no meat in
them. I wold ruther be heir than to be in camp with the Regement. We
los one man out of our company. He died las Sunday at Adams Run with
the typhoid fever. His name was Marion Branion. He live about
Donelsville S C. You want to no if R McAdams pad me for that tobacco.
He did not. He tole me that lizzy ann wold pay you for it. He sed tha
war two ponds of it. You ot to have eighty sence for it but I don't exspect
you will ever git it but maby tha will pay you for it. I will be sorow if
you don't git pay for it after your trobel of raising of the tobacco.
    [unsigned — probably written by Fenton Hall]

Next we hear from Daniel on December 19, 1862, a few days after the

Battle of Fredericksburg which the Seventh South Carolina took part in from December 11 through 15. The regiment was under the command of Lieutenant Colonel Elbert Bland and was assigned to Brigadier General Joseph Kershaw's brigade on Mayre's Heights during the battle.[32]

Around 2:30 on the afternoon of December 13, the Seventh South Carolina along with the rest of Kershaw's Brigade was positioned at the base of Telegraph Hill. While repulsing Union assaults they began running short of ammunition. From behind the wall, the soldiers pooled their ammo by forming relay chains where those in the rear loaded and handed rifles up to those at the wall. The federal troops on the other side had ground to a halt and were hunkered down behind rocks and swales. One member of the brigade recalled, "The muskets became so foul that they frequently had to be wiped." The men used their shirts to wipe down the weapons. The constant firing left the soldiers sore; one reported that "our shoulders were kicked blue by the muskets." Kershaw had departed for the sunken road and soon sent for his brigade to follow. The Seventh South Carolina was second in line behind the Third and followed by the Fifteenth. They dashed down the Telegraph Road under heavy artillery fire. They charged up the backside of Mayre's Heights and regrouped behind the Willis family cemetery. The brigade was then ordered to occupy the crest; the Seventh taking up its position behind the Mayre mansion.[33]

The Third South Carolina in the lead went through seven commanders in a matter of minutes, "the dead of the Third Regiment lay in heaps, like hogs in a slaughter pen." The Seventh moved up to the Mayre house and relieved part of the Third South Caroina and the Fifteenth North Carolina. They took cover behind the fence which ran along the front of the house and halted there. They stood to fire then lay down to reload.[34] *Lieutenant Colonel Elbert Bland would praise the valor of his men, saying that they lived up to the high standards expected of Palmetto State troops.*[35]

Daniel gives a description of the battle along with the names of the wounded from his company. He explains he had not been able to write because he had been on the battle line for the previous seven days. James Alewine had not yet returned to the war as Daniel had expected in his previous letter. He speaks of getting a letter from Alewine as well as one from his father. Also in this letter he mentions the death of James Crowther (referred to as Old Man Crowther). James Crowther was born in 1787 in Yorkshire, England, and immigrated to America in 1819. He was a leading citizen in the community and the father of William Crowther, Mary Ann Boyd and Hannah Boyd, as well as the grandfather of James H. Alewine.

Fredericksburg
December the 19 1862

Dear father,

I am happy to inform you that I am still among the living yet, and ar well. Well I hav ben through another big battle at Fredericksburg last Saturday and it was a hard one. We gave the yankees the worst whipping that they got since the war commenced. Curshaws Bregaid and Cobs fought three divisions. We drove them back five times. Cobs bregaid was in front. The battle lasted all day. We kild more yankees than I ever saw on one battle field. The field was covered with dead yankees and they lying all over the town. We captured a great meney prisoners. Our loss on our side is about 18 hundred kild and wounded. The yankees loss is about twenty thousand. We gaind the greatest vicktory since war has commenced. We lost five kild and fifty is wounded in the Reg. William Harkness was kild. Our loss is very lite. We had four wounded in our company. I will give their names. A Watts, G W Johnson, A M Shooe-maker, B F Hutchason was the wounded. General Cob was kild and General Gregg was kild. Their was nine yankee generals kild. We hav took a larg amount of small arms and annunition and blankets and overcoats, canteens and bacon. The yankees hav all crosst back over the river. The town of Fredericksburg ar badly riddled with canon balls and a deal of it burnt. Som houses ar tore down. It is the worst distruction I ever saw. I wold hav rote to you before now but we hav bin in line of battle for seven days and I had no chance to rit to you. I received your letter and was glad to hear from home. I received one from James Alewine the same day. I was glad to hear that he is well, but I was sory to hear that old man Crowther was ded. I want you to rite to me and let me know how you ar getting along and wheather they hav got you out in the army or not and if Andrew is at home or not and J T Boyd hav got hom or not and if you hav herd from him since you rote before. I wold like to get hom to see you all if I cold but the chance bad. There is so much fighting going on that their wont be iney chance this winter. I want to no if you hav got the watch that I sent to you by James Carlisle or not. If you hav not got it I want you to get it and I want you to send them things by James Alewine, but tell him to not be in a hury about coming back for the weather is vey cold. Rite soon and give me all the news. I wil half to close for the want of something to rite. Give my respects to all my friends and tell them to rite to me.

Daniel Boyd to Robert Boyd

1863

The next letter came from Fenton Hall to his wife, Mary Jane. It was written over January 8 and 9, 1863. Writing from Charleston, he gives details of who his mess mates were and talks of the health of his horse. Several names of locals from the Abbeville area are mentioned.

January the 8 1863

Camp neir Charleston

Deir wife,

I seet myself this evening to let you no that I am well hoping when this com to hand it may find you all well. I reseve your kind leter this evening. I was glad to heir from you all an to heir that you was well. I was glad to heir that Daniel Boyd had com thru saft in the last batel.

January the 9. you want to no how my horse look. He look ondly tolabry well. All horses git plnty to eat. Senc we com heir my horse dos not eat his fed. We git corn and foder for our horses. We git beef an corn meel rise and shugar. You need not send me eney clothin. We hav drawed pants. I have three shirts. I have tow par of good socks yet, tow par of drours. You want to no hoo is in my mess. W N Hall, Peter Burton, Meikel Alewine. We all do a litel coocking. John Lee dos som of it. We git a long to gether very well. I wroat you a leter a bout the last of desember. You seven or eight invlops and forty cents wirth of stamps in the last leter I wroat to you. I want you to send me sum tobacco by James Rampy and a bunch of shage. You need not send me iney thing to eat. I can make out withutthot you sending me iney thing to eate. You had beter keep what you have at home. I fourgoten to writ to you in my last leter about the cotton. If you can git it gind an put up on linen [indecipherable word] you had as well have it don. Peter Burton has just now recev a leter from home. His wife wroat to him that James Rampy was sick. We ar camp at the same plase. I do not no how long we will say heir. We may stay heir a good while. I have nothing mutch to writ to you at this time. Thir has bin a good del of stelin with the trups. Sum of the trups com back from Noth Carolina. Tha say Stevens regiment has com back to the island. I want to go to see them sum of this time. I want to go a Sunday if I ant on gard. We have bin drawing our provishions an hors feed from Charleston senc we have bin heir.

We have had sum cold wether heir. We have had sum of the heveis frost heir as I every saw at home. I have sun rise heir from morning till night. Well I have just com of drill. We have to drill twise a day. I wold rather be heir than to be in the regment. We dont have to keep up camp yard heir but thir is sum talk of ous having to go back to the regment but it is onsurtin. John Lee ses tel his mouther he is well an harty. The health of our company is tolrabel good except sum cases of sunderes. I wold like to heir from Tennessee an to heir how the bois did com out. I hope tha com thru saft. Thir was grat rejoising about Charleston last Friday, shutin canion over the grat victory in Tennessee but I am afrad it is a deir one. We git the news heir every day from Charleston. The bridel that I wroat to you in the last leter is still at the [indecipherable word] Glens. Tha will be sent to James Thompson. I sent them by Glen when he went up home. Glen will writ to his pepel to sen them to James Thompson. Then you can git them. Well Mary you mus not think I have fourgoten you. The last thing I think of at night an the first thing I think of in the morning is you an the children. I will send you sum stamps in the next leter I writ to you if I can git them. I sent you half of the stamps I had in the last leter I sent to you. Well Mary I will have to close my leter so nothing more at present but I remind your loving husband until deth.

Fenton Hall for Mary Jane Hall

My love to you an the children. May the lord be with you an the children. Tel Essa to be a good girle. When this you see remember me.

On January 13, 1863, Daniel Boyd wrote his father again. He gives more details about his combat at Fredricksburg. He speaks of all the illness and death in the camp and speaks of furlohs being given. Two men had been furlohed from his company in the first round and Daniel expressed his hope and expectation of being in the next round.

Daniel speaks of getting a letter from Thomas near the end of December. He passed along that Thomas was well and back in camp at that time. Sadly, Daniel did not know that Thomas had been killed at the Second Battle of Murfreesboro, also known as Stone's River, on December 31.[1]

The Nisneteenth South Carolina had also lost their commander, Colonel Augustus J. Lythgoe. Lythgoe was born in Aiken February 6, 1830, and was a civil engineer building railroads. He married a woman from Abbeville and moved there where he was partners in a mercantile operation with his brother-in-law. At the outset of the war, he joined Company G and was elected lieutenant. From there he rapidly rose to command of the Nineteenth before their first major action at Corinth, Mississippi. The February 1900 edition of The Confederate Veteran Magazine had this to say about Colonel Lythgoe and the Nineteenth's actions at Murfreesboro: "Murfreesboro was one of the bloodiest battles of the war, and here again and for the last time Col. Lythgoe led his regiment with great skill and valor into the thickest of the fight, his brigade capturing a battery of four guns. This exploit was so daring and brilliant that the commanding general of the army by general order directed that the chief officers, Col. Lythgoe being one, should have their names inscribed upon the several pieces. The regiment went into action with two hundred and thirty men, and lost eighty-two. It was here that Col. Lythgoe received a mortal wound, from which he died in a few hours."[2] The four cannons captured were sent back to South Carolina where they were used during the battles opposing Sherman's invasion.[3]

In his report, Colonel Arthur Manigault, who was commanding the brigade that the Nineteenth South Carolina belonged to, stated that at 4 o'clock in the morning on December 31, 1862, he got the order for battle. The firing began at 7 o'clock when McCown's and Cleburne's divisions took the enemy by surprise on the extreme left end of the Confederate line. Manigault said that by the time their turn to enter the fray came, the Yankees were somewhat prepared for them. They were to attack the Federal forces to their front. They advanced, each regiment about fifty yards apart; the Nineteenth was positioned between the Twenty-fourth Alabama and the Tenth South Carolina. They were met with heavy fire as they cleared the woods and advanced into the cotton field. They drew the fire of the Yankee troops and two batteries to their front, which were otherwise unengaged. To the front of the Nineteenth was the Eighty-eighth Illinois regiment. Each regiment of Manigault's brigade managed to break through the first line of the enemy, but was unable to defeat the second line and was forced to retire. Maney's brigade of Tennesseans was supposed to reinforce them, but did not show up when expected.[4]

After falling back, Manigault rallied his troops and mounted a second attack with Vaughn's Brigade. He sent an officer to General Maney to inform him of their pervious failure and again request his support in the next attack. With Maney's assurances, Manigault advanced again once more overrunning the enemy's first line. Therein, "suffering and losing many men from the fire to our right which we could not return." Their reserves were still

*tardy and Manigault was once again forced to withdraw along with Vaugn
when his right flank was hit by a counterattack by Roberts's brigade. Their
third assault, this time with Maney as well as Vaughan, managed to take
the second line.*[5]

 *Records show that John Thomas Boyd was 20 years old and stood 5'9"
tall. He served in Company G of the Nineteenth South Carolina Infantry.
The January 30, 1863, edition of The Abbeville Press newspaper stated that
Captain Robert N. Chatham reported among his casualties: "J.T. Boyd, shot
in head early in action, died instantly."*[6] *He is likely buried in the mass
grave in Evergreen Cemetery in Murfreesboro where a number of the Confederate dead now rest, but this is uncertain. Of the four Boyd brothers who
had entered the Confederate service, 1862 had claimed three of them. Now
only Daniel was in the war along with brother-in-law Fenton Hall. Seven-
teen year old brother Andrew remained at home.*

January the 13 1863
Camp near Fredericksburg

Dear father,

 I take this opportunity of riting you a few lines to let you know how
I am. I am well at this time and hope when thes few lines coms to hand
they may find you well. I received your letter that was dated December
30 and I was glad to hear from home and that you was all well and all
my friends. I was sorry Robertson McAdams was dead and that they hav
so much sickness in their camp. The health of our regiment is tolerable
good at this time. There has bin a great deal of sickness in our regiment
and a great meney deaths. We hav lost five men out of our company
since the fight at Sharpsburg. Their is a great meney coming in every
day that has bin home on furlow. They all look well and harty. There is
a great talk of getting furlows now. Their too to go now from our company at a time. They hav sent out their furlows to get the general to sine
them. I do not wheather they wil get them or not. I wil not get to go the
first time but I am agoing to try to get of the next time if eney body gets
to go. They get 27 days. A J Barnes and J B Alen is ons that gets to go
first out of our company. I wanted to go first but I had to giv way for
them to go first as they hav don mor duty than eney of the rest. I think
my time coms next. I turn the subject.

 Well you wanted to no how I com out the Battle at Fredericksburg.
I com through safe. I was struck twist with spent balls but they did not
hurt me. Our company did not suffer much. We had three men wounded.

A Watts, G W Johnson and A M shoemaker was ons that was wounded. Watts was wounded in the leg. I herd from him the other day. He is suffering very much from his wound. He will not be able to go home under a month. We had five kild and fifty six wounded in our regment. We was exsposed very to the fire of the enemy but we pored in such a hot fire to them they cold not stand it. We kild more of them than eney fight that we hav ever bin in yet. The enemy is still on the opisit side of the river to us yet. We picket in cite of each other. They are one side of the river and we on the other. Their is talk of us going to North Carolina but I do not no it to be so. You wanted to no if I got them things that you sent me. I got all of them but the bottle of brandy. The gard took it him on the cars. I got the one that was in the cloths. I like my sherry verry well. The coat is most too small but I can war it. It wil be larg enough in summer time. I received a letter from Thomas about the last of December. He was well at that time. He had got back to camp. Rite to me as often as you can and giv me all the news in general. Nothing more. Rite as soon as you get this.

Daniel Boyd to Robert Boyd

On January 15, 1863, Robert Boyd received the following letter from Captain Robert Chatham informing him of the death of his son Thomas. Chatham expressed deep sorrow at the loss and assured Mr. Boyd that Thomas's final pay would be forthcoming. The payment of the remaining $62.31 to settle the account would not be paid until August 8, 1863.[7] Thomas's body was buried on the field along with his personal effects.

Camp 19th S C Regt near Shelbyville Tenn
Jan'y 15 1863
Mr Boyd,

Dear Sir,

It becomes my painful duty to announce to you the death of your son, a member of my company (G). He fell in the battle of the 31st ult., nobly battling for his country's rights and yielded his life a cheerful sacrifice on the altar of his country. I deeply sympathize with you in this bereavement. Thomas was a noble boy and splendid soldier. He never munnured-let his duties be what they might. He met the foe with soldier like bearing and manliness and fell in the thickest of the fight, discharging his duties with perfect coolness. I was not permitted to visit him after he fell, there being strict orders for shielding me. But he received as decent a burial as the place and circumstances would permit. His personal effects he had with him, and were interred with him. His pay will be duly attended to and full arrangements will be made for your receiving it. I regret his loss as a valuable member of my company and hope you may receive consolation from the Giver of all good.

Again expressing my sympathy, I remain his captain,
Robert N Chatham

Also on January 15, Fenton Hall wrote to his wife, Mary Jane, from his camp near Charleston. Fenton had seen the list of casualties and knew about Thomas. He expressed his sorrow at Thomas's death and his concern about how Mary Jane was taking it.

He speaks of an ongoing dialogue with Mary about how she will work the farm without him there. Options with her father, Robert Boyd, are discussed and mention is made of an earlier oat harvest taken up by his brother Davis Hall, who was now with the Twenty-Fourth South Carolina, which is the Stevens' Regiment he frequently mentions. The regiment of then Colonel Clement Stevens included a number of his cousins as well as his brother.

He mentions an earlier trip home and having borrowed money from James Taggart, a Lieutenant in his company. In this letter Fenton celebrates being blessed with good health since he has been in the camp.

Camp neir Charleston
January the 15 1863

Deir wife,

I take my pen in hand to let you no that I am well hoping when thes com to hand it may find you an the children all well. I reseved your kind leter yesturday evening. I was glad to heir from you and to heir that you an the children was well. I seed the casualitys of the nineteenth Regiment and I am sorrow to say that I seed the name of J T Boyd in the list that he was killed. Mary I want you to bar with this as well as you can. I no it heirt you. This can not be help now. I am sorow to heir it. H Hall was wounded in the shoulder. I will stop writin this evenin an write more to morrow.

January the 16. This mornin is cold an winday. Las night was the wirst night we had sinc we bin in camp. It rain an the win blowed hard. It blowed over several tents. We have our tents heir with ous. Thir is not mutch news heir to writ a bout. Neirley all of the trups a bout heir is gon to North Carolina. Stevens regment has never com back heir yet. Thir was several regment com back heir but tha ar all gon back to North Carolina. Thir is not miny trups a bout heir now. Tha ar exspectin a fight in North Carolina. Mary you sed you did not no wht you wold do a bout makin of a crop. I do not no my self what you will do. I wish it was so that the groun cold be wirked. Mary if davis has not taken them oats a way try to get them savd. If you can not get the groun wirked if your farther can wirke iney of the groun let him take the oats an sow them down on the river or he can sow them at home whar he lives an if tha do iney good he can give you what is right. I will try to satisfy Davis a bout the oats. I do wish the war wold close so I cood com home. I no you need me at home. I hop the time will son com when we will git to com to stay with you an the children an to wirke for you an the children. Thir is som talk of ous haven to go to North Carolina. You wanted to no if we wold git to stay heir. I do not no. We do not no what we will have to do. We may stay heir all this winter an summer an we may not stay heir one week. I hop thir will be no need for ous thir nor no whar elce. You want to no how my clos hol out. Tha hold out very well. You want to no what sort of far we hav. We have tolerable ondly we git corn meel an beef, rise and shugar. We drawed money yesturday. We drawed forty eight dollars but James Tygret git half of it an ten dollars for that I bared from him when I went home. I will send you a litel money if I have the chanc. I will send you tou ritin pens in this leter.

I wold send you sum stams if I had them but I have ondly a few at this time. I will send you sum the first chanc I have. Give my resepts to all of the frends. Tel them to writ to me. This leves me well an I hope it may find you an the children well. I fele thankeful to the lord for I have bin blest with good helth senc I have bin in camp. We mus loke to the lord for protecson. So I will have to close so nothing more at present but I remain lovein husband till deth.

Fenton Hall to Mary Jane Hall

Daniel wrote his father from Fredericksburg on January 27, 1863. This letter gives some insight into camp life there and Daniel's travails in trying to get a furlough to come home. He expressed sorrow at Thomas's death of which he had been informed by his father's letter of January 18. He says that he had first found out a week prior from Samuel Pingen Haddon who had received word in a letter. He laments that "It seams like all of us wil half to fall in this war."

It also sheds light on the practice of substitution within the army. Daniel states that the only way he can come home is if his father finds someone to come as a substitute for him for two months. He offers $50 to anyone willing and even suggests James Colwell as a candidate.

Camp near Fredericksburg Virginia
January the 27 1863

Dear father,

I take this oppertunity to rite you a few lines. This leaves me well at this time hopeing when thes few lines comes to hand they may find you enjoying the same blessing. I hav no news of eney importance to rite to you. All is quiet on this line at this time, but I am afraid it wont be so long. We are looking for another big battle here. Jenerall Burnside is going to make another attempt to cross the rapperhannock by the way of Falmerth which about four miles from Fredericksburg. But the wet weather has prevented him from crossing. If he crosses now he will half to leav his artillery for the ground is very wet and it is raining now and looks like it mite rain on for a day or too. The health of our regtment is some what better than it has bin for som time. We hav but one sick man in our company. W R Clinkscales is sick. This morning he has the chills but I think he wil soom get well again. We had one death in our company last weak. It was William C Baty. He died at Richmond. He had just got from the hospital and took sick and started back to the hospital and died by the time he got ther. I received a letter from A Watts the other day. He is still in the hospital. He is confined to his bed yet. He cant walk eney on his leg without his crutch. The rest of the boys is getting well that was wounded at Fredericksburg.

You wanted to no if I had got R P money. I hav not got it yet. I can not get it til I get the chance to go to richmon. I can not get it here. You said you wanted me to come home and bring it. I tell you there is no chance for me to go for they wont let us off. They promised to giv us furlows but they ar all maet up. If I cold get someone to take my place for a month or too I cold get to go. I wish you wold try to get som of the boys to come and tak my place. Try James Colwell. I wil giv him fifty dollars if he wil take my place for too months. That wil be the only chance for me to get off. I want to go home wors now than I hav since I hav bin hear. I wil get that money the first chance and send it to you for I hav no use for it for I hav got enough to do me. I hav got one hundred and thirty dollars in my pocket and I hav got about forty dollars owing to me. I received your latter that was dated Jan the 18. I was glad to hear from you but I was sory that Brother Thomas death. I heard of it about a weak ago. S P Haden got a letter a few days ago and he told me about it. It seams like all of us wil half to fall in this war. But if it is my lot to go in that way I am wiling go but I hope that this war wil soon end so we wil get back home again. Try and get someone to take my place. Rite soon as you get this and let me no if you can eney one to come. So nothing more at present. Rite.

D Boyd to Robert Boyd

Next Fenton Hall writes to his wife from Rantowles, South Carolina, about 10 miles east of Charleston along the Charleston and Savannah Rail Road. He began writing on February 4 and concluded it on February 6, 1863. He references recent fighting on the Stono River and at Charleston. As always rumors of where they might be going, is a topic of the letter. According to Fenton, they were hearing that the Sixth South Carolina Cavalry might be destined for Kentucky. Also, there was great anxiety of an expected fight looming in Charleston.

He had apparently gotten a letter from Thomas prior to his death in Tennessee because he promises to send it home to Mary Jane. He extends his respects to all the family and admonishes them to trust in the Lord.

Camp Ranetowle
Febuary the 4 1863

Deir wife,

I take my pen in hand to let you know that I am well at this time hoping when this com to hand it may find you an the children all well. I have not got nary leter from you not in three weeks. I wold like to heir from you an the clildren. This makes the forth leter I have written to you senc I have got one from you. I shal look for one from you to night. I recken you have heird of the fight don heir. Tha have bin fiting at savannah an heir on the stono river an at Charleston. Tha taken one gun boat on the stono river. Tha takin severiel prisoners. Tha have sunk one of the blockead vessel an all that was on it. Tha sed the rest of the blockead got a way. Our men clame the best of it at all the plasis.

I can not tel you mutch a bout the fite. We heir more a bout it thn

is so. Thir has bin sum talk of ous havin to go to canetuckey but I do
not no for serten whether it is so or not. I want you to writ to me an let
me no if you got the money an the stamps an pens I sent to you. Glen
is at home now. I exspect he will send the bridels down to Major James
Topson. I want you to git sum one to go and git them. I found one of
them. It is a good bridel. I want you to writ to me an let me no sumthing
a bout it. Thir is sturin news com heir. We have just reseve orders to
bein redeness at a minint warning. Tha say tha ar looking for a fight at
Charleston or sum whar a long the cost but this may sone all blow over.
I will writ more to night.

Febuary the 5 ... I have just riten a leter to Davied Murdock. I did
not git a leter from you las night. I lovd to finish my leter las night but
as I

did not git one I will not finish it until night. The news we got yesterday I think it is all a false a bout the fight coming on at Charleston
although tha may fight heir before long. This has bin a cold windy an
raney day. Captin Miot is a gointo advertis James Rampy as a dissurter
an ofer twenty dolers reward for him.

Febuary the 6 ... I resev your leter las night. I was glad to heir from
you an to heir that you an the children was well. I wold be the gladis in
the wirld to be at home with you an the children. You sed you wanted
me to com home the first chanc I had. I will be surtin to com home the
first chanc I have. You can tel John Lees mouther that he is well an harty.
He has groad a hep.

We ar camp clost to Rantule stashion on the suvanah raleroad ten
miles from Charleston. Tell Essa to be a good girle. I am glad to heir that
our litel children is do well. Cis them for me. Mary try to rase them as
ny right as you can. Give Ant Saley an Jane an your father Sara Andrew
my respects. Tel them to writ to me . tel mouthers pepel to writ to me.
It is cold wet wether heir now. I do hop this war will end an let ous all
returne home. I will send you that leter of Thomas to you. I wold be
glad that Daniel cood git a furlow to com home. I no you all wold be
glad to see him. I will have to com to a close for this time so nothing
more at present but I remainds your loving husband till deth. This leaves
me well an I hop it may find you and the children the same. Put your
trust in the lord.

Fenton Hall to Mary Jane Hall

At the same time, February 5, Fenton also wrote a letter to a friend named David Murdock. David Murdock was a 45-year-old member of Company I of the First South Carolina State Troops, which was also engaged in the defense of South Carolina.[8] *Fenton tells that his unit had been engaged guarding two bridges on the Ashley River.*

Camp Rantowles House
February the 5 1863

Dear frend,

I take my pen in hand to let you no that I am well hoping this com to hand it may find you well. I have nothing mutch to writ. I wold like to see you all. I wold have come down to see you all but I cood not git the chanc. I have not got narey leter from home in three weeks. I heir that all you that is over forty yers old is about to git off. I wold be glad that you an your frends cood git off. I wold be glad this war wold close an let all of ous go home. We git corne meele an beef to eat. If you git off I wold like to see you before you go home. We ar camp in sit of rantowle stshion. If I noad wen you was going home I wold com out to the raleroad to see you all.

We have to gard tow bridges on the Ashley river. We have to go a bout twenty miles to them. We have to drill twise a day. I reckon you have heird a bout the fight on the Stono River an at Charleston. I reckon you have heird that Thomas Boyd was killed in the fight at Murfeesboro. I was sorow to heir of it. I want you to writ to me an let me no how you are giting a long. I will have to come to a close so nothing more at present but I remains your frend till deth. I had to writ this in a hurry.

Fenton Hall to David Murdock

Next Fenton wrote his wife, Mary Jane, on Febrary 12, 1863. Not much of note is discussed, but several people from the area are mentioned.

Camp Rantowl
Febuary the 12 1863

Deir wife,

I take my pen in hand to let you no that I am well hoping when tis com to hand it may find you an the children all well. I reseved your kind leter last night. I was glad to heir that you was all well. I am glad that you have som one to git wood for you. I am glad that your farther can do such turnes for you. Old Beny Adams stad night before lase with ous. He left hir yesterday morning. He is coming to this company when his regiment is dis banded. He saed Daved Murdock an all the rest was well. He saed that tha wold all be disbaned nex tusday and he saed that William Furgurson was being sick at Jamesville an was very low. I have not mutch news to write at this time. Their has bin a good miney trups pasing heir going toward Savanah. Thir is no news heir.

It is quit warme heir now. James Rampy has not returned yet. Tha will half to wirke on him if he comes back heir. I was glad that David Murdock cud git to com home. I wish we all cood git to go hom to stay. Give William an Sara my respects. Tel them to write to me. Tha ar look-ing for a fight heir or that has bin the talk. I wold send you som more stamps if I had them an I wold send you som paper if I had iney way of sendin it to you. If I git to see D Murdock if [I] git of I will tri to git him fetch sum hom to you. I will haft to close for the want of sumthing to write. God be with you an the children. I remain your loving husband till deth. My love to you an the children.

Fenton Hall to Mary Jane Hall

Fenton wrote Mary Jane again on February 18, 1863. He said that his company would be leaving Rantowles and returning to Adams Run. He talks of conditions in Charleston and various individuals known to the family.

Camp Rantoule
Febuary the 18 1863

Deir wife,

I take my pen in hand to let you know that I am well hoping when this com to hand it may find you an the children all well. We will leve heir to marow morning to go back to Adams run. Thir is a company com heir to night from our regment to take our plase heir an we will have to go back to the regment. Tha ar looking strong for a fight heir. Bouagard has orded all the women an children out of Charleston. I was over to Charleston the outher day. I seed Waid and all the rest of the bois. Tha war all well. The twenty forth reg. is going down to night to Pocataligo. Thir is 75 vesels in sit of Charleston. Nex Sunday is the day the yankeys has set to attack Charleston. There is more talk of fiting heir

now than has bin senc we have bin down heir. No one nous what tha ar
a going to dow. Mary Glen has com back. He sed them brideles will be
sent to James Tompson. When you write direct your leters to Adams
Run company G Aikens regment of cavlery. John Burton lef heir las Sunday with out promishion an has not return. I have just reseve your kind
leter to night. I am glad to heir tha you an the children was all well. Your
har looks netcheral. I will take car of it. James Barnes is gon to the guver-
ment shop at Greenville to wirk. I am sorrow to heir of sickness in the
nabor hood. It makes me feel onesey but I hop the lord will proteck you
an the children an I hop that he will proteck me an tha I may return
home to you an the children. I will write to you a gane when I git to
Adams run. Your loving husband till deth.

Fenton Hall to Mary Jane Hall

On February 21, 1863, Daniel Boyd wrote to his father from Fredericksburg. It contains the usual rumors of moving out. This time speculation
was that they were bound for Blackwater, Virginia, or Charleston. Daniel
expressed hope that they might go to Charleston. Many individuals are mentioned along with a first-hand account of watching 26 Federal regiments
departing on trains across the river from their position.

Camp near Fredericksburg
February the 21st 1863

Dear father,

I take this oppertunity of droping you a few lines to let you no that
I am well at this time and hope when thes few lines comes to hand they
may find you all well and doing well. The health of our regiment is very
good at this time and the boys ar in good sperits. All ar quiet on this
line. Their ar some talk of ous moving from hear. We hav bin under
marching orders for the last weak. Their ar som talk of us going to Black
Water Va or to Charleston South Carolina. I wold like to go to Charleston
very much. Our army is moving now. They are going towards Richmond.
We hav got orders to send of all the heavy baggage that we cant cary
with us. We will go soon. Jenenral Jackson army going to stay hear to
guard this line. The weather has bin very bad. We hav had a big snow
and rain after. We hav water and mud til we cant hardly get about. But
it cleared of now and we wil hav dry weather now. We had to go on
picket about a weak ago and stayed six day. We cold see the Yankees

leaving. We saw twenty six regments get on the cars. They hav bin burning in their camps. We saw smoke. Their has bin agood meny men gon
home on furlow. There is four gon from our company. I do not no
whether eney more of us wil get to go or not. If there is eney more furlows
given I am going to try to get one. But I do not think that their be eney
more given. But if there is I am going to do my best to get one. I want
to go home very bad but it like I never wil get the chance to go. James
Alewine is well and harty. He says for you to tell his mother to send him
a pack knife with W L McCury for we cant get eney thing the sort hear.
I wish you wold send me one also for they cost ten dollars hear. I want
you to rite to me as often as you can. I hav not heard from hom in a
month or mor. I want to no if David Murdock has got hom or not. I
heard that they wold be dismissed and tel him to rite to me and I want
to no how the too Marys and their children ar geting along. I want to
no wher Fent Hall is and tell him to rite to me. Tell Mary to rite to me.
I want to no if N C McCury has started back for I heard that he has a
notion of getting him a wife before he coms back. I wold like to hear
how him and Miss Lieucinda is getting along. I am out of something to
rite. Nothing more at present, but I remains son to death.

    Daniel Boyd to Robert Boyd

----

*The next letter to Robert Boyd is nearly a month later, on March 17,
1863, again from Daniel. He is still in Fredericksburg, so the earlier word
that they would be moving on was incorrect. Once again, Daniel writes of
being frustrated in his efforts to obtain a furlough. He was next in line, but
from his account someone objected and lots were drawn for it and he lost.
His bitterness is transparent. He even names three individuals he blames
for blocking his chances to go home for a visit and pledges to have "satisfaction out of them" if he does not get a furlough and calls them liars.*

Camp near Fredericksburg
March the 17th 1863
Dear father,

    I take this opportunity of droping you a few lines to let you no how
I am ageting along. I am well at this time and hope when thes few lines
coms to hand tha may find you enjoying the same blessing. I received
your kind letter that W L McCury fetch to me. I was glad to hear from
home and that you was well. I hav no news of importance to wright to

you at this time. As for war news I hav nun. All is quiet on this line as fare as I no. We are ly about in camp doing nothing. The times is very dull. We hav bad weather. We hav rain and snow. We had a hail storm the day it covered the ground about one inch deape. All the boys has got back to camp on the 15th. I got them things that you sent to me. I was glad to see the ham of meat com for we dont such hear. We hav been living fine since they com back. They all look well and harty. N C McCurry is talking about his girl. He is rather down. I am sorry to inform you that I cant get to com home this time. I was in hopes that I wold get of this time but I am mistaken. I wold hav got to go but som of the company got mad and kicked up a fuss about it and we had to draw for it and I did not get it. There is too gon home now and too mor wil start in a day or too. I dont think that they treated me rite for they all promised me that I shold go first and when the time come they don all they cold against me going home.

It is doupt foull about me getting one when they get back for I am afraid that they wil stop giving furlows. If they continue giving them I think I will get one in about a month for there is no one to draw against me unless they put the conscrips against me. You need not look for me til you see me coming for it looks like they don't in tend for me to get home but if I get ther I'll make it count for too for the way they treated me. I don't think that Capton Allen don rite for he sed that he intended to let me go when John Allen com back but there is four to go before me. I reckon when all the rest of the company goes I wil get off. Capton Allen wil start home in a day or too. I am getting very much dissatisfied. If I don't get to go I intend to hav satisfaction out of them that nocked me out of going home. D Clark, J P Black and J E Shaw is the ones. They ar the grandest lyars in the 7th regment for they wil say one thing one minit and do another the nex. Wel I wil turn the subject. J T Campbell was up to see us the other day. He sed that D Cleoland was well and all the rest except Thomas Hampton. He has bin sick for a weak or too but he is getting better now. Well I am about out of something to rite. I want you to right to me every chance you hav and giv me all the news. I wil not rite eney more til I see wheather I get go home or not. I wil rite Mary Jane another time. Giv my best respects to all my friends and tak a portion to your self. Nothing at present.

Daniel Boyd to Robert Boyd

March 19, 1863, found Fenton Hall back at Adams Run outside of Charleston where he wrote to Mary Jane. He mentions the arrival in Charleston of his younger brother, Davis Hall, and his nephew, William Newton Hall, Jr. W. N. Hall would serve in the Sixth South Carolina Cavalry, Company G, along with Fenton,[9] but records indicate that Davis Hall served in the Twenty-Fourth South Carolina Infantry.[10] Judging from this letter, the issue of which unit Davis would serve in had not been settled at this point as he speaks of trying to get him into their mess.

As he often does, he thanks her for sending provisions to him, but expresses concern that she and the children are doing without by sending these things to him. He mentions her asking about what must be lice in the camp, referring to them as "Jerusalem Travelers." Fenton says that he has heard about it from others, but had not seen any himself.

He mentions several individuals, asks after Daniel Boyd and expresses a strong desire to see his brother-in-law. Daughter Essa has sent more pies and biscuits to her father and Fenton said that they "eat mity good."

Camp Adams Run
March the 19

Deir wife,

I take my pen in hand to let you no that I am well at this tim hoping when this coms to hand it may find you an the children all well an all of the kin as well. W. N. Hall an Davis got heir yesterday. I reseved your kind leter that you sent by W. N. Wich I was glad to heir that you an the children was well. I reseved the pack of pies an biscit and the ham of meet an the buter an potatos an the tobacco witch is very exseptebel heir. I thank you for your kines but I am afraid that you have discomfit yourself an the children in sending the provishion to me. Tel Davy that I was glad to heir from him. Thir is not mutch news heir to write to you about, it is cloudy heir now but it is very dry an dusty heir. A shower of rain wold do good heir to lay the dust. You wanted to no if we had iney Jrusalam travelers heir, I have not seen eney yet but tha say tha ar heir. Hi heird sum of our men say tha have cetch sum of them on their close tha say tha ar the bodey lise. I exspect we will git sum of them sum of thes times you wanted to no how our mess was giting along senc the recruts com in to it. We git along about as usual. Davis is not in our mess, he is in a mess with the old man Adams. Adams went in to a mess with Bill an Davy McCleland there is six in our mess. We had no objection of his coming in to our mess. I have not heird him say iney thing about what mess he wants to go into he was heir an in the tent before I noad it. I was not looking for him but maby we will all git in th mess together yet. I wold like for Adams an Davis very well to be in our mess

March the 21. It is cloudy an raning today we ar all tolrabel ondly. Bad colds Mikel Alewine has the cold very bad. I wold have finish this leter before but I had to quit. I had to go on gard Mary I did not no that the salt that yu got wold cost so mutch. I did not think that it wold cost more than eight dollars peir bushel to git it hom. I sent a pack of old leters by Samuel Shaw. I want to no if you got them. I have just reseve a leter from Waid Eldirdge, he was well. I want you to write to me an let me know if you have heird from Daniel Boyd sense tha have moved. You sed in sum of your leters that he had moved on. You did not no whar he was gon. I wold like to see him.

March the 22, it is clear today. I expect Miekel Alewine will have to go to the hospital. He is no beter today. Thir is a hep of bad colds heir

I have the cold myself, but I am abel to eat my alowence. Tel Essa that heir pies an biskit eat mity good. I hop the time will son com when I will git home to eat pies an bisket with you all. I wold like to see you an Essa and Thomas the best in the wirld. We had pretchin heir las Sunday an today. The pretcher name is Gillard. Tha hav not commence furlow iney heir yet, it has bin stop for sum time. I wish tha would commence furlowing agane. I wold ruther tha wold make pese an let us all go hom. I never noad the good of a home an a loving wife an children till I com into camp, but I hop I will live to see that time agane. I will have to close so nothing more at present, but remain your loving husband til deth.

Fenton Hall

To Mary Jane Hall

Fenton wrote Mary Jane again a few days later, on March 26, 1863. He tells of much sickness in the camp. His brother Davis had left with Captain John R. Miot headed to Columbia. Fenton said Captain Miot would try to get a discharge for Davis. He encourages Mary and their neighbors to plant foodstuffs rather than cotton.

Captain Miot had been Company G's captain from the time it had been formed. Apparently popular with his soldiers, Miot got drunk with some of the privates in his company in October 1863 and was charged on October 29 with drunkenness while on duty and conduct prejudicial to good order and military discipline. He resigned on November 4.[11]

Although his service record does not reflect a furlough, Fenton mentions a recent trip home and having to pull guard duty for overstaying his leave. All rolls in that time frame show him as present. It is likely that he was allowed a short trip home rather than a full furlough due to the relative closeness of Abbeville County to Charleston, which is a little over 200 miles away as opposed to the 500 miles to Fredericksburg where Daniel was encamped. That and the fact that Fenton had a horse, would have made this possible.

Camp Adams Run
March the 26 1863

Deir wife,

I seat myself to drop you a few lines to let you know how I am getting along. I am tolarible well. I have the cold but I am abel for duty. I hope when this com to hand it may find you an the children all well thir is three of our mess sick Mikel Alewine is heir at the hospital tha say he has the Bronchitis. I seed him yesterday. I think he is a litel beter. Robert Tucker is at the hospital he has the messels, he is doing very well. Peter Burton is sick. I think he will have to go to the hospital. I do not no what ailes him he has a very bad enough thir is a hep of bad colds heir an bad coughs. Davis left heir yesterday he is gon to Columbia. Captain Miot went with him he is goin to try to get a discharge turn over.

Mary, Peter Burton tole me just now not write hom tha he is sick, he sed tha his pepel wold be uneasy, but I have don writon to you alred in this leter tha he is sick. Mary I have just reseve your kind leter this evening. I was glad to heir from you but sorrow to heir that the children was not well, but I hop tha will son git beter you sed tha you had heird that tha had put me on sentry duty for staing over my time at home, tha did put me on gard once for it but I wish tha wold give me the chance to go home again. I will stan gard ten or twelve times if tha will let me go home again an think noways hard of it. W. N. Hall sed tell you to tell Margret tha he reseved the leter that she sent to him, he has don ritten one an close it up. He won't write non now.

Mary, you sed that your farther was goin to sell the coton I suspect it wold be well not to sell it. I want to no if you have paid your farther the money that I borrowed from him when I started to camps, if you have not he can pay himself when he sells the coton. you sed you was looking for Daniel hom I wish he cood git hom you sed thir was some talk of pese but I am afrade that it will be good wille before it come, but

I hop an trust to god that it will not be long. I hop that joifull day will soon com, you sed that you had no plowing don if you get iney thing planted let it be sumthing to eat. I think the nabors all aught to plant sumthing to eat an let coton alone. Them that has to by tha will no how tha will git it.

Mary, you sed you was goin to sell the old sow if you cood git a good prise for her. Let her go if you can git a good prisé for her an have another sow a coming on you sed that the naborhood was goin to have the mail fetch to diamond hill three times a week. I will be glad if tha will do it.

March the 27, we ar all tolerable this morning. Peter is no beter. I have not heird from Meikel Alewine or Robert Tucker this morning.

Mary I want you to write to me an let me no all the news an if R. D. Tucker has got hom. I have not got time to write to David Murdock this morning. I will have to close so nothing more at present, but I remain your loving husband till death.

Fenton Hall to his loving wife and children

Mary Jane Hall

Tell Davy not to think hard of me not writing to him tell them all to write to me my respects to all.

Fenton wrote Mary Jane again on April 6, 1863, again from Adams Run. He acknowledges that his brother Davis did not get into his unit and was instead in Stevens's Regiment (Twenty-Fourth South Carolina) and talks of another nephew arriving for service, John W. Hall. John W. Hall would not end up in the Sixth South Carolina Cavalry with Fenton either. Instead he would serve in the Nineteenth South Carolina Infantry, Company G — Thomas's old unit.[12] Once again, like with Peter Burton in the previous letter, Fenton had written about someone before being asked not to and swears Mary Jane to secrecy. He talks of seeing 36 to 40 Yankee boats on the Edisto River.

Camp Adams Run
April the 6 1863

Deir wife,

I take my pen in hand to let you no how I am giting along. I am ondly tolerable well. I have the cold mity bad and I have had it for sum time but I have never stop for it. I have a mity bad cough. Peter Burton

is at the hospital heir he has the pneumonia. He is giting beter. Mickel
Alewine has got back to camp. Robert Tucker is still at the hospital, he
mends very slow. John W. Hall got heir today he sed that he seed Davis
at Charleston, he is in Capt. Hill's company, he sed that Stevens regment
was moving back to James Island. I have not heird from Davis since he
left heir till today. Mary, I have no news mutch to write to you about
the war tha say the Yankees is giting very pleny heir along the east. I was
on picket las Saturday at White Point. I cood see the Yankees vesels tha
war about thirty six or forty of them. Their vesels is being in Edistow
river. I do not no whether John will get in to this company or not. Davis
and cood not join it. Mary, John tole me not to name him in my leter
you, sed not say iney thing about him he was tow late a telen of me not
to name him as had done rote sumthing about him in this leter.

April the 7., Mary I have just reseve your kind leter. I was glad to
heir from you an to heir that you have as mutch money as you have.
Your wanted to no if I was willing for you to pay the debts. I am willing
if you can spar iney of the money if you pay iney be shure to keep anuf
to do you if you pay iney I want you to pay unkel Ezikel Hall five dolars
that's borrowed from him to git corn with.

I want to no who you sold the old sow tow. I want to no how miney
shoats an pigs you have lef an how tha look. I want to no if you have got
the potatos planted an if you can git the grown wirked. You sed that
Daniel was still at Fredricksburg. I am sorrow to heir that he has not
come home. I want to know who it was that com home. I want no how
you like the salt that you got an if you got them old leters that I sent by
Samuel Shore.

April the 8, there is still no news this morning they keep us busy do
duty. Thir is ondly seven companys heir in this regment. We have to go
on picket every seven days. I wold as soon go on picket as to be on camp
gard. We have to keep our camp gard yet was in hops tha wol quit keep-
ing up the camp gard sumtime we have very miser wether heir now.
Ondly sum what dusty when we all git out to drilling we kick up a mity
dust. We git corn meele to eat an sum times beef an sum times bakin an
a litel shugar. John Lee ses tel his mother that he is well. Mary I am about
out of sumthing to write, I wold be glad to see you and the children the
best in the wirld. Thir is no one giting furlows heir now nor thir is no
talk of furlowing heir. The old man Biley Clinkscales came down heir
yesturday, he ses thir was a mity stur in Columbia an in Charleston as
he com down. I will have to quit for the want of sumthing to rite. This

leves me beter than I have bin. Hoping when this com to hand it may find you an the children all well, so I will for this time nothing more at present but still remaining your loving husband till deth.

Fenton Hall to Mary Jane Hall

Mary, kis the children all for me.

Excuse my bad writing.

Next, on April 26, 1863, Fenton writes to Mr. Boyd, addressing him as "father." He had gotten a letter from Daniel and talks of observing 14 Union vessels in the river from White Point. There are the usual rumors of Beauregard's troops heading elsewhere; this time west. He discusses the poor health of the horses and says that his "looks very bad."

It seems that the main point of the letter is to thank Mr. Boyd for working Fenton's land for him while he is away at the war. He passes along the usual regards to the family.

Camp Adams Run

April the 26 1863

Deir farther,

I take my pen in hand to let you [know] that I am well hoping wen this com to hand it may find you an the rest of the famley well. I reseved a leter from Daniel Boyd las tusday it was rote the twelf of this month he was well thir was not mutch news in his leter he rote like he wold like to come heir to this company if he cood git a exchang he ses it is rumerd thir that the yankes is all goin south but he ses he don't think tha ar. He think tha will have to fight before long. Well thir is not mutch news heir. I com off picket yesterday evening. I was at white point thir was ondly about fourteen vesels in sight. Thir has bin as high as forty seen at this plase. It is rumerd heir that ten thousand troops under Buaguard command is orderd to the west but I don't think that we will have to go if we do I don't think we will git this maney horses we lost tow horses in our companey yesterday. Horses have all kind of deses heir my hors looks very bad. We don't git iney thing, but corn to feed on the helth of this regment is tolrabel good. I not got quite shed of my cold yet but I have got beter. Mary ses that you have planted parte of the ground and was goin to plant the rest of it. I am glad that you have taken charge of the ground that I had to wirke. I did not no when she wold git to wirke it if you did not wirke it for her. I no you have a bad have to wirket it an wirket your one. I wish I was at home to wirke my one I am afraid that the famleys that is lef at hom will see hard times if this war go on mutch longer. I will have to com to a close for the want of sumthing to write. Write to me when you git this give Sarah an Andrew my best respects an exsept the same to your self.

    Fenton Hall to Mr. Robert Boyd

    The next letter comes from Daniel Boyd to his father following the Battle of Chancellorsville. It is dated May 7, 1863, two days after the battle. He reports that his brigade was in reserve and they were only involved in light skirmishing.

    Lt. Col. Elbert Bland had been in command of the Seventh South Carolina since Colonel D. Wyatt Aiken was wounded at Sharpesburg in the same campaign in the same action in which Pressley Boyd was killed. A doctor from Edgefield District, South Carolina, Bland was greatly admired by his men for his courage. He had graduated with distinction from the Medical College of New York and had been assistant surgeon for the Palmetto Regiment during the Mexican War. At the beginning of the war, Bland was the Surgeon with Gregg's First South Carolina. Not satisfied patching up the wounded, Bland helped Thomas Bacon organize the Ninety-Six Riflemen, which soon became Company H in the Seventh of which he would be captain. He was considered the ideal soldier and a fighter "par excellence." Possessed of eyes described as penetrating and a strong, commanding voice, Bland had a gift for inspiring in his men a courage which rivelled his own. Noble and generous, "[h]e was idolized by his troops and beloved as a comrade and commander." He was also known for his sense of humor of which this interesting anecdote arises following this battle. He was sent as a "bearer of orders" to General Hooker across the Rapahannock under a flag of truce. He was met by some officers and a crowd of curious onlookers. Some of the officers were confused by the Confederate rank insignia. His collar bore the two stars of a Lieutenant Colonel. One officer asked of Bland, "I can't understand your Confederate ranks; some officers have bars and some stars. I see you have two stars; are you a Brigadier General?" Bland replied, "No sir, but I ought to be. If I was in your army I would have been a Major General, and in command of your army." Then he added with a chuckle, "Perhaps then you would not have gotten such a damn bad whipping at Chancellorsville." This drew a laugh all around.[13] Apparently even the enemy appreciated his humor.

    Early in the war, while a captain, Bland had wounded Major Emett Seibles in a duel. The two had been engaged in a friendly chess game in which thoughtless insults escalated until a challenge was issued. Major

Seibles was seriously wounded in the chest, while Bland was unhurt. Seibles
would recover only to be killed the next year in battle.[14] *In this letter, Daniel*
gives a few details and reports the wounding of Stonewall Jackson and A. P.
Hill along with a few from his unit. He reports that they took prisoners and
confiscated a great many provisions from the fleeing enemy.

Camp 7th South Carolina Regment
May the 7th 1863

Dear father,

I have the pleasure of writeing a few lines to let you know that I am
still on the land of living and ar tolerable well at this time. We have just
got back from eight days hard marching and fighting. the seckond battle
of the Rappahannock has bin fought. We have whipt the enemy at every
point. our Bregaid was not engaged, only in skermishing and loss is very
light. We had two men wounded in our company. N. C. McCurry shot
himself in the foot accidently. J. M. Brooks wounded with a shell can
not give no correct statement about the Battle. We have taken a large
number of prisoners. it is reported that Jeneral Jackson is wounded and
A. P. Hill and W C Jameson ar all wounded. The yanks maid the poorest
out at fighting that ever don. We drove them one knight on four miles.
I never saw Yankees runn before they plunged into the river. when they com
to it their was a great many got drownded. they left everything they had.

We got a great many blankets, oil cloth knapsacks, coffee, shugar,
tea and most eney thing that you can name. We have gained the greatest
victory that bin gained since the war commenced. The prisoners say that
they never intend to fight again an their time is out now. they was the
worst scared men I ever seen. the loss on the enemies side must have bin
heavy from the number of prisoners we took. Well I wil not try to give
you a true statement about the fight. we have lost everything we had. I
have lost my cloths but what I have on my back. I want you to send me
sum the first chance you have a shirt and pair of drawers and socks for
I don't know when I can get eney hear. The health of our regment is
good and in fine spirits. I wil half to close for the present for I am very
tyard of marching. I wil rite as soon as I can lern more about the fight.
I thought I wold rite a little lest you hav coment. I want you rite soon
as you can and give me all the news. Excuse my short letter, nothing
more at present but remain your son til death.

Daniel Boyd to Robert Boyd

Fenton wrote to Mary Jane on May 13, 1863, from Adams Run. He reports of recent fighting on nearby John's Island. James Rampey who he had mentioned in several recent letters had finally returned to camp and was in the guard house. He asks for clothes and about his children.

Camp Adams Run
May the 13 1863
Deir wife,

I take my pen in hand to let you no that I am well hoping when this com to hand it may find you an the children all well. I have bin looking for a leter from you for the last weke. The last leter that I reseved was wroat the twenty-six of April. Thir has bin a right smart sture here for the last fore or five days. All the trups here is over on Johns island and a parte of our regment is over their. Tha went over thar to attack the yanks but tha have not don it yet. It is reported that tha have give it out but our trups has not returned yet. About one oclock yesterday we had hevy firing down at white pointe. We sune got orders to go down thar. We went down ther in a hurey but the yankes was all gon. Tha had run up to white pointe with tow gun boats.

Tha sheled the woods an run our pickets back but don no damage. We picket over the woods but found no yankes. Tha did not stay long. Tha soon returned back to the blocked. Every thing is still as far as I no this morning.

May the 14 ... James Rampy got back hear yesterday morning. The capt. had him put right strate in the gard house. He will be apt to stay thar a while. Thar is all wase a bout fourteen or fifteen in the gard house. James Barnes has got back to camp. He com yesterday morning. Well Mary I have just reseved your kind leter. I was glad to here from you an to here that you an the children was well. I am glad to here from all of the frends. I am glad to here that wheet looks well. You sed that you was a goin to by sum flower and send it to me. I dont want you to send me all you have got. I want you an the children to live well and let me dou a thought if iney one has to do a thought. You wated to no if I wanted iney close. I have tow good shirts and the same douers that I fetch from home. I have tou par of woolen pants. I am not a needing iney at this time. I wold like to have a par of cotton pants to war but I have as meney close as I ought to have in camp. Tel Jane that I will try to git her sum palmetto if I can an send it to her. It is hard to com at. I have not saw but very few trees of it yet an tha had nothing on them. Tha war all trimed.

May the 15 ... Tha have give out the fight on John island at this
time. Mary I want to know if Essa and Thomas has groad eney an if tha
ar as purty as tha was when I lef home an if Thomas has got to talking.
Tel Essa to be a good girle. I do wish I cood be at home with you an the
children if it is the lord will. I will put my trust in the lord. I want you
to do the same. I will have to close for this time so nothing more at present but your loving husband.

Fenton Hall to Mary Jane Hall

---

*Fenton wrote again two days later on May 17, 1863. He reported that
the planned attack on John's Island didn't happen. The word in the camp
was that the enemy was tipped off by a deserter.*

Camp Adams Run
May the 17 1863

My deir wife,

I take my pen in hand to let you no that I am well hoping when thes
few lines coms to hand tha may finde you an the children all well. I have
no news to write to you at this time. I thought I wold drop you a few
lines as W N Hall was writing an put it in with his. I have not heard from
the fight in veirgenna. I have heard from Capt Harpers company. I heard
that the los in that company was seven killed and twenty one woned. I
heard that William Robertson was killed. It looks like it is a hard mater
to hear from thar. I want you to write to me an let me no if you have
heard from Daniel Boyd or eney of the rest of the bois. Every thing is
still hear at this time. Most all the trups is gon from hear. Tha say the
reson that our men did not attack the yankes on John island was that
one of our men desearted the night befor tha was to attack them an went
to the yankes. Yesterday was a very wet day but it is clear an warm to
day. Mary if you send me a shirt or a par of drours sow down the seams
close like the seams in a wagon cloth. But I am not needing iney at this
time. I am on gard to day. I will finish my leter in the morning.

May the 18 ... I will put my short leter up to it self. Thar is nothing
new to write to you this morning. It has bin reported hear that all the
frut is killed. I want you to write to me an let me no if it is so. Let me
no if you have heard from Davis sence he lef Charleston. I want to no
how long Waid got to stay at home. Give me all the news in genral. Let
me no how the wheet looks. I do wish it was so that I cood be at hom

to cut the wheet for you if thar is iney wheet to cut but thar is no chance to git home now at this time. Lord send the time may soon com that I can get to com hom to see you an the children an this war may close and let ous have pese. I will have to close so nothing more at present but I still remain your loving husband til deth. Fenton Hall to his loving wife an children Mary Jane Hall Essa an Thomas. Give my best respects to all the friends.

We next hear from Fenton on May 23, 1863. The letter does not have the year, but 1863 may be deduced from events in the letter. He once again is concerned that Mary Jane is being too self-sacrificing in sending items to him. This letter, like many between Fenton and Mary Jane, illustrates the financial hardships posed on the families by the war. There are many discussions of money borrowed and owed between family and friends and whether said debts have been collected.

He speaks of getting a letter from another of his nephews in the war, Hezakiah Hall, who was the brother of W. N. Hall.[15] In this letter is the first mention of a fight between Peter Burton and Michael Alewine. News had apparently made its way to Abbeville County, but Fenton seems reluctant to discuss it. First Creek Baptist Church records indicate that Burton and Alewine joined the church on the same day during a revival that ran from September 25 to October 23 of 1841. Ninety-six people joined along with them that month.

Camp Adams Run
May the 23

My deir wife,

I seate myself to drop you a few lines to let you no that I am well hoping when this coms to hand it may find you an the children all well. [Crossed out text: I am sorrow to hear that Thomas is not well] I reseved your kind leter this morning that you sent by R. A. Tucker. I was glad to hear that you was well. You sed that Thomas was not well. I am sorrow to hear that he was not well but I hop that he will not be bad. R. A. Tucker got here las night. He got here with all the things safe we have opin the box but have not taken all the thing out yet. I eate a mity good diner of pies an buter today. Robert Tucker sed that he put all that you tooke to his house in but the flower. I mus try to make out with what I draw here. I am afrad that you disappoint yourself an the children. I don't want you to do it. I had mutch ruther do a thout myself than to here of you an the children a doing a thout. Robert brout a box for Peter Burton. I saw a par of pants with my name on them. I have more close than I no what to do with we all drawd pants and coats today. Michel Alewine is sick he went to the hospital yesterday. I do not no what ailes him. You wanted to no how mutch we paid W. N. Hall for John Lee a month. We pay him one dolar a month a pese. You wanted to no if W. N. Hall had paid me my part for fixin of the bridg. We have don setel that. He took it in the way of what I oud him for John Lee. Mary I sent a leter by John Hall to you an ten invelops eight of them had stamps on them. Well Mary tha ar given sum furlows now. All that has not bin hom an all that went before me will git to go hom before I do but I will com hom as soon as I can git the chance. Tha ondly low tow to go hom from the company at a time. I fourgot to turne you my thankes for your kindness for sending me sum provishion. Mary if I had noad that we was gine to draw clothing now I wold ruther you had not sent me the pants. We heird today that the yankes has got vickesburg an forty thousand of our men. I will write mor tomarow. I will drop a few more lines this evening. We don't have to drill iney now tha keep us bisey on gard an picket. The men about here is cirse now to what tha war. I reseved a leter Heskiah Hall today he is well, he is still in Tennsee yet. He roat like he thought tha wold have to go to Mississippi. Mary I want you to write to me an let me no if you have heard from Davis sence he left Charleston.

Sunday morning, May the 24, there is nothing new this morning to write. We git plenty of blackbureys now to eat by paing ten sense a quart. The nigros fetches them in every day now to sel to the men. The helth of this camp is tolrabel good. Their has bin sum talk of ous moving our camp but I do not no whether we will or not. I wish the war wold end an let ous all go hom. Well Mary, R. A. Tucker tole me that you had heard of the fus that had bin in our mess between P. S. Burton an Mickel Alewine. I don't want to say iney thing about it. I hardley no what tha did foul out about so I will just let it pas without saing iney mor about it. I am about out of sumthing to write, so I will close for this time. This leves me well hoping this may find you an the children all well. Nothing more at present, but I still remanes your loving husban till deth.

Fenton Hall to Mary Jane Hall an children

On May 28, 1863, Captain Robert N. Chatham, Thomas's commanding officer, sent Robert Boyd a letter instructing him how to claim Thomas's final payment from the Confederate government.

Chatham had been elected First Lieutenant in May 1862 and was promoted to captain on June 19. He was severely wounded in the shoulder at Chicamauga in September 1863, about four months after this letter was written. He would recover from this wound, but one year after writing this letter to Mr. Boyd, Captain Chatham's own appointment with eternity would arrive. The early morning hours of May 29, 1864, Company G's picket line was overrun by a Federal line of battle at New Hope Church in Georgia. Chatham was the company's only casualty having been accidentally shot in the abdomen by one of his own men. He died the next day in the division hospital. Chatham's death was considered a great loss to the regiment.[16]

Three days later, on May 31, Rev. J. G. Richards, the chaplain of the Tenth and Nineteenth South Carolina Regiments, would write to Chatham's brother from the field hospital he describes as being "fifteen miles West of Marietta, Ga." Chatham's father had died earlier and his mother was remarried to Edmund Cobb. The Cobbs had both died during the first year of the war, so Robert Chatham's death left young James M. Cobb truly orphaned.

Richards states that he was with Chatham from the time he was wounded at 2 o'clock the morning of May 29 until his death that afternoon at 5:30. He says that Chatham "while endeavoring in the darkness of the night to get the men in position, received the fatal ball in the pit of the stomach, which passed out at his back." He states that Chatham did not appear to suffer much and was conscious until the end. Richards details his final moments:

> *His last words were: "Mr. Richards, write to my brother. Tell him I have no fears of death. I am sorry to leave him without a protector, but I leave him in the hands of our merciful, heavenly Father. Tell him to prepare for eternity; to live a sober, righteous, and godly life; to meet me in heaven; to remember my instructions, and our mother's dying request."*
>
> *This message was uttered with difficulty, and we thought all was over with our dear friend, but after a few moments he rallied a little and said: "Tell my Company and my Regiment to put their trust in God, and never desert the glorious cause in which they are battling, until God, in His goodness and mercy, shall give us the victory. As they are noble soldiers in their country's cause, so let them be true soldiers of the cross, and if it is permitted, I will watch over them as a guardian angel."*
>
> *When he had said this, he turned to the doctor and said: "Loosen the bandage around my body, and I think I will die easier." He then folded his hands and breathed his last. Thus passed away a Christian and a soldier.*

Richards said of Chatham, "In the army all had confidence in him— all loved him." Chatham's wish was to be returned to South Carolina for burial, but Richards states that this was not possible considering the situation so they buried him there: "as decently as possible, under the circumstances, and marked the spot so it can be easily found." He also says that Chatham wished his brother to have his sword and other personal effects and promised to send them as soon as possible.[17]

There was, however; some controversy as to whether the official account of Chatham's wound being the result of an accidental discharge from one of his own soldiers was correct. John Abney Chapman of Company D, who was wounded by the same bullet, would later write:

> Occasional firing was going on all that night, and, in fact, nearly all the time, day and night, for we were nearly always in the presence of the enemy. We were lying, at the time Captain Chatham was fatally wounded, in line of battle. I was in the rear rank lying upon my left side with my right leg a little drawn up, so that the foot rested upon the left just above the ankle. Captain Chatham, a little in the rear of the rear rank, was lying upon his right side within a few feet of me. I was about half asleep when suddenly a gun fired, which seemed to be very near. The ball passed through my right leg about an inch above the ankle, tearing out the smaller bone without touching the larger, and struck Captain Chatham in the stomach and lodged in his body. We were both carried together to a little house not far away. On the afternoon of Monday, May 30th, I was lifted into a wagon and transported to Marietta over the roughest road, it seemed to me then, that ever wagon travelled over. Captain Chatham was alive when I left him, but he died that afternoon, as I was told afterwards. He was an amiable and good man, a brave and good officer, and loved by his men. I saw Colonel Shaw at Newberry in 1867, and talking about the events of that night, he said he had come to the conclusion, and the general conclusion was, that the gun was fired by the enemy. I thought at the time that, being so near, it must have been the accidental discharge of one of our own guns, but the ball passed diagonally across our line, so that the man who fired the gun must have been in our front, though near.[18]

In either case, Captain Robert Chatham was clearly a man who was loved by both his troops and his commanders. This letter to Robert Boyd is illustrative of the lengths he would go to in seeing to the best interests of his men.

Camp 19 SC Regt
Shelbyville Tenn.
May 28 1863
Mr Boyd,

Dear Sir,

Enclosed I send you a final statement of amount due your son by the government, which if you will send to Richmond Va to W H S Taylor 2nd Auditor of the Treasury, you will as soon as the matter can be attended to, receive the pay. This statement will have to be accompanied by an oath that your son had neither wife nor child and that you are the lawful heir; also an oath from a creditable person that knew both of you and that he was your son. These are taken before some lawful magistrate and then the paper has to receive the seal of the Clerk of Court with a certificate from him to the effect that the magistrate is one duly appointed and authorized by law to act. Some of the district officers at Abbeville can give you the desired information if this is not sufficiently explicit. I hope that you will soon obtain the same.

Your friend,
R N Chatham Capt.
Co G 19th S C Regt.

The next letter dated the following day, May 29, 1863, was written by Fenton Hall to Mary Jane. To compound his worries about the war and the fact that there was a wheat crop — a good one based on this letter — to bring in, his children were ill. They were apparently quite sick, enough so that he commented, "if you an the children should live you wold need it" in regards to the wheat crop. He talks again of the fight between Peter Burton and Michael Alewine and diminishes the severity of it calling it a little fuss. Fenton then turns to using a war metaphor to describe the dust-up between the two, saying that Alewine "tried to storm Peter Burton's battery but did not make narey charg on it." He then mentions the positons of their pickets. In his closing you can see that Fenton Hall had a touch of the poet in his soul.

South Carolina Adams Run
May the 29, 1863

My deir wife,

I take my pen in hand to let you no that I am well hoping when this coms to hand it may find you an the children all well. I reseved tow leters from you today I reseved the leter that you sent by John Hall he gave it to a man that belong to thir company at Hodges Depot. I reseved one also at the same time by mail. I was glad to here from you. I am sorrow to here that the children is not well. I hop tha will sone git over their bad coles you sed that our weet looks very well. I am glad to hear it. I wish I cood git hom to cut it but thar is no chance to git off now. I no you wold be glad to see me I do not no how you will git the wheet cut. Every body I reckon has as mutch as tha can do at hom but I hop that you will git it cut an saved. I no if you an the children should live you wold need it. I wish this war wold com to a close an us all go hom. I wold like the best in the wirld to be hom with my loving wife an children and I hop an trust to god the time will soon com when I will get to be with you an the children you sed that thir was sum talk of the old men being orderd off but I do hop tha will not have to go. Mary when you pay Wickliffe git that noat I give him what I owe him is on a noat what I owe Wackfield an Bason is on Book account you can pay Dany Murdock. I owe him for sum iron I do not no how mutch it is. I reckon he knows. Our mess is all well but Mickel Alewine, he is at the hospital yet. I do not no whether is iney beter or not. Thir was one man out of our company died today at the hospital his nam was Whitfield Stricklen. He was from Anderson District. Well Mary you wanted to no if Peter Burton an Mikel Alewine had a fight tha had no fight tha had a litel fuss. Michel Alewine tried to storm Peter Burton's battery but did not make narey charg on it. I think tha will git right we had a heap of rain yesterday an las night an it looks like it will rain more. I am sorrow to hear that Stevens regment had los thir men. I heird that Captain Hill company was neirley all taken prisoners if tha ar taken it is beter than to hear of them being killed. Thir is no news mutch here to write everything is still here. Mary I fourgoton to tel you that I oad R. T. Tucker a litel it is a litel note that I give him for sum sewing but I want you to keep anuf of money to by what you need. I will give you the names of our picket portes. I will commence at the nies one to Charleston an go west first lerochers; litel Briton; white point; Edestow ferey; Pineburey; grimbels; Willtown. I will drop a few mor lines in the morning as I have wrote all that I can think of now.

May the 30, it is still cloudy an looks like it will rain mor today. You sed that you wanted me to git a feurlow if I cood an com hom to cut the wheet if thir was iney chance to git hom to cut it I wold com. Mary I want to no how mutch ground was sewd in wheet an how mutch of that old ground was sewd. I want to no if you got the yale wheet an the white wheet boath sewd, let me no if you have iney garden comin on an how the potatos com up. I am about out of sumthing to write. I paid tow dolars a quivar for this paper that I am a writing on. I sent to Charleston by Captain Miot for it. I will have to close for the want of sumthing to write. Give my best respects to all of the frends so nothing more at present, but I still remain your loving husband til deth.

Fenton Hall To his loving wife an children Mary Jane Hall.

When this you see remember me with my loving wife an children I want to be. Mary Jane, Essa an Thomas Hall

Fenton wrote Mary Jane again on June 4, 1863, from camp in Adams Run, South Carolina. The children were well again. There is mention of a raid by Union forces on Pocotaligo, South Carolina, about 40 miles from his location. Fenton and Daniel Boyd were at that time still talking of trying to get Daniel transferred to the Sixth South Carolina Cavalry.

Camp Adams Run
Thursday June the 4

My deir wife,

I seet myself to drop you a few lines to let you no that I am well hoping when this coms to hand it may find you an the children well. I reseved your kind leter today was glad to hear that you was all well there is no news mutch to write to you it is reported here that the yankes com out down about Pocotaligo an burnt a good meney houses an destroyed all thir provishion an captured a good meney nigros the report ses that tha took one thousand negros. This was don las Monday. Mary I reseved leter today from Daniel Boyd, it was wrout the 30 of May. He was well he sed that tha was under marchin orders he sed it was reported this that the yankes was all goin west. He still right like he wold like to com here if he cood git a exchang. There is a man heir ses that he will go thar an take his plase if he cood git off. Daniel ses tha lost everything tha had ondly what tha had on thar back. I wish Daniel cood git heir. I will write him a leter tomorrow if I am not on gard tha keep ous bisey heir sumtimes on picket three or fore dais ham running. Mary you sed to tel Peter Burton that Felix Burton was about today. Peter heird yesturday that he was ded. Our mess is all well but Mickel Alewine, he is still at the hospital. He walked up heir yesturday to camp. It is about three hundred yards from camp to the hospital. John Hall got here night before last. You sed that you wanted to no what tha had don with James Rampy. He is still in the guardhouse. He has plenty of compney in thar with him his brouther Frank was down hear the outher day to see him. James peirs to be very well satisfied. Tha have not cortmartel him yet

Well Mary I have just undon the pants that you sent to me. I did not no thar was iney tobacco in them. I found the tobacco in them I have sum that you sent to me before. Well Mary we have bin paid of this evening. I have paid W. N. Hall all that I owe him but one dolar. I have forty dollars but I have to pay James Taggret out of it yet. I owe him sum thirty or thirty five dollars yet. My horse is out in a paster . Thar was a good meney of ous took our horses out to the paster. Tha ar in the charg of a old niger we have to pay him tow dollars a month a pese. W. N. Hall tooke his hors out thar today. He sed that my hors looks sum beter than he did my hors has bin out thar neirley a month. I am neirley out of sumthing to write. I am sorrow to heir of Captin Hix Company A giting cut up so I am afraid tha will be cut up a heap wirses sum of thes times thar. I have never heard Davis sence he lef heir. I will send sum of my close hom the first chance I git. I am glad to heir that you have got your corn clen. I will write a few mor lines in the morning.

June the 5, well Mary I am well this morning. Thar is nothing new this morning I wish I was at hom with you an the children. I have not got Janes palmetto yet. Mary wold have tried to get you sum an sent it to you but I did not no that you cared iney thing about it let me no if you want iney give my respects to all inquiring friends. I will close for this time so nothing mor at present but I stil remain your loving husband.

Fenton Hall to Mary Jane Hall

When this you see remember me with my loving wife an children I want to be

---

Next Daniel wrote his father from Culpeper on June 8, 1863. The Seventh South Carolina had left Fredericksburg on June 3 and had arrived in Culpeper on June 7. He reports that they were only to stay there a short time and word in camp was that they would soon depart for Pennsylvania.

Cullpeper C. H.

June the 8, 1863

Dear father,

I take this opertunity to drop you a few lines to let you know how I am getting along. I am well at this time and hope when these few lines reaches you they may find you all well. I have no news of importance to rite to you. We left Fredericksburg on the third and got to Cullpeper on the 7th. We have stopt hear to cook a few rashings as we got orders to cook three days rashing it is reported hear that we ar going to pennsilvania but for my part I don't know wher we will go cos the yanks hav left Fredericksburg and ar going to manassas and ar fortifying their. I hear that General Hill gave them another whipping at Fredericksburg but I can't say wheather it is so or not. I can't tell you wher we wil go to but I think we wil go to Warrenton, Va. I think we will half to fight before long.

I received a letter from Mary yesterday. I was glad to hear from home. I thought I wold rite you a few lines to let you know wher I am for I don't know when I will hav the chance to rite again for I don't know wher I wil be in a weak from now. I will rite every chance I get. I want you to rite to every chance you get. Wheather I rite or not. Rite soon as you get this and give me all the news. Tell Mrs. Alewine that James is well. I must bring my short leter to a close you must excuse my short letter. So nothing more at present. Rite soon and give all the news. So fare well for the present.

D. Boyd to Robert Boyd

The next surviving letter was not written until August 29, 1863. It was composed in the hospital in Petersburg by Daniel Boyd and sent to his father. Much had happened to the warriors since then.

Fenton Hall had been killed July 10 in a skirmish at Willtown Bluff near Charleston, South Carolina. Company G — along with Companies B and D — had acted as support for the Washington Artillery. There the artillery engaged an armed Federal steamer, the John Adams, and two smaller boats, the transport Enoch Dean and the tug Governor Milton. They sank the Governor Milton in the battle.[19]

On the afternoon of July 9, 1863, 250 black soldiers with the First South Carolina U. S. Troops departed on the three boats: the John Adams — an armed ferry boat steamer carrying two Parrott guns, a 20-pounder and a 10-pounder along with two howitzers; the Enoch Dean — a transport with one 10-pound Parrott gun and a small howitzer; and the Governor Milton — a tugboat armed with two 12-pound Armstrong guns. They were headed up the South Edisto River, then also known as the Pon Pon River, with the goal of burning a rail road bridge about 30 miles up the river. They travelled under a dense fog which made their journey difficult, but also shielded their movements from the Confederate pickets set up along the river. About 4 A.M. they anchored at Willtown Bluff near the Morris Plantation. There they found the bluff defended only by the Chestnut Artillery and a handful of cavalry. The Confederate guards spotted the encroaching federals at sunrise and engaged them. The outnumbered battery commanded by Lieutenant Thomas White was soon forced to retreat leaving the bluff to the Union troops.[20]

Colonel Hugh Kerr Aiken ordered 50 of his Sixth South Carolina Cav-

alry to support the force at Willtown Bluff under Lieutenant Colonel L. P. Miller. The remainder followed under Major Thomas Ferguson. Aiken deployed his entire force against the Yankees on Willtown Bluff where they skirmished throughout the day. When the tide became high enough for the John Adams to proceed, it was ordered forward. However it ran aground on its first attempt, becoming hopelessly stuck. The Milton and the Dean were able to press on without the Adams. Further upstream, the Chestnut Artillery under Lieutenant Thomas White had reformed near the Barnwell Plantation and subjected the Dean to a heavy fire. The guns of the two boats finally driving White's battery back. The Dean kept running aground, but managed to push up the river until it finally became stuck about two miles short of the bridge they wished to destroy. The Milton was ordered to continue without them.[21]

At a point opposite Dr. Joseph Edward Glover's plantation, about a quarter mile from the bridge, the Milton encountered a battery of Walter's Light Battery which was part of the Washington Light Artillery under the command of Lieutenant Samuel Gilman Horsey. The battery subjected it to a furious fire and disabled the engine of the Milton. The Milton — now 30 miles upstream from the mouth — attempted to float back down river to safety. At this point Colonel Aiken ordered the Marion Artillery to reinforce White at Gibbe's Plantation, where they attacked the Dean and the Milton as they moved back downriver. Under fire, the Milton again ran aground. The Adams had managed to dislodge and was now moving freely again. The Dean had worked its way back down to Willtown Bluff to attempt to pick up the federal infantry there. The Adams moved upstream to the aid of the Milton, but was unable to free it. Subsequently the Milton was abandoned and set afire to prevent the Confederates from capturing it. At sunset Colonel Aiken ordered the Sixth South Carolina Cavalry to move on Willtown Bluff to find it abandoned by the enemy. A section of the Sixth pursued the federals downstream with part of the Chestnut Light Artillery to a point below Morris's Mill, but to little effect.[22]

Colonel Hugh Kerr Aiken was a brother of Colonel D. Wyatt Aiken of the Seventh South Carolina. He was born on July 5, 1822, in Winnsboro, South Carolina, and like his brother attended Mt. Zion Academy and South Carolina College. Prior to the war Hugh K. Aiken had been elected major general, commanding the state militia. Aiken would remain in command of the Sixth as they moved to the Army of Northern Virginia under Wade Hampton's cavalry corps and General Matthew C. Butler's brigade. Aiken would distinguish himself at Trevillian Station on June 11, 1864, in a struggle that was often hand to hand. Aiken was shot through the body while leading a charge. The bullet grazed one of his lungs. The severity of his wound forced the Confederate troopers to leave him in the hands of the enemy. The Yankee *surgeons considered his situation hopeless and also left him behind. Friends of Aiken's found him and removed him to Louisa Court House to the home of a Mr. Hunter who frequently took in wounded Confederate soldiers. Aiken would partially recover and was offered softer duty in Richmond due to his health. He would decline opting instead to return to the field where he would continue commanding the Sixth. Aiken was witness to the death of Preston Hampton, son of General Wade Hampton. He would briefly command the brigade as they moved back to South Carolina in the wake of Sherman's march to the sea. On February 27, 1865, Butler ordered Aiken down Lynch's Creek to determine if any of the Federals had crossed into Darlington, South Carolina. During this mission Colonel Hugh K. Aiken was mortally wounded and died in the arms his nephew, William Cloud Aiken, who served as his courier.*[23]

Aiken's wife, Mary Rees Gayle Aiken, was a daughter of the former governor of Alabama, John Gayle. In 1837, while Gayle was serving in the U.S. Congress, Mary's favor was pursued by a number of army officers. Among them was a young lieutenant named William Tecumseh Sherman. It was during this time that she met and married Aiken. When Sherman's forces were passing near the Aiken home in Winnsboro, the general stopped by to pay his respects. Mary met him on the front porch, unwilling to allow him into her home. Sherman spoke of happier days in Washington, D.C., and expressed regret for the suffering inflicted on the South during the war. It was a short time thereafter that Aiken was killed. While examining his remains for intelligence, the Yankee soldiers found his final letter to Mary on his body. Some time around 1880, General Sherman would give this letter to his brother, Senator John Sherman who in turn delivered it to U.S. Congressman D. Wyatt Aiken, Hugh Aiken's brother. So 15 years after it was written, Colonel Aiken's last letter to Mary found its way home to her.[24]

All Confederate records had listed Fenton Hall as having been captured, but no record could be located of his being taken prisoner or his body being recovered. It is likely that he was mortally wounded and died in the hands of the federal army. Also, being captured by an enemy who was under heavy fire and in the process of withdrawing, it is entirely possible that the federals were in no mood to deal with handling prisoners and simply shot him. In any event, his remains probably rest in an unmarked grave — quite likely a mass grave at that — like so many of his brothers in arms.

Fenton was the eldest of the letter writers, having perished in the defense of his country at the age of 29. The man who exuded such warmth in his letters to Mary Jane and often lamented that his greatest desire was to return home would never see Diamond Hill again. His family would not know his ultimate fate. On Oct. 23, 1917, at the age of 85, Mary Jane Boyd Hall would *state in a Confederate widow's pension application that Fenton "was captured and never heard of any mor."*

Days prior to the loss of Fenton, the Boyd family had nearly lost another son. Daniel sustained a severe wound to his thigh at Gettysburg on the second day of the battle, July 2.

The official record states that Company D returned from picket duty at Guilford, Pennsylvania — about twenty miles from Gettysburg — on July 1 and joined their brigade at neighboring Fayetteville, Pennsylvania, then marched across the mountain at Cashtown Gap about 2 A.M. July 2. It further states that the company "Took our position and participated in the hottest engagement of the war 3 & 4 days."[25]

On the second day of battle, the Seventh South Carolina, as a part of Kershaw's Brigade and McLaws Division, came down from Seminary Ridge to support Hood's troops in the Wheatfield around 4:30 in the afternoon. The Seventh under Colonel D. Wyatt Akien — along with the Third South Carolina — were formed on the right wing of Kershaw's Brigade. With the regimental officers leading on foot, Kershaw's soldiers — about 1,800 strong — advanced across the field and over the Emmitsburg Road under heavy fire; then wheeled left parallel to the Wheatfield Road. Heading toward the stoney hill to the left and rear of the Rose barn intending to swing the left wing against the left and rear of the Peach Orchard, a storm of shot and shell cut down 400 of their men. At Kershaw's orders, the Third passed between the Rose barn and house and the Seventh advanced to the right of the house. After clearing the farmyard, the Seventh and Third descended into marshy ground along Plum Run in front of the gap between the stony hill and Rose's Woods. Here the two regiments became bunched together and Kershaw ordered Aiken to move the Seventh to the right; once untangled they were ordered to attack the federal positions on the hill. The South Carolinians closed in so close they could see the expressions of the canoneers. As success seemed assured, a miscommunication occurred that proved disasterous.

Someone, apparently misinterpreting Kershaw's shouted orders to Aiken "and construed them wrongly, shouted a command that turned the well-disciplined infantry toward the right flank and away from the guns." Before this could be corrected, the Federal guns pounded the Seventh and the Third, destroying their effectiveness. Kershaw would bemoan that "hundreds of the bravest and best men of Carolina fell, victims of this fatal blunder."[26]

The Third and Seventh then drove the Federal troops from the stony hill and Kershaw directed the Third's left wing against Union batteries on the Wheatfield Road just west of the stony hill. The Third's right wing and Aiken's Seventh were in the woods on the hill. The Federal troops had fallen

*back to their north. Other Federal brigades advanced to the South Carolini-
ans' right. The right wing of the Seventh was pulled back to face them. Kershaw placed Lieutenant Colonel Elbert Bland in command of this action.
Kershaw had just arrived back at the stony hill from directing the actions
of his other regiments as the Union troops halted about 200 yards to Bland's
front where they fired a volley then assaulted his position. Kershaw would
comment, "They were handsomely received and entertained by this veteran
regiment, which long kept them at bay in its front."*

*The Federal brigades pressed the attack; the South Carolinians holding
the high ground, many firing from behind boulders in the western part of
the woods. They were far enough up the slope that their feet were at about
the same level as the attacking Yankee troops' heads. Strangely the angle
worked against the Seventh, requiring them to expose themselves above the
tops of the rocks in order to fire on the enemy. This allowed the Federal soldiers to get in particularly close. The Federals worked their way into a gap
in a hundred yard long ravine along their right side and forced the Seventh's
right wing back toward its left wing. Despite attempts to reinforce them
with the Second South Carolina, the Seventh finally was forced to retire.
Kershaw wrote, "These men were brave veterans who had fought from Bull
Run to Gettysburg and knew the strength of their position, and held it as
long as it was tenable." He ordered Colonel Aiken to retreat across Plum
Run's marsh and position the Seventh behind a wall near Rose's farmyard.*[27]

*Colonel Aiken's earlier wound would flare back up and prove to be too
much for him. Aiken was reassigned as commandant of troops and defenses
in Macon, Georgia. He remained in this position until July 21, 1864, when
he would be retired under the Invalid Officers Act.*[28]

*Daniel tells of being wounded in the right thigh near the knee with
buckshot. Since he gives no details of the incident surrounding his wounding,
it is unknown at what point in this action he was wounded. The nature of
the wound would possibly indicate that it likely happened during the latter
part of the action on the stony hill. The earlier mass of woundings seemed
to have been due to artillery as the Seventh and Third South Carolina Regiments were advancing on and capturing the stony hill.*

*After the third day of battle, General Robert E. Lee would withdraw
his army south back into Virginia. The conditions of many of the wounded
were too dire to evacuate them home with Lee's Army of Northern Virginia,
so they were left behind for the enemy to tend to. This was the case with
Daniel. Records indicate that Daniel was transferred to the Provost Marshall
then was sent to DeCamp General Hospital on Davids' Island in Long Island
Sound off the coast of New Rochelle, New York. He was paroled from the
hospital on August 24 and turned over to the General Hospital at Culpeper
Court House, where he stayed until August 26. On August 28, he was admit-*

ted into the Episcopal Church Hospital in Williamsburg, Virginia.[29] *In this letter he recounts his wounding and treatment while being held prisoner.*

Petersburg Va
August the 29 1863

Dear father,

I have the pleasure to drop you a few lines to let you know that I am still on the land of the living and ar getting a long pretty well. I was wounded at the battle of Gettysburg Pensylvania on the back end of July. I was wounded in the right thigh near my knee with a buck shot. I cold not walk eny for a weak. I was left to the mercy of the enemy. I was taken prisoner. I staid their until the eighteenth and then I was sent to Baltimore. We stayed ther one day and knight and then we was sent to new york. I was put on Davids Island a bout 80 miles from new york and their we was kept until the 24 of August. I was peroled and sent to Petersburg va. I am in the South Carolina hospital at Petersburg. My wound is doing tolerable well. It still running yet. It wil bee som time before it wil be well. It is wers than it was three weaks ago. The Yankees treated us very kind. Was at the best hospital in the United States. Ther was 26 hundred of us their. I met up with som of my old friends their. Thomas Hampton and John McCury and J M Hill is all their. They hav all lost a leg. Hampton is nearly well. McCury was very sick and I dont think he ever will get well. His leg has not heald eney yet. Hill was nearly well but he fell down and hurt it but I think wil soon get well.

Hill requested me to rite to you to let his sis no how he is. He is a brother to Robert Bells wife. You can tel them that he is getting along very well. I left him at Davids Island new york. You can tel Hamptons mother that he nearly well. I think he wil get home soon. McCury has the fever. Their was but one of my company with me that was B F Hutchison. He is nearly well. There is a great meney more ther that you no. S W Calaham is dead and John William Wakefield is dead. He was wounded. I recon you have herd from the rest since I hav. I hav not herd the regment since they left me. I am going to try to get a furlow to go home. The Yankees burnt all my cloths and shoos but they giv new ons in their place but they sent me back barfooted. I got a pair to day. I had to pay 25 dollars for them. Every thing is high hear. I am goin to an other hospital at Farmville Va. I want to get home but I am afraid I never will get home again. I want to hear from home. I want you to right soon as you get this and giv me all the news. Direct your letter to Petersburg

Va S C hospital ward third. I cant go to the regment til I am exchanged. This leaves me tolerable well and hope when you get this it may find you all well. I hope to hear from you soon. Nothing more.

Daniel Boyd to Robert Boyd

The next letter was written to Daniel Boyd on September 30, 1863, from the camp of the Nineteenth South Carolina Infantry near the Chicka-mauga battlefield. The author was John Calvin Alewine — brother of James H. Alewine. Due to his wound at Gettysburg, Daniel had finally gotten the furlough he had so long sought. So Daniel was not there to witness the loss of their beloved commander, Lt. Col. Elbert Bland, who was killed during the Battle of Chickamauga.

Alewine talks of the battles and movements around the Chickamauga campaign. Many local individuals are mentioned, including his brother James Alewine and Fenton Hall's brother Davis.

Camp near Chicamauga Tenn.
Sept the 30 1863

Dear Freind,

I take my pen in hand to drop you a few lines in answer to your kind leter that I recivd to day. I was glad to hear from you and to hear that you was getin well and had got back hom one time mor. Theas few lines leaves me in good health and I hope tha may find you injoying the same blessing of health. I have not got mutch news to rit at this time. The yanks is still in Chattanooga but I think tha want to git out of thar if tha can. Our men has got them surrounded on their side of the river but our cavrly is gon round in tha rear but I am a fraid tha cant do mutch with them for the mountains. Well Daniel, Brouther James com to see me yesterday. I was glad to see him. He looks very well but it is a nuff to kill a mule to stay in this war as long as you and him has been in it. When you com out hear if we ar close to geather you must com and see me. I cant git to leave my wagon to go to James Regt. You must go and see all of the girles befor you leav home. I have bean trying to git home for a long time but I cant git of. You must go and see sweat Linda for me. H Hall and S T McAdams com thrue the fit saife. I will give you the naimes of the wounded in my company. Tha was non kill in my company. Capt was wounded. Lut. Carlisle wounded. He lost his rit leg. He is a brouther to that Carlisle in your com. Sargent Jordan, Sargent H Wilson,

Isaac Canedy, Lou Young, Moss Bell. I beleave them was all that was wounded. You can tell H Hall and S T McAdams people that tha ar well and harty. Davis Hall Regt is out hear but I have not sean him yet. The Yankees sent thar ambulances after thos wounded. Our men pairold them and let them go back. Long Strates men surprised the Yankees when tha sean them in thos blue coates and pant. It is very dry and dusty out hear but it look like it will rain to knight. I am out of nues to rit so excus my short leter.

Tell Andrew to fly a round the girles. Direct your leter to John C Alewine Com G 19 Regt S C V Chattanooga Tennesee.

So good evening to you all.

John C Alewine

1864

The next surviving letter was not written until February 16, 1864.
Daniel Boyd was writing his father from Bristol, Tennessee. Andrew had
joined the Confederate army on February 10[1] and was now en route with
Daniel back to the Seventh South Carolina, which, as part of Longstreet's
Corps, were in winter quarters in eastern Tennessee. Daniel states in his
letter that he understood they were at New Market, Tennessee. There Andrew
would become a member of Company D along with Daniel who was seven
years his senior. They were now the last two remaining Boyd brothers. The
others, along with Fenton Hall, were now dead.

In this letter, Daniel briefly details their travels including being robbed
and experiencing railroad derailments.

February the 16 1864

Dear father,

I take this oppertunity to drop you a few lines to let you no how
we ar getting a long. We ar well at this time. We had to ly over at Collumbia one knight and day to get Andrews papers but I got him through
with out eney truble. We hav not got to our regiment yet. We hav bin
eight day on the road and hav one hundred ten miles to go yet. The cars
riun of the track too or three time but did not eney one get hurt. We hav
had to ly by too or three days. The cars missed connection every place
we change but one. We ar at Bristole Tennessee. We wil leave hear to
morrow. We lost our bag of pervision. Som body stole it at Raleigh. We
hav a days rashions to day. Longstreet is at New Market. He is moving
on to wards the enemy. They ar excspecting a fight there soon. The
weather is very cold hear. It snowed al day yesterday. The ground covered
one foot deap. Well I believ I have rote all I can at this time. I wil rite as
soon as I get to camp. I wil close for the present. I forever remains your
son.

D Boyd to R Boyd

*By February 21, 1864, Daniel and Andrew were at New Market, Ten-
nessee, from which Daniel again wrote their father. They had arrived on
the February 18 to find the Seventh in winter quarters, where Daniel reports
they were well fed and well supplied. Despite being in winter quarters,
rumors of moving soon were rampant. Daniel reports that desertion rates
were high at that time and that the countryside in which they found themselves was highly Unionist. He reports of the deserters that, "They ar a shooting them every weak or too."*

Camp near New Market Tennessee
February the 21 1864

Dear father,

I take this oppertunity to drop you a few lines to let you no how
we are getting a long. We ar both well at this time. We landed in camp
on the 18th. I found the boys all well and doing well. They are in winter
quarters. They ar all looking well. We ar getting plenty to eat now. The
boys looks fat and sassy. The regiment is larger than it has bin for the
last year. We hav 20 men in our company for duty. Every day the men
is doing better than I expected to find them. They have good shoos and
most of them hav tolerable good cloths. There is som of them that is
nearly naked but not meney of them in that fix. The men is in good
spirits and ar ready for a fight eney time. We ar expecting to move eney
minute. I do not think that we wil stay hear long. There is som talk of
us going back to wards bristole but I hope that they wil stay hear til
could weather is over. We hav had som of the couldest that I ever saw. I
thought I wold freez to death fore I got hear.

They ar fur lowing a great meney men hear. J H Masters started
home yesterday. I wil get a fur low be fore long. I hav got it rote out. I
hav not sent it up yet. I wil send it up in the morning. I saw James Little
to day. He is well and harty. You can tell Miss Stoks that James is well.
I herd from him to day. You can tel L Murdock that if he wants to com
hear he can git hear with out eney truble. I wold like to get an other
recruit. I think that I wil be home in a month or so. Andrew is very well
satisfied with camps. Tell James Crowther that James Alewine wants him
to com hear and let him go hom. We wil take all the recruits that we can
get. There is a great meney men disserting from hear. They ar a shooting
them every weak or too. The peoples in this country is all union men.
Well I believ I hav rote about all that I can at this time. We wil close for

this time. Direct your letter to 7 Regt S C V Kershaws Bregaid Longstreets Company. Rit as soon as you can and giv me all the news. Far well.

D Boyd to R Boyd

On March 17, 1864, the first letter from Andrew in the collection was written. He lists the location as "East Tennessee." He tells of his unit marching within four or five miles of Bulls Gap, Tennessee, the previous Monday expecting a battle, but that the enemy turned back upon their arrival.

Even though Daniel's service record does not reflect it, he apparently had gotten the furlough he had spoken of in the last letter. Andrew talks of Daniel being home with their father and sends along several messages from friends and neighbors to their families.

East Tennessee
March 17 1864

Dear father,

I take this oppertunity of ansuring your kind letter that I received this morning dated the 6 of March. I was glad to hear from you. This leaves me well and harty and I hope these lines may find you in the enjoyment of the same. I am tolerable well satisfied better than I expected to be. We marcht last Monday in 4 or 5 miles of Bulls gap to meat the yanks but when we got down there they turned back. It is said they ar back at Marestown. They onley made a cavalry rade and then went back. I cant tell whether they will attack us or not. We have a strong forse down near the gap. Some thinks we will go back to Greenville in a few days. You may tele Daniel we ar not living as well as we was when we at Greenville for we cant get chickens and gees as we did up there for this forest is entirely eat out. Me and T C Milford and P Huckaby went out yesterday to get dinner. We went about 5 miles before we get it and it wasent mutch when we got it. We got bread and dryed beef the tufest you ever saw and they charge us $2.00 a peace but they caud not change our money and we onley pade them a dollar a peace and that was a naugt. I hav not got mutch nuse to rite. Daniel can tell you more than I can rite. Tell Dan that J Alewine says to fly round the girls for him and give them his respects. Tell his mother he is well and harty. You rote to now I am most with Danal can tell you. If you sea any of T C Milfords folks tell them that he is well and harty. At the request of T C Milford he wishes you an Daniel to sea T B Milford and tell him that T C want him to sea to the paying of his tacks. He says that his sisters has got soame of his money. He can get it from them and it will ablidge him vary mutch. I will close as I have rote all the nuse I can think of. So nothing more but remains your true son till death. So farewell.

Andrew Boyd to Robert Boyd

Andrew writes again on April 22, 1864. The Seventh had now moved to Gordonsville, Virginia. Daniel had not yet returned to the camp. Andrew said that he was expected in another week. Andrew indicates that the Seventh South Carolina had termporarily moved to the brigade of Brigadier General Samuel McGowan — a fellow Abbeville County resident who practiced law in the county seat of Abbeville before the war.[2]

Camp near Gordonville Va
April 22 1864
Dear father,

I seat myself to write to you. I have not recd eny letter as yet from you or Brother Daniel in some time. I hope to get one soon. News is scarce. My health is very good. We hav got back to the Army of the Potomac. We landed at Scharlote on the 19th. We hav moov near Gordonsville. We will probla stay hear a week ar more as we are cleaning up camp. That is if Genl Grant dosent rouse us up. We had a heave snow storm on the 16th and 17th. That was while we was near Bristol Tenn but ther is a grate change in the weather since we came hear. It is like spring but two or three hundreds miles make a diferance. It seems as Corps is known far and wide. When we came to Scharlotsvil we wer met by the ladys of the town to cheer us and the yong girls from the coledge came running to meet us. We are ruff weatherbeeten lookin fellowes dirty and raged but the womans and yong girls seems to say stand of you clean shirts hospitle rats the town is fild with such but a few more week will tell the news whether we shall bee free or fight a nother year.

Father I would like to bea at home to healp you. I think how loansom you must bea no one to help you plow or feed the stock in mornings. Brother Daniel will leave you soon but our Cuntry call us for healp and we have to obey. I hope you ma have the good shower to help make corne which will doo mor good then me. I will look for Dan to bea comeing back in a nother week and he will tell me all of the news. I wish it was so that he could stay and help you make a crop. We have got better rashions since we have come hear. We draw very good corne meal bacon rice coffee shugar soap. We can live very well an thas if they continew to ishue such rashions. I shall go to see some of my old friends if we stay hear longenouff in McGowens Brig. I hear that they are camp near Orenge C H. Every thing is qite backward hear. Wheet begins to make a show. People is commence planting corne. I will close my few lines. Write soon. Give me the news. I ever remains yor truly son till death.

Andrew Boyd to Robert Boyd

The next letter — dated April 28, 1864, from Gordonsville — is unsigned. The content and references strongly indicate that it was written by Daniel Boyd and is addressed "Dear father." He says that he arrived back with his regiment on April 26.

Camp near Gordonsville Va
April the 28 1864

Dear father,

I take the opertunity of riting you of a few lines to let you no that I hav arrived at the regt safe on the twenty sixth. I found all my mess well and doing well. Andrew is well and harty. He stands the camp fine and is very well satisfied. He looks as well as he did when he lef home. James Alewine is well and harty. T C Willford is well but he looks rather thin. He grieves about home too much. The health of the men in our regimen is not as as it has bin for som time past. There is not much news as boring here. It is the opinion of the men that we will fight soon but as for myself I cant tell. It looks very much like we will half to do something soon. The Yankees is a bout 20 miles from here. I dont think that we wil stay here long. It is thought that we will go to Richmond or to Fredericksburg but it is uncirtin wher we wil be sent too. We wil half to go wher the most fighting wil be don.

Their is a great meney troops coming her from South Carolina an other places. I met up with a great meney of my aold friends in Collumbia. I saw W N Hall and a good meney others from our neghborhoods. I started to rite a letter when I was at Collumbia biut cars was about leaving and I did not get through. I sent them papers too all four of you. I got then for four dollars a peace. I sent the receipts and one dollar in money in the letter that I sent. You may pay Mr Crowther and unkle

William one dollar apeace. I wold hav sent it to you but I did not hav the chang. I did not get eney money at Collumbia. I wil draw som in a day or too. The regiment has not bin payed of yet. Money is the scercest that I ever saw it in camp but it aint much use here for there aint eneything to buy. We get plenty to eat. We get corn meal bacon coffee and sheugar. We wil live for a while. I got my box through safe. Me and Hagis come to geather all the way. I wil send this with J T Campbell as he is going home. Well I believ I hav rote about all that I can at this time.

[Unsigned presumed to be Daniel Boyd to Robert Boyd]

The next letter was written May 24, 1864 by Andrew from the hospital in Lynchburg, Virginia. He had been wounded in the Battle of the Wilderness on May 6.

On May 4, Grant's army crossed the Rapidan River at Germania and Ely's Fords. They began moving towards the turnpike coming out of Orange Court House and leading to Fredericksburg through the Wilderness. The first engagements began on May 5 along the turnpike and one mile away on the plank road. At nightfall both armies had held their own and halted hostilities for the night. Longstreet's Corps, including Kershaw's Brigade with the Seventh South Carolina, was not involved. They had received orders to march early that morning; having received reports of firing coming from the Confederate cavalry skirmishing with Grants army at the river fords along the Rapidan.[3]

They marched all day along unused roads and through fields and thickets "taking every near cut possible" to reinforce their comrades in Ewell's and Hill's Corps. Pushing through barely pausing for a rest, they had marched 28 miles by 5 in the afternoon. They stopped there with orders to march again at midnight. Here Daniel, Andrew and their friend James Alewine would have stretched out on the ground, not even bothering to pitch a tent, as did the rest of Kershaw's men. They moved out promptly at midnight as ordered. In the dark they moved along "blind roads, overgrown by underbrush, through fields that had lain fallow for years, now studded with bushes and briars." The men floundered and fell as they moved along, often wandering off the path and having to backtrack to find their way again. The exhausted troops reached the plank road at daybreak. From there they headed down the plank road. Kershaw's Brigade took the lead with the Seventh South Carolina being the third regiment in the line behind the Second and the Third. They marched at a quick pace for two miles down the plank road passing Hill's Field Infirmary along the way. The wounded from the previous day's battle were being treated. They prepared for battle here with 40 rounds in their cartridge boxes and twenty more in their pockets.[4]

Upon hearing firing of muskets, they picked up their steps and hastened to the crest of a small hill and deployed across the road. The Second South Carolina set up on the left of the road and the Third South Carolina on the right. The Seventh was positioned to the right of the Third. Kershaw's Brigade with Wofford's Brigade of Georgians forming to their right in the undergrowth beside the road had not fully formed into line of battle before "a perfect hail of bullets came flying overhead and through our ranks." Heth's and Wilcox's battle weary men retreated through their lines. They had held on from the previous day's fighting, nearly out of ammunition, lying on the battlefield waiting to be relieved. Under the impression that they would be relieved before daylight, they had not dug in or constructed breastworks as Ewell had. Now they were in a dangerous position. The enemy, however, had reformed their lines and thrown up breastworks that now lay 200 yards to the front of the Boyd brothers and the other unsuspecting Confederates. Hancock ordered his Federal soldiers to advance at sunrise. After a feeble defense, Wilcox's and Heth's skirmish lines gave way and the Yankee forces broke through to Kershaw's lines. The South Carolinians and Georgians were unprepared for this onslaught. Some were cooking a hasty breakfast, others were still asleep. Bullets flying all around, General Kershaw himself dashed to the front of the column. "[H]is eyes flashing fire, sitting his horse like a centaur — that surpurb style as Joe Kershaw only could," wrote D. Augustus Dickert, Kershaw's biographer. Kershaw addressed his men saying, "Now my old brigade, I expect you to do your duty." His men seemed greatly inspired and determined to not let their general down, knowing that his ascendency to major general commanding the division would be assured by their good performance.[5]

Under a heavy fire they marched down a gentle slope into a withering fire from the enemy who was still concealed from their view. While men collapsed all about them, they were ordered to hold their fire. As they neared the bottom of the slope, Kershaw's Confederates came into full view of the enemy, lying just 40 yards ahead of them. The battle was on in full force now with Kershaw's guns blazing away face to face against Hancock's. New troops were being added to the fray to replace the fallen. "Men rolled and writhed in their last death struggle; wounded men groped their way to the rear, being blinded by the stifling smoke." Many officers were killed or wounded. Colonel Franklin Gaillard, the commander of the Second and Colonel James D. Nance of the Third were both killed. Captain E. J. Goggans, commanding the Seventh was wounded as was Colonel John D. Kennedy, who was commanding Kershaw's Brigade that day. The battle continued unabated, however. "It seemed for a time as if the whole Federal army was upon us — so thick and fast came the death dealing missles." Kershaw's ranks were being decimated by the fire, neither side backing down. To Kershaw's right was Humphrey's men and to their left were Hood's old Texans. It was reported to General James Longstreet the "deadly throes of battle" in which Kershaw's Brigade was engaged. To relieve this, Longstreet ordered a flanking movement against the enemy. Four brigades were ordered around to attack the left flank of Hancock's men. Kershaw's Brigade remained at the front of the enemy. Hancock's men gradually began to retire and Kershaw's Brigade was replaced at the front with Bratton's (Jenkin's old) Brigade. It was during this action that General Robert E. Lee moved up to personally lead Hood's men into the battle. The flanking movement was succeeding and Hancock's men were soon put to flight. Generals Longstreet, Kershaw and Micah Jenkins rode down the plank road with their staffs. Through the heavy smoke, a Virginia regiment attempting to cross the road to rejoin their brigade opened up on a Federal brigade just as Longstreet's assembledge crossed between the two. General Jenkins was killed and General Longstreet fell seriously wounded. Several from their staffs were also killed or wounded.[6]

Kershaw's Brigade was credited by many for saving Lee's army that day. Captain J. F. Caldwell of McGowan's Brigade paid tribute to their actions: "Kershaw's Brigade was extended across the road, and received the grand charge of the Federals. Members of that brigade have told me that the enemy rushed upon them at the double quick huzzahing loudly." Wilcox's and Heth's brigades were plunged in disarray. "Yet Kershaw's Brigade bore themselves with illustrious gallantry." Not only did they have to deploy under fire, "but when they were formed, to force their way through crowds of flying men, and re-establish their lines. They met Grant's legions, opened a cool and murderous fire upon them, and continued it so steadily and resolutely, that the latter were compelled to give back. Here I honestly believe the Army of Northern Virginia was saved!"[7]

The brigade surgeon, Dr. Salmond, had established his field hospital near where the fighting had begun that morning. D. Augustus Dickert — who was wounded in this battle himself — had this to say of the scene: "In the rear of a battlefield are scenes too sickening for sensitive eyes and ears. Here you see men, with leg shattered, pulling themselves to the rear by the strength of their arms alone, or exerting themselves to the utmost to get some place where they will be partially sheltered from the hail of bullets falling all around; men, with arms swinging helplessly by their sides, aiding some comrade worse crippled than themselves; others on the ground appealing for help, but are forced to remain on the field amid all the carnage going on around them, helpless and almost hopeless, until the battle is over, and if still alive, await their turn from the litter-bearers." He says that the next day was devoted to burying the dead "and here lay the dead in greater num-

bers than it was ever my fortune to see, not even before the stone wall at Fredericksburg."[8]

This was the predicament in which Andrew Boyd found himself. In his letter to his father, he gives the exact details of his wound and says that he is otherwise in good health. This letter tells of several of their neighbors who were killed or wounded in the fray.

Lynchburg, Va.: General hospital Ward 3
May the 24, 1864

Dear father,

I sit myself this morning for the purpose of riting you a few lines to let you now that I am in good health but I am wonded. The ball went in close to my back bone an came out just above my hip bone. It is a flesh wond, it did not gow to my insides. My wond is dooing very well. I was wonded the sixth of this month. I have not herd from brother Daniel since the seventh of this month. Their was five wonded the first day we was in the fight. Liutenant Carlile, Liutenant Davis, Bill Campbell, Lockbridge, T. C. Milford was wonded an died the next day. I can not tell you mutch about the fight. I have not herd mutch about the fight since I left. I get very litel news from the army. I think I will get a furlow as soon as the bord meets. Thay ar gowing to meate in a few days. I have met with some of my old friends James Blanchet, John Blanchet, William Campbell. Thay ar all wonded. Whit McCurrie is here sick. I herd that Caton Milford was killed. Now nothing more at present. But remains your son untill death.

Andrew Boyd to Robert Boyd
You nead not rit to me till I rit again to you.

From May 23 through May 26, 1864, following Spottsylvania Court House on May 20, the Seventh was involved in the battle of North Anna River. Colonel Henagan of the Eighth South Carolina was commanding Kershaw's Brigade during this time. Kershaw's adjutant Y. J. Pope said, "How many times, as soldiers, have we crossed this stream, and little did we imagine in crossing that on its banks we would be called upon to meet the enemy.... Soon after [Spottsylvania Court House] General Grant though baffled by its result, renewed his effort to reach Richmond. By a rapid march, General Lee was before Grant's columns at the North Anna River." They had hoped to be attacked there. On the south side of the river along the road leading to Hanover Junction, they completed heavy works while on the north side a fort "of inferior proportions" was built to protect the bridge from raid-

ing parties. All parts of the army had crossed except the Third South Carolina, the James' Battalion and our boys in the Seventh, who had been left
to man the aforementioned fort. Pope said, "We had no idea that anything
serious was intended; but after a while it leaked out that General Lee needed
some time to complete a line of works from one point on the river to another
on the same stream, on the South side, and that it was intended that the
bare handful of men with us were intended to hold the approach to the
bridge in face of the tens of thousands of Grant's army in our front." The
Seventh was stretched thin along the left corner and it was seen that they
could not occupy "even by a thin line" their territory. Artillery support was
promised from the other side of the river.⁹ The attack opened to the right
and the center, but the badly outnumbered Confederates repulsed the attack.
A second attack on the same position was likewise repelled. Then the third
attack was launched against the left of the Seventh's location. Pope wrote,
"and although the Seventh Regiment did its whole duty, gradually our left
was seen to give way." This prompted the enemy to make another attack on
the center and right again, but with no success. With the sun setting and it
appearing likely that the Union troops would soon be in their rear, they
"made a bold dash to cross the river" in their rear bringing down "the
enemy's fire of shot and shell, as well as musketry." They ascended the long
hill on the south side under heavy fire. Once they reformed at the top of the
hill, the soldiers broke the tension with jokes as detailed by Pope. "War has
its humorous as well as its serious side, and many a joke was cracked in battle, or if not mentioned then, the joke was told soon afterwards."¹⁰

Five days later, on May 29, Daniel writes his father from Mechan-
icsville, Virginia. He says he has not heard from Andrew since he was
wounded. He gives details of the Seventh's participation in the Battle of
North Anna River on May 23. Daniel makes an interesting statement at the
end of the letter. He refers to a letter he had just received from his father
bearing unexpected news that he does not expressly elaborate on. He says,
"but you surprised me very much about morning but I hav no objections. I
like for ev one to plas them selves." Could this be the news of Robert Boyd's
marriage to Hannah Crowther? The timing would make sense as now with
Andrew gone to the war, he was probably feeling more alone. Out of his
seven progeny, the only one remaining at home now was Sarah. Perhaps the
solitude while doing the chores alone he once had Andrew to help with turned
his thoughts to remarriage.

Camp Machanicksville
May the 29th 1864
Dear father,

    I take this opportunity of droping you a few lines to let you no that

I am still on the land of the living yet. I am unwell at this time. I have the diarear but I am beter to day. We hav bin I hav bin in line of battle for 20 days. All is quiet to day as far as I no. We hav bin marching and fighting for 23 or four days. The 7 regimen was in a fight on the 23rd. We was left to gauard a bridg across the North Anna River. The Yankees flanked ous on our left. You ought to a saw us running. We only had one place to get out or wade the river. Som went to the bridg and the rest took the river where they com to it.

We lost one man of the company. Eastus Olliver he was wounded. We lost 26 out of the regtment 73 wounded and 13 taken prisoners. Som of the yanks crossed the river after us but they did not get back. We covered the ground with them. We hav had the hardest fighting that we ever had and it aint over yet. I hav not herd from Andrew since he was wounded. J H Alewine is well. All my mess is well and harty for the chance we hav had. Well I believ I wil close. I received a letter the other day. I was glad to hear from home and that you was all wel but you surprised me very much about morning but I hav no objections. I like for ev one to plas them selves.

[Unsigned — Presumedly by Daniel Boyd]

The next letter was written by Daniel to his sisters, Mary Jane and Sarah, on June 9, 1864. He is writing from Gaines Mill, Virginia, where the battle of Cold Harbor had recently taken place. He details the skirmishing and trench warfare following the battle. Daniel was also either unaware of Fenton's fate or was more likely under the assumption that he was a prisoner as he asks his sisters if they had heard anything from him.

Daniel expresses concern at having not heard from Andrew. Unfortunately due to the fighting his regiment was engaged in, Daniel was unaware that his last surviving brother had died from his wounds several days earlier. Andrew Boyd's wounds from the Battle of the Wilderness on May 6, 1864, claimed his life 24 days later on May 30 at the College Hospital in Lynchburg, Virginia.[11] The College Hospital was located at the corner of Wise Street and Twelfth Street. Dr. Edward A. Craighill, a Lynchburg physician assigned as surgeon at the College Hospital, was likely the doctor who attended to Andrew's wounds. There were 50 military surgeons staffing the thirty hospitals in Lynchburg. Dr. Craighill entered the army at the age of 17, making him the youngest physician in the Confederate medical service.[12]

Andrew is buried in the Confederate section of the Old City Cemetery of Lynchburg. Burial records indicate that he was buried on May 31 in a coffin constructed for him that measured 6 feet 3 inches long by 22 inches wide.[13] The excellent records kept of the burials were thanks to the man who almost certainly prepared and buried — or at least oversaw the process — Andrew's remains; George A. Diuguid. Diuguid was the son of Sampson Diuguid, who co-founded the Diuguid Mortuary in 1817. Diuguid, from his workshop, oversaw the preparation of over 3,000 bodies during the war, including the 2,200 Confederates in the cemetery. His meticulous records allowed the removal of the Union prisoners buried there to National cemeteraries or back north following the war. The Diuguid Mortuary continues operation and is the second oldest funeral home in the United States.[14]

Camp near Gaines Mills
June the 9th 1864

Dear sisters,

I seat myself this morning to respond to your kind letter which I have just received dated June the first. I was truly glad to hear from you and that you was all well. This lieves me and James Alewine both well and I hope when thes few lines reaches your home it may find you all well. I hav not herd a word from Andrew since he was wounded. I am very uneasy a bout him but I hope that he is doing better than we think for if eney of you hears from him pleas let me no and let me no how he is. I was very sory to hear of the death of D Cleland and James Millford and James brother. There has bin many a fine fellows fell in the last 40 days to rise no mor. Ther is not a day no not a hour but there is someone falls.

We hav bin fighting this mishin every day since the sixth of May. We ar in line of battle now. We hav bin in line of battle ever since the fight commenced. We ar about three hundred yards from the yanks. We keep up constant fireing at them. I went out on picket yesterday. We was in about 75 yards of the Yankees breast works. I tell you we had to ly lowe for every time they us poke our heads up they wold shoot at us but we returned the same compliment with them. They half to ly lowe as we do. There is not a minute in a day but there is a bullet flying over our head. I long to see the day when this fight is over so we can get some rest. We half to be up half the knight ever knight to watch for the Yankees. I think that their wil be a fight som wher on the line in a day or tow for we cant stay so close to geather with fighting. We hav bin in six or eight battles since I left home. Our boys has bin fighting in most of the fights. We lost ten out of our company. J. S. Gibert got wounded day befor yesterday in the head slightly. I believ I named all the rest my other letters. We hav bin successful in every ingagement. We hav kild and wounded five to one. If they continue to fight us behind our breast wirks we wil whip them ever time. We hav got the 20th Regment in our bregaid. It has twelve hundred men in it. There is a good meney men in it that I know saw James Ashley. He is in it. We seam in great nead of officers in our regment. Their has bin so meny kild and wounded and them that is hear is playing out of it. Som of them wil half to off their stripes soon as this fight is over for commissions.

I want you and Sarah to rite often and giv me all the news that is stirng. I want to no if you hav herd eney thing from Fenton. Sarah I want to no how you and doctor little makes it now. I wold like to no what has become of my mule Shony if she is still living yet. I wold like very much to hear from Miss Lucinda and all the rest of girls. I want som of you to rite every to weaks if you can. I hav not got but to letters from home since I left home. Tell Mary Boyd I wil rite to her be for long. When I rite one I rite to all of you. I hav not had the chance to rit as often as I hav don. We ar getting plenty to eat. We get bacon corn meal coffee shugar. I hav four in my mess. They ar all well. I must bring this to a close by saying rite soon. Nothing more at present but remains your affectionate brother.

D Boyd to Sarah Boyd and M J Hall

July 7, 1864, finds Daniel writing from Petersburg, Virginia. The letter is unsigned, but as usual gives enough clues for the reader to conclude that Daniel is the author. He talks of marching from Chaffin's Bluff, Virginia, on June 17 to Petersburg to fight Grant's forces, opening the Petersburg campaign. He discusses the trench warfare about Petersburg and general conditions of the town.

Camp Petersburg, Va.
July the 7th, 1864
Dear father,

I seat myself to drop you a few lines to let you know that I am tolerable well at this time and I hope when these few lines coms to hand they may find you enjoying the same great blessing the health of the troops is not as good as it has bin. We have a great deal of sickness hear.

I have not got much news to rite at this tim. We left Chaffin's Bluff on the 17th inst and marched to Petersburg to meet Grant. We met him in a mile of the town. We went to work on our breast works. We soon put them up but before we got them done the Yankees maid a charge on front of our line. We pourd heavy fire into them and drove them back. Their has bin several fights around hear but our division has not bin engaged. Everything has bin quiet for several days with the exceptions of heavy shelling and picket fighting which has become as common as a man's voice. They have bin shelling the town but they not done much damage yet. The citizens has moved out of town to get out of the way of the shells. They have wounded some few weman and children. It was thought that they wold tare the place down on the fourth, but we was deceived. It was the quietest day we have had since we have bin hear. We have lost one man since we came here he was wounded in the leg. His name is Frank Edwards. Our lines is about four hundred yards apart. A man can't put his head above the breast work without being shot by the sharp shooters. The have kild a great many of our men. We pay them back in the same kind of corn. Our division has bin resting for beter than a weak. We have bin running after rading parties. We have run them back to their gunboats. There is sum talk of us goin on the lines to knight but as for my part I can't tell wheather we will or not.

I saw John Logan early last weak. He came over to me two or three times before I got see him he looks wery and he says his health is very good. He has bin in the army two years. His brothers is in the Western army, he is in co. F, eight Ga. Regment. O. Fowler and O. Parnel is in the same company. I did not see them he says his mother is living yet. Will McCoy is dead. I believe them is all that he mentioned. We have drawed money. I drawed one hundred and 71 dollars. We got two months wages and clothing money. We did not get it before we needed it. I was out for the first time since I hav bin in the army. Every thing is very high hear flour 2 to 3 dollars a pound, corn meal 2 dollars a quiart, Bacon 8 dollars per pound, peas 2.50 a quart, Beans 4 dollars a quart, pies 50 cts a pie, onions 1 dollar apeace and every thing else in perportion. Whiskey 3 dollars a drink.

The weather has been very hot and dry for the last month the crops is nearly burnt up in Va. If it don't soon rain they won't make seed in this country. Corn looks like it will dry up in few days, I am afraid. We will see harder times than we have every saw yet. The Yankees has had our railroads tore up an the cars culd not run. We have not had a mail in ten days. We wod get the mail in day or two. I received a letter from you about two weaks ago. It was good to hear from him and to hear that you ar all well. I want you to rite every chance you have and let me no how you ar getting along with your crop and how much wheat oats you maid and how crops, leaks and the price of red onions and the news in jeneral. We ar faring tolerable well for sumthing to eat. We got corn meal, bacon, coffee, shugar, peas, rice. some times they have cauld on us to help the sufferers of Petersburg. I thought that it best to keep my money in my pocket. I don't giv them iney thing. I hav giv my last to Such folks.

[Unsigned probably written by Daniel Boyd]

The next letter from Daniel is dated August 20, 1864, from Culpeper County, Virginia. He says that they are camped on the site where Jackson fought the Battle of Cedar Run. The Seventh had transferred to the Second Corps commanded by Lieutenant General Jubal Early and was now in the Shenandoah Valley. One of the most significant elements of this letter is a discussion of the Battle of the Crater when northern forces, using an abandoned mine, attempted to blow up Confederate lines by igniting barrels of gunpowder underneath them.[15]

Camp near Mitchel Station Culpeper county Va
August the 20th 1864

Dear father,

I take this oppertunity of droping you a few lines in answer to your kind and welcome letter that I received a few days ago. I was truly glad to hear from you and that you are all well but I am sorry to hear that aunt Jane an Emmy is so lowe but I hope that they wil soon recover and get well again. The of our regiment is not so good now. We have a good deal of sickness in the army. As for my self I hav bin enjoying tolerable good health since we left Petersburg. Every thing has bin quiet for the last five or six days. We left Chester Field on the 6th and got on the cars and went to Richmond and from there to Mitchel Station Culpeper county Va.

Ther has not bin eney fighting since the fourth as I know of [indecipherable words]. The Yankees breast works up on the [illegible word] whitch caused great confusion ther. We hav paid them for blowing up our line. J W Calaham was kild by the blowing up of our breast works.

He was buried with the dirt. When they found him he was standing strait up the ditches. There was one hundred kild and buried with the explosion. They had six drums of powder under our works. They got so badly whipped at their own tricks I dont think they try it eney more. The Yankees hav bin sending troops from to the valley. Ther has bin too divisions of our cavalry sent to reinforce erley. It is thought that we ar on our way to Pennsylvania.

We ar waiting for our wagons to come up. If we go on we wil force the Yankees to leav Petersburg. Jeneral is in Mairland now and if we go ther we wil hav a hard time of it but the boys says that they wil mak the yanks feel the war. If I half to go ther I intend to live while I am ther but I hope that wont half to go ther for the wether is so warm that we cant stand to march. We hav had som of the hottest weather that I ever saw and very dry and dusty. The crops is the soryest in virginnia that I ever saw in this part of the country. Ther is nothing growing. I think that we wil half to go to Pennsylvania or som wer els to get pervisions for another year. Jeneral erly is haling wheat, corn and bacon and every thing that he can get away with out of Mairland and Pennsylvania. He is taking all the horses cows hogs sheep that he can get hold of if he hold on to wil lay in enough to do his army all winter. They ar faring better than we ar. We hav got wher we cant buy eneything but I dont think we wil stay hear long. We ar going move camp to day. We ar campt on the oald battle ground of cedars runn wher Jackson fought. I believ I hav rote all the news that I hav at this time. I received a letter from Sarah a day or too ago an one from S W Bowen. He wants to settle up with me for the wirk that I don. They can pay it to you eney time. If they pay you giv them a resipt. It is $15 or 20 dollars. Nothing more at present but remains your son til death.

D P Boyd to Robert Boyd
August the 20th

A week later Daniel writes his father again from near the town of Charlestown in what is now West Virginia. He gives more details of the actions in the Shenandoah Valley. A number of individuals are mentioned as well as a cave exploration that Daniel took part in. That is an interesting aspect to personal letters and diaries that show the tourist emerge from these soldiers when they get a break from the conflict. We often discount the fact that these farm boys are seeing parts of the country they had never visited prior to the war.

Camp near Charlestown Va
August the 28th 1864

Dear father,

I seat myself this evening to drop you a few lines to let you know
that I am tolerable well at this time hoping that thes few lines may find
you all well. I hav not got eney thing of importance to rite. We left
Culpeper on the 14th and came to Shanandore river and campt too or
three days and then started for Winchester. Wafords Bregaid had a fight
near frunt royal. We lost three or four hundred men. The most of them
was taken prisoners. We drove the yanks all day but did not get up with
them. Erleys attacked them at Winchester. We drove out of town the
next day.

We past through Winchester and found Erley. We campt at Winchester too days. On the morning of the 21st we started in persuit of the
yanks. We marched eight miles and near took them. The 7 regiment and
the second and fifteen was sent out as skirmishers. We soon commenced
firing. We soon rowsted them and drove them eight miles. We lost three
men in our regiment. One in my company. His naim is Hyram Cowan.
They was all wounded. The other regiments loss was lite. On the 22 we
sarted after them again but Erley got ahead of us and pitched in to them
at Charlestown and drove to Harpers Ferry. We ar campt three miles
from Charlestown.

The weather has been very warm. It was the worst marching that I
ever don. It is som cooler today. We had a fine rain yesterday. It is thought
that we will be in Mairland in a few days. The yanks is burning all the
wheat as they go over ther. Our officers tel us to git boys. We ar out of
officers in our company. Lieutenant J C Carlisle has resigned and gon
home. Its every fellow for him self. It seem that Co L has all the cowards.
He had to resigined for cowardice. I believe I hav giv you all the news
of interest. I and W Clinkscales J B Allen visited a cave in the mountain.
We went to the end of it distance of three hundred yards. It was dark as
knight. It was the grandest site I ever saw. It had rooms and steirs like a
bar room. It is as cauld a place as I ever saw for the season. I will turn
the subject to something else. I want you to rite to me. I hav not herd
from hom in too weaks. I want to no if Aunt Jane has got well and all
the news. My mess is all well at this time. We are faring very wel in the
way of something to eat at this time. I beliv I hav rote all that can at
this time. J H Alewine is well and harty. I wil close for this time by asking

you to rite soon. Nothing more at present but remains your affectionate son til death.

D Boyd to Robert Boyd

Fare well til you hear from me again.

Daniel writes Robert Boyd again on September 1, 1864, from Winchester, Virginia. There are two primary topics of this letter. First he writes of a battle around Halltown in western Virginia or modern West Virginia. Next he tells his father that he is sending home papers needed to file a claim against Andrew's belongings at the time of his death.

Camp near Winchester

September the 1st 1864

Dear father,

I seat myself this evening to drop you a few lines to let you know how I am getting along. I am well at this time and hope when thes few lines comes to hand they may find you all well. I hav no news of interest to rite to you only that we had a fight on the 26th. We got the worst of it. The 7th, 2nd and 15 regments was out on picket. The Yankees saw our line was weak and they massed their force in a peace of woods and charged our lines with cavalry and infantry. The cavalry charged the 15th regment and broke their lines and captured about 75 of them.

We had to do som of our best running. I tell you it was a rite close place. We lost about 25 men in our regment 2 kild and 20 wounded. Ther was too of my company wounded on the 25th. They was going after water when they was wounded. Their naims Warren Cochren and Curren Jones. The fight tok place between Charlestown and Harpers Ferry. We left their the next morning and came to bruce town. We campt their til the 31st. We campt in the same place that we did too years ago. We left their yesterday and came to Winchester. We ar campt one mile from town. I dont no how long we wil stay hear. I think that we wil get back to Petersburg before we stop.

I wil sende you a paper to draw pay for what things Andrew left at the hospital when he died. I wil send it with Harison Campbell of company H. He is going to start home in the morning on furlow. It is the best chance that I get to send it for we keep moving about so much. Som thinks that we wil go to Tennessee. I dont think that we wil go their. I dont car wher we go so we dont go to Petersburg. I dont want to get back their. We ar living better hear than we did their. I believ I hav rote al the news I have at this time. I want you to rite to me and let me no how Unkle Williams family is getting and all of the neighbors is getting along.

I want to no if you hav herd wheather J C Alewine is prisoner or not. We hav not herd from him in a long time and let me no if C B Willford has got home or not. Giv me all the news. I wold like to hear how friend Stuckey is getting along and what he is doing. I herd that Henry Burton and Francis Young is going to marry let no if it is so or not. If is so I think it is an unequal match. I hear that Spauldion is having a big meeting at his Schall house. Let me no he joined the church and so forth. Tel Mary and Sarah to rite soon. Thes lines leaves my mess well. I wil calose my letter by asking you to rite soon as you get this. Nothing more at present but remains your son til death .

D Boyd to R Boyd

A week later, on September 9, 1864, Daniel writes his sisters Sarah and Mary Jane from Winchester. In this letter he tells of his units actions at the Battle of Berryville, Virginia, on September 3.

Camp near Winchester
September the 9th 1864

Dear sisters,

I take this opportunity of droping you a few lines to let you know that I hav not forgotten you. My health is tolerable good at this time and I hope when thes few lines comes to hand they may find you all well and doing well. The health of our regment is very good at this time. I hav no news of importance to rite to you at this time only that we had another fight on the third near Berryville. We had three bregaids of our division engaged in fight. It lasted about one hour. Our bregaid had to charg the yanks breast works. We took them with out eney trouble. Our loss in our regment was very light.

We lost 5 or 6 wounded in the regment one in my company. Rastes olliver was wounded and died the next day. He was the only one that was kild in regemnt. Jeneral Humphrey of Mississippi was wounded. His bregaid suffered severly. We drove the yanks about half a mile. They fel back that knight. We left their the next day and came back to Winchester. We ar looking for a fight. Every day we get orders to move every or too. We start out to meet the Yankees every too or three days. We hav had three fights since we left Petersburg. We hav had men wounded in our company and no kild. Our company hav lost more men than eney company in the regment.

We do not stay at one place more than three days at a time. We half to rium after the yankee cavalry to keep them of our waygons. I dont think that we wil stay hear long for we hav nearly eat out this part of the country. We hav men thrashing out all the wheat that they can get. They hav got near about all they can. We dont get as much to eat as we did when we first com hear. The Yankees is burning all the wheat where they go and everything that is useful to the army. They ar trying to starve us out and they cold get far enough into our country they wold do it. This part of Va dos not look like the same place. Everything is scarce heare.

We cant buy eneything with confederate money here. They wont hav eney thing but yankee money. We jenrly get what we want without buying. We hav eat all the roasting ears that is reach of us and everything els. I believ I hav rite all the news. Sam Davis has got back to camp at last. Ben Campbell is not back yet. I recon he has catched the heart each from some of the girls he is trying to get a first love. I want you to rite to me as soon as you get this and giv me all the news and let me no how the neighbors is getting along and what sort of time they had at the big meetings. Who joined the church and if eney boddy has got marryed. Tel father to rite to me. I hav not had a letter from him in some time. Tel John I wil rite to him soon. I wil close by asking you to rite soon.

D Boyd to M J Hall and Sarah C Boyd

Daniel's next letter is dated September 21, 1864, and is written to his father from Rapidan Station, Virginia. They had departed from Winchester on September 15 and had therefore missed the Third Battle of Winchester. He gives his opinion of their new brigade commander, General James Connor of Charleston. Connor had been the District Attorney for the state of South Carolina who had prosecuted the captain of The Wanderer — long believed to be the last ship to disobey the law banning the importation of African slaves.[16] Daniel said that Connor was the hardest of all the generals they had served under.

He talks of being tired of war and expresses a dim view of their chances believeing they will soon be starved out. He says of the Yankees, "They burn everything wher they go."

Camp near Rapidan Station, Va.
September the 21, 1864

Dear father,

I seat myself morning to drop a few lines to let you no how I am geting along. I am tolerable well at this tim and I hope when thes few lines coms to hand they find you all and doing well. I received your letter of the 12. I was truly glad to hear from home and that you ar all well but I was sorry to hear of the death of cosin William and to hear of little Pressly being sick but I hope they will soon get well. I no they hav had a hard time year for they hav had so much sickness in their famleys. Well I will give you what little news I hav. We hav not had eney fighting since the 13. The eight regment had a little fight with the cavalry. The eight regment was nearly all taken prisoner. Colonel Henigan and one hundred an four men was captured. We left Winchester on the 15 we hav bin marching ever since. We ar on our way to Petersburg or to East Tennessee. I don't know wher we wil go to. We have got a new Brigadier General, his name is Conor he is a hard customer he makes the officers fly round. He is the hardes on us of eney General that we ever had camp. John Nance has bin in command of the 7th Regment for som time. Our Bregaid is getting very small. We have left nearly too regments since we hav bin the valley and am afraid that we wil go to wars place before long if we get to Petersburg.

We have an election for legislature and tax collector. I don't know hoo will be elected. Pressly is making a good run, hear Bradly is ahead for legislature. I want you to let me hoo is elected. I want you to rite to as soon as you get this and giv me all the news and let no if you got that paper that I sent by Campbell to draw pay for Andrew's things that he left when he died and I want you to send me two pares of socks the first chance you hav for I am needing them now. I recon that we wil draw clothing in a few days. Their is great meney men barfooted and if thay keap us marching about wil soon all be without shoes. We ar fairing very well in way of rashings but I am afraid that wil get to a bad place yet. Som thinks that we wil go to Georgia but it is hard to tell when we wil go to. I think that I wil hear tomorrow. I wil half to close for the men is bout leav. I wold like to get home this fal but won't be eney chance this Winter. I am tyard of the war. It looks like the Yankees wil overrun us yet. If they keep on they wil starv us out. They burn everything wher they go. I want you to rite as soon as you can and do same. I wil close for the present so nothing more but remains your son til death.

D. Boyd

To R. Boyd

Daniel next writes his father on October 25, 1864, from New Market, Virginia. He gives great detail of the battle at Strasburg, Virginia, a few days earlier. It began as a total rout of the Union army at dawn then once the federals were reinforced the tide turned and the Confederates were routed in an equal fashion. In his postscript to this letter he also gives some details from the Battle of Hupps Hill on October 13.

Camp 7 S C V near New Market Va

October the 25th 1864

Dear father,

One more time I hav the oppertunity to drop you a few lines to let you no that I am still alive and enjoying good health hoping when thes few lines comes to hand they may find you enjoying the same great blessing. I received your letter of the 9th. I was glad to hear from home and you ar all well and doing wel. That is more than I can say. We hav had another big fight near Strasburg. We left camp on the knight of the 19th marched all and attacked the Yankees on morning of the 20th at day light. We captured all their pickets and then marched in to their camps and fired in to their tents wher they was sleeping. We kild a great meney of them a sleep. We drove them out of their breast works. They went flying all over the country leaving everything in camp. We drove them six or seven miles. It was a charge all the time. We captured 38 peaces of artillery from 1500 to too thousand prisoners and blankets and tents enough to souply the army and eneything that you can call for. Every thing went rite til after twelve oclock. We had the completely routed but to our mis fortune they got reinforcements and made a charge on Gordon's division and broke their lines. They was on the left. They run of and left Kershaw's division to fight it out. We fought them til they got in our rear and then we had to do som of our best running and the Yankees after us. Their was no such thing as rallying our men. They went swarming like bees. They drove us back over the same ground that we drove them in a bout as big a hury as we went. They got all their artillery back and nearly all of ours and a good meney wagons. We had one of greatest victories won on the war if we cold of held it. We had cut too corps to peaces. If our men had done their duty we cold hav whipt then easy enough. I hav bin a hearing of fights but I never witnessed such a one before. I thought that they wold get in spite of all I cold do but I kept runing. The yankee cavelry got us cut off. We crossed the river twist and our way to Fishers hill. About half of the men went to the mountains. A great meney throwd guns a way. There is thousands of them in the mountains yet. They coming in every day. Our loss is quite lite. The 7 Regt lost too kild twenty four wounded ten or fifteen missing. I do not no how meny the bregaid lost but it lost heavey. The colonel and lieutenant of the 20th Regiment taken prisoners.

The major of the 3rd regiment was wounded. Company J lost one man wounded. It was K W Cramer. He was left on the field. All that was wounded after started to fall back fell into the hands of the enemy. We rallied at Fishers hill fel back to New Market the next day a distance of 27 miles. We marched it a day. We cold scercly drag one foot after the other. I never was as tyrad in my life but the thoughts of being a prisoner moved us on. We was looking for the Yankees to com on us every minute. They did not follow us. They was too badley cut up to follow us. Tha hav not come theis side of Strasburg. I dont think that their will be eney mor fighting in the valley this winter. I got me a good blanket. I did not hav time to get eney thing els. I was thankful to get out without eneything. I run about five miles. It was the worst stompead that has bin since the commenced. I hope we never wil hav another such. I believe I hav giv you about all that I can at this time. I wil giv you a little mor the next time. I want you to me every chance you hav and giv me all the news. Let me no how much corn you made and how all Unkel William and David's folks is getting along and all the neighbors is getting along and how meney has gon to the army. You sed in your letter that you wold send me some socks the first chance you hav. I hav got me too pair. They wil last me til you get a chance. I drawed a pair of shoes the other day. Them that I wore from home lasted me til now. I hav got cloths enough to do me. Bill Campbell hav got back to camp at last. He lost the socks you sent with him. I believe I hav rote all that I can this time. Tel Unkel William and D Murdock to rite to me. I must close for the sun is getting low. Nothing more at present but remains your affectionate son til death.

D Boyd to R and Hannah Boyd

PS I forgot to tell you about the fight we had on the 13. My friend B Hutchison was kild. He was the only one that was kild. They was about 320 wounded. Jeneral conor lost a leg. Colonel Rullfurd was kild. That is all that no. We ear on picket to day. Your boy til you hear from me agin.

1865

On Febrary 3, 1865, Daniel wrote to his sister, Mary Jane from the South Carolina coast. The location given in the heading is "Salkahatchie River," where they had been attached to McLaws Division and the corps of Lieutenant General William Hardee beginning the Carolinas Campaign.

Camp on the Salkehatchie River
February the 3rd 1865

Dear sister,

I take this oppertunity of droping you a few lines to let you no that I am well at this time and I hope when thes few lines coms to hand they may find you all well and doing well. The health of the army is tolerable good at this time. We hav som sickness in the regment. We hav one man sick in the company. I havent eney news of interest to rite at this time. We hav not had eney fighting yet only a little picket fighting. The third regment and third battalion had a little fight the other day. They had too men kild and eight or ten wounded. They whipt the Yankees and drove them back. We ar on one side of the river and the Yankees on the other. I dont think that we wil hav eney fighting at this place. It is reported that the Yankees ar going towards Branchville but I cant tell wheather it is so or not. I dont think that they get ther unless they get reinforcements. Jeneral Hamptons cavalry has come from Va. The 6th regment is at Greenpond. I hav not saw eney of them yet. We hav got wher we cant see or hear eney thing. We hav bin saronded with water for the last weak. We hav had a great deal of rain and some very coald knights. I am afraid that it wil be a sickly place when the water fals. There is nothing but swamps down hear. We half to use the river water to drink. It is very bad but it is the best we can get in the country.

I hav not heard from home since we left Carleston. I hav not had but one letter since we left Va. I received your letter dated December the 19th. We hav not had eney mail from Abbeville in a month. It looks like we wil never get eney more letters. I want to no if you all hav quit riting or what is the reson. Some of the boys says that their folks hav turnd to unionist and that they need united states stamps to cary their letters through. I wold like to hear how you ar getting along and how the girls is getting along and how meney weddings their has bin this winter. I hear that there is a good meney soldiers at home now. It looks like there is a chance for som of them fast widows that you speak of in your letter. You sed that it is no use to com home unless intendes to marry. I dont think there is eney danger of them capturing me but their might be a chance for som of them to get badly fooled like one that undertook to capture me onst in time. I dont expect to get home this year. There is good meney getting furlows for ten days. There is ten or twelve to go befor me but I am very wel satisfied to stay here. We ar fairing very well. We get plenty to eat now. We get flower corn meal rice pork beef. I dont no how long it wil last. I want you too let me no if you got the money that I sent to you with James McGee. I sent 20 dollars with him. I believe I hav rot all the news that I have at this time. I red a letter from J E Crowther the other day. He is well. He is at Florence S C. I wil half to close my short letter. Nothing more at present but remains your brother til death.

D Boyd to M J Hall.

Direct your letters to 7 Regt Connor's Bregaid Charleston S C.

This is my last til I get one from you.

Hardee's Corps reached Florence and then Cheraw, South Carolina, on March 3, 1865, and crossed the Pee Dee River on March 5. General P. G. T. Beauregard had expected that Sherman would be attempting to capture Charlotte, North Carolina, and had positioned his forces there. Sherman, however, had other plans and turned east, shadowing Hardee's retreat along the coastal plain into North Carolina where General Joseph Johnston awaited. Governor Zebulon Vance had placed all state forces, mainly junior reserves, under Johnston's command.[1]

Sherman's command had expected to discover a hotbed of Union sentiment upon crossing into North Carolina. They were wrong in this assumption. Major Nichols of Sherman's army wrote after a week in the old North State, "Thus far we have been painfully disappointed in looking for Union sentiment in North Carolina, about which so much has been said. Our experience is decidedly in favor of its sister states."[2]

Hardee's Corps had retreated through Fayetteville, where Lieutenant

General Wade Hampton's cavalry would soon engage Federal cavalry under Judson Kilpatrick on ground which is now part of Fort Bragg. Hardee's infantry crossed the Cape Fear River with Hampton's men close behind. Confederate forces then burned the bridges once across. Now in control of Fayetteville, Sherman's men took the opportunity to send the valuables they had plundered from the citizens of the Carolinas to their homes in the north. They also burned the Fayetteville Arsenal and the offices of the local newspaper, the Observer.[3]

Across the river, Hardee was taking the road leading to Smithfield and Raleigh. On March 16, Hardee's forces would engage Sherman at Averasboro, North Carolina. Here Daniel with the rest of Hardee's men would repulse charge after charge from the Federals before falling back to Smithfield leaving General Joseph Wheeler's forces at this position. As Hardee retired toward Smithfield he was headed to roll his corps into the command of General Johnston. The other scattered Confederate forces throughout the Carolinas and Georgia were marching toward the same goal. Johnston knew that he must strike a blow to check Sherman's advance and prevent him from joining with Grant's forces. Once he had done that, Johnston knew that the Confederacy's only hope lay in him moving his army north to join with General Lee's forces.[4]

Johnston planned to do this halfway between Raleigh and Fayetteville in the town of Bentonville. So with the forces of Hardee, Hampton, General Braxton Bragg and Major General Robert Hoke now under his command, Johnston prepared to do battle. On March 19, Hoke's division, which included the North Carolina Junior Reserves, engaged the enemy in the woods and thickets along the county line between Johnston and Sampson counties. Johnston's army with Hoke in the lead would repeatedly repulse Sherman's men. The bloody battle would rage for three days, until March 22. Confederate losses were: 223 killed, 1,467 wounded and 653 missing. They took 900 prisoners and Federal losses were otherwise estimated to have exceeded 4,000. On March 21, Johnston began retiring his forces toward Raleigh. He had attained his first objective of retarding Sherman's movements. Sherman attempted to follow, but was prevented by a swollen stream he could not cross so he retired his forces to Goldsboro where they occupied themselves plundering and burning houses along the way.[5]

On March 29, 1865, Daniel wrote his last wartime letter in the collection from Smithfield, North Carolina, to his father. He talks of the battles of Averasboro and Bentonville.

Camp near Smithfield NC
March the 29th 1865
Dear father,

I take this oppertunity of droping you a few lines to let you no that

I am well at this time hopeing when thes few lines coms to hand they may find you all enjoying the same great blessing of health. I hav not got much news to rite at this time. We had a fight on the 16th and 19th 20th 21st. This time we loss but one man on the 16th. On the 19th we lost a bout 20. Four kild and the rest wounded. Beard Taylor lost his right leg. He is the only one that was hurt in company D. The loss in the Bregaid is about 75. We whipt Sherman at both places. The first fight was between Cape Farrer and Black River and the other near Bentonville Johnson county. Shermans gon to Gouldsburrough to rest his men. We ar 20 miles ther. We ar in camp near Smithfield Station. I do not no how long we wil stay hear. It is thought that Sherman wil back through S C. It matters not which way he starts. He will go wher ever pleas for we hav no body to keep him back. There is about one third of the men gon home. Their has bin 7 thousand left hardees camp since we left Charleston. There is 8 hundred left one regment. It looks like the poor little Confederacy wil soon go up if it has to go. I dont car how soon. All the western army is hear. I saw the 19th regment a few days ago. Saw Wes Bowen, Eellick Robertson and good meney more of the boys. J Alewine has not got hear yet. He is with the wagons. They was at New-bery the last hear of.

You wanted to no if I got the things that you sent with Naris. I did not get eney thing. He left them on the road. He cold not fetch them. He had to walk 40 miles. I wold like very much to hav got them for I am nearly out of socks. There is great meney of the men bare footed and som with out cloths. I hav got very good cloths my self. We are fairing very well in the way of rashings with what we steal. They are pressing every thing in reach of the army. They are only leaving the citizens three months rashings. I dont see how they ar to live. When this is don I dont see how the army is to live hear long for this very poor country. There is hardly enough to do the citizens. We wil half to leave thes parts. I hear that thay ar putting the negras in the army. It wont do to put them with the white men for they wont stand it. We are nie enough on equality with them now. There is a great meney talking about diserting. They ar leaving every knight. I wold like to get home very much but there is no chance unless I run away. I wold hate to giv it up after fighting four years but it seems like them that stays at home get mor honor than them that stays and fights. I wil turn the subject. We hav a good deal of sickness in camp at this time. James Alewine is not very well today. I heard that Jessy Campbell is on his way home. He was very sick. He had stayd on the road. The doctor did not think he would live to get home. I wil half to close for this time. I want you to rite soon as you get this. Giv me all the news. Tell the rest to rite. I wil close by asking you to rite soon. Nothing more at present but remains your affectionate son til death.

D Boyd to R Boyd

Direct to Connors Bregaid Hardees Corps Smithfield Station N C

As Daniel noted, Sherman's army had retreated to Goldsboro and Hardee's Corps was camped at Smithfield. They would soon withdraw to Raleigh, where the women of the city were busy nursing the wounded from the Battle of Bentonville. Churches and schools had been turned into makeshift hospitals and the people were sharing the last of their food with the starving boys in gray.[6] Meanwhile, President Jefferson Davis had evacuated Richmond late on the night of April 2 and had stopped in Danville, Virginia. He was now working his way through North Carolina, stopping in Greensboro on the morning of April 11. Davis would remain there until the afternoon of April 15, when he would depart destined for Abbeville, a mere 15 miles from the Boyd farm.[7]

By this time, the Confederates had abandoned Raleigh to the enemy — Sherman having taken possession of the state capital on April 12. On the morning of April 14, General Hardee with his corps met with General Johnston at Hillsborough. They continued on to the Haw River Bridge and later that day withdrew on towards Greensboro. It was on this day that General Johnston first made arrangements for an armistice and the meeting with Sherman at the Bennett house near Durham. After signing the terms of surrender with Sherman on April 26, Daniel Boyd and James Alewine were paroled at Greensboro along with the 36,971 men remaining in Johnston's army. The men of Company D, 7th South Carolina — like Daniel and James, who had stayed until the end—would depart in the company of their comrades for home on May 3.[8]

Daniel had entered the army at the beginning of the war with James H. Alewine and his brother Pressley. They had marched through Virginia, Maryland, Pennsylvania and the Carolinas together. Now Daniel and James would return to Diamond Hill together having left Pressley resting beneath the earth of Harpers Ferry. The preceeding four years had redefined the world in which they lived. Many friends and most of Daniel's family were now gone. Diamond Hill would not be the same place they had departed in April of 1861 and they, no doubt, were far different men from the ones who had marched away to the fields of glory.

After the War

The final letter in the collection was written several years after the war on July 31, 1871. A Boyd cousin — Eunice Cleland Boyd — writes to Mary Jane Hall from Pope County, Arkansas. Eunice and her husband, Samuel A. Boyd, had moved there from Laurens County, South Carolina, prior to the war. The Alewines mentioned in the letters had all relocated there following the war.

This letter has interesting details of life working on the farm in Arkansas for a woman, but it is significant to this collection for a far sadder reason. It mentions the death of the last of the main letter writers and our only survivor of the war; Daniel Boyd. Despite having survived hunger, disease and enemy lead, Daniel was still destined to a short life.

Pope County Ark
July 31 1871

Dear cousin,

I seate myself to write a few lines to you to let you know that I have not forgotten you. This leaves myself and family well and I hope will reach your hands and finde you all enjoying the same greate blessing. We hav unsettled wether tho tolerable warm. We havent had very much coald wether since about Christmas but I think we will hav more coald wether yet. If we do not we will hav the fowerds spring that we hav had since we hav bin here. Mary you wanted to kno about the womans work here. I hav bin so neglectful I never answered you. I am almost ashamed to write but I hope you will excuse me. I alwase hav so much busyness to attend to I hardly ever have time to write. But I will say to you say to you that "greate many of the women who works in the field in cotton hoeing time and picking time and tha are not ashamed of it. Women that work out here is as much thought of by the people here as them that never did wok out. They can make more by working in the field than they can in the house. As for weaving ther is not many that hier it don. Cloth has come down and the most of them buy cloth. I was sory to hear of the death of your last brother. I know how harde it is to parte with a friende but we hav to give them up. I would be glad to see you and your sister. I ofen think of you. You must live a lonsom life and see a harde time. I want you to write to me every chance and tell your sister to write to me. Give my best respects to your father and mother. The connedtion here is all tolerable well as fare as I know. Cousin William Murdock and Gracy was down to see us last knight was a week Sunday. They are getting along very well. He made a good crop last year. Cousin William got a letter from his sister Elizabeth. She wrote that Aunt Jane Plunkett was still living. My daughter thet is maryed is living close by me now. She has bin very bad with a pain in her head and teeth but has got some better now. I will bring my letter to a close. Give me all the news. You must excuse my bad writing and spelling. I send my best respects to all inquiring friends if there be any. No more but remains your affectionate friend until death.

Eunice Boyd to Mary J Hall

Epilogue

Robert Boyd died on January 17, 1875, at the age of 70, having out-lived all five of his sons. Hannah Crowther Boyd, Robert's second wife, whom he married probably during the war, but possibly before, died September 8, 1903, at the age of 84. Daniel Boyd, who had endured so much pain and loss, married Hannah's niece Lucinda Crowther following the war — the Miss Lucinda he refers to in his letters. Lucinda, born April 5, 1840, was the daughter of William Crowther, who was a veteran of the Fifth South Carolina Reserves. Daniel had dodged death for the entire four years of the war, but his eventful life was destined to be short nonetheless. He died on September 27, 1870, less than a month after his thirty-fourth birthday. His stone gives his birth date as September 6, 1836. No obituary or other documentation of a cause of Daniel's untimely death could be located, but in searching the newspapers for an obituary, there was ample discussion of a cholera epidemic at the time. Along with Lucinda, he left behind a young son, James Robert Boyd. Lucinda would die September 28, 1891, and lies buried beside Daniel in the cemetery at First Creek Baptist Church. First Creek is situated along the county line between Anderson and Abbeville counties, just on the Anderson side.

W. N. Hall, nephew of Fenton Hall, like many in South Carolina, was driven into financial ruin during Reconstruction, and advertised the bankruptcy sale of his property on October 9, 1868. The *Abbeville Press* stated: "I will sell on the 19th day of November next at T. B. Mill-ford's Mill in Abbeville District, the real estate of said bankrupt, con-taining 75 acres... on Prickly Pear Creek, waters of Rocky River... bounded by lands of Wm. Crowther, Robert Boyd, and others." His was but one of a number of properties being sold at auction during November of 1868. The auction place — as with W. N. Hall's — was at T. B. Millford's Mill. Incidentally, one of the properties being sold that month was that of T. B. Millford himself.[1]

Michael Alewine, mess mate of Fenton Hall, had married his first cousin, Emmaline, who was the sister of James Hyley Alewine and John Calvin Alewine. John C. Alewine was known by his middle name of Calvin. He with his wife, the former Emmaline Milford, was the first to move. They settled in an area near Atkins, Arkansas, in 1869. Their son, Reece, learned to walk on a steamboat during the long trip. The next year Michael and Emmaline Alewine also moved, bringing along the matriarch of the Alewine clan — Sarah Crowther Alewine. Her husband, also named Michael Alewine, had died April 3, 1845, and is buried at First Creek Baptist Church. James Hyley Alewine arrived in Arkansas on New Year's Day 1871 with his wife and their two children. They had left Abbeville November 20, 1870, less than a month following the death of his good friend Daniel Boyd. They journeyed in a covered tobacco wagon with two teams of horses and all of their possessions. The first winter in Arkansas, the entire Alewine family lived in a one-room house with a shed that Calvin and his brother-in-law, David Milford, had built. Family tradition states that the women and small children slept in the house and the men and the "big boys" slept in the covered wagons.[2]

The Alewines were to become renowned as pioneers of that section of western Arkansas. Michael and Emmaline had seven children. Michael died December 17, 1913, at 76. James H. Alewine — known as "Uncle Jimmy"— died June 19, 1918, at the age of 79. The family is buried in the Atkins City Cemetery.

Sarah Catherine Boyd, sister of the letter writers, married Samuel A. Purdy after the war. Samuel Purdy was born June 6, 1843, and was a veteran of Company G, First South Carolina Rifles Regiment — William's company. Sarah, born March 23, 1841, died February 24, 1918, at the age of 76. Samuel outlived his wife by 18 years, following her in death November 7, 1936, at the age of 93. They are buried at Rocky River Baptist Church.

Thomas A. Hall, son of Fenton and Mary Jane, was born shortly before January 9, 1862, as stated in the letter from his uncle Pressley Boyd. His grave, however; incorrectly states his birth as 1863. He died in 1932 and is buried at Rocky River Baptist beside his wife, Rossie. In the 1920 census, Mary Jane was living with her daughter Essa Mitchell in Diamond Hill. It states that Essa L. Mitchell 60 years old was living with her children: Leida Mitchell, 37, and John K. (or R.) Mitchell, 23. (Conflicting records put his age at 27.) Mary Jane Hall died June 30, 1923, at the age of 91. She was the first born and the last to die of Robert and Catherin Boyd's children. Her death certificate lists the cause of death as "Angina pectoris." It was attested to by her grandson, J. R. Mitchell. It is from this document that we know that the Boyd's mother was Catherin Phropet (or perhaps Prophet) Boyd. It also lists the place of burial as Rocky River; however, no surviving stone can be located for her grave. A number of stones in the cemetery are broken beyond recognition or are missing, with only simple unmarked foot stones signaling the existence of a grave.

Although the collection at Duke University does not say so, the editor believes it is thanks to Mary Jane that these letters exist today. All of the letters were either written to her or her father and were probably left to her after his death. For this, history owes her a great debt.

Editor's Afterword

When you write a biography, you basically live with that person for about three years. In this case, I felt that not only did I live with them, but I became a member of the family. The tragedy of this family grabs the heart and refuses to let go. Sharon Strout, who transcribed a large number of these letters, would write a note with letters she had finished that revealed the news of the death of one of the brothers to the effect of: "I was sorry to hear of [William's] death." It was as if we had just read in the newspaper of the passing of a close friend who expired the previous week. Finally, after Andrew's death, she wrote me, "Please tell me that at least Daniel survives the war!" Daniel did survive. He went off to war with four brothers and came home alone.

The closeness brother-in-law Fenton Hall shared with the Boyd family is clear. It looks like they considered him the eldest brother and that he shared those feelings. Another thing that touched me deeply was the bond between Fenton and Mary Jane. I can imagine how these letters gave her something to hold onto through the years she should have spent with him. How Essa must have smiled as she would read of her father's enjoyment of the pies and biscuits she made for him. The father she almost certainly could not clearly remember.

History has not recorded if Daniel kept his word about looking after Mary Ann and her children after William's death, but it would be hard to fathom that the man who wrote these letters would have done anything less during the limited amount of time he had left on this earth. I can't help but believe that during those last five years of his life that "Uncle Dan" was a mentor and protector that William's children would cherish for the remainder of their lives.

This collection is unusual in that it gives a flavor of all the theatres of the war. Several names are given in these letters for which no surviving Confederate service records exist. This would tend to validate their service to their country and claims the descendants of these men make.

Appendix A: The Boyds, Crowthers, Halls, and Alewines and How They Are Related

The interconnecting family trees governing the lives of these families practically require an organization chart to understand. So a rundown of how some of these people are related to the others is in order:

1. Robert Boyd—father of the Boyd brothers, Mary Jane Boyd Hall and Sarah Boyd; husband of Hannah Crowther Boyd; father-in-law of Fenton Hall, Mary Ann Crowther Boyd and Lucinda Crowther Boyd.

2. William Boyd — son of Robert Boyd; brother of Daniel, R. Pressley, J. Thomas, Andrew and Sarah Boyd and Mary Jane Boyd Hall; brother-in-law of Fenton Hall; husband of Mary Ann Crowther Boyd; brother-in-law of William Crowther; brother-in-law and step-son of Hannah Crowther Boyd; brother-in-law and uncle (by marriage) of Lucinda Crowther Boyd.

3. Daniel Boyd — son of Robert Boyd; brother of William, R. Pressley, J. Thomas, Andrew and Sarah Boyd and Mary Jane Boyd Hall; brother-in-law of Fenton Hall; husband of Lucinda Crowther Boyd; son-in-law of William Crowther; step-son and nephew (by marriage) of Hannah Crowther Boyd.

4. R. Pressley Boyd—son of Robert Boyd; brother of William, Daniel, J. Thomas, Andrew and Sarah Boyd and Mary Jane Boyd Hall; brother-in-law of Fenton Hall.

5. J. Thomas Boyd — son of Robert Boyd; brother of William, Daniel, R. Pressley, Andrew and Sarah Boyd and Mary Jane Boyd Hall; brother-in-law of Fenton Hall.

6. Andrew Boyd — son of Robert Boyd; brother of William, Daniel, R. Pressley, J. Thomas and Sarah Boyd and Mary Jane Boyd Hall; brother-in-law of Fenton Hall.

7. Fenton Hall — husband of Mary Jane Boyd Hall; brother-in-law of Boyd brothers and their sister Sarah Boyd; brother-in-law of William Boyd (brother of Robert Boyd); son-in-law of Robert Boyd.

8. James Hyley Alewine — son of Sarah Crowther Alewine and Michel Alewine; brother of John Calvin Alewine, Emmaline Alewine; brother-in-law and first cousin to Michael Alewine; nephew of William Crowther, Hannah Crowther Boyd and Mary Ann Crowther Boyd; first cousin to Lucinda Crowther Boyd; grandson of James Crowther.

9. John Calvin Alewine — son of Sarah Crowther Alewine and Michel Alewine; brother of James Hyley Alewine, Emmaline Alewine; brother-in-law and first cousin to Michael Alewine; nephew of William Crowther, Hannah Crowther Boyd and Mary Ann Crowther Boyd; first cousin to Lucinda Crowther Boyd; grandson of James Crowther.

10. James Crowther (Old Man Crowther) — the patriarch of the Crowther family was the father of William Crowther, Sarah Crowther Alewine, Hannah Crowther Boyd and Mary Ann Crowther Boyd.

11. William Crowther — father of Lucinda Crowther Boyd; father-in-law of Daniel Boyd; brother of: Hannah Crowther Boyd, Mary Ann Boyd, Sarah Crowther Alewine; brother-in-law of: Robert Boyd and William Boyd (son of Robert Boyd); uncle of James Hyley Alewine and John Calvin Alewine.

12. Hannah Crowther Boyd — second wife of Robert Boyd; stepmother of the Boyd brothers and sisters; sister of: William Crowther, Mary Ann Crowther Boyd and Sarah Crowther Alewine; sister-in-law and stepmother of William Boyd; aunt of James Hyley Alewine and John Calvin Alewine; aunt and stepmother-in-law of Lucinda Crowther Boyd.

13. Mary Ann Crowther Boyd — wife of William Boyd (son of Robert Boyd); daughter-in-law and sister-in-law of Robert Boyd; sister of: William Crowther, Hannah Crowther Boyd and Sarah Crowther Alewine; sister-in-law to the Boyd brothers and sisters; aunt of James Hyley Alewine and John Calvin Alewine; aunt and sister-in-law of Lucinda Crowther Boyd.

14. Sarah Crowther Alewine — mother of James Hyley Alewine and John Calvin Alewine; sister of William Crowther, Hannah Crowther Boyd and Mary Ann Crowther Boyd.

15. William Boyd (brother of Robert Boyd) — uncle of Boyd brothers and sisters; brother-in-law of Fenton Hall.

16. Sarah Hall Boyd — wife of William Boyd (brother of Robert Boyd); sister of Fenton Hall; sister-in-law of Robert Boyd.

Appendix B: Company Rosters for the Boyd Brothers

South Carolina 1st Infantry Regiment Rifles

FIELD STAFF AND BAND

Ahrens, William H.— Rank in Private. Rank out Sergeant Major.

Benson, Thomas B.— Rank in Private. Rank out Quartermaster Sergeant.

Brennan (Brenneke), Augustus— Rank in Musician. Rank out Chief Musician.

Cleveland, Francis M.— Rank in Private. Rank out Private.

Clinkscales, Silas W. (W. S.)— Rank in Private. Rank out Band Musician.

Crayton, B. F.— Rank in Quartermaster. Rank out Acting Quartermaster.

Cromwell, Benjamin M.— Rank in Surgeon. Rank out Surgeon.

Evans (Evins), Thomas A.— Rank in Surgeon. Rank out Surgeon.

Hadden, William M.— Rank in First Lieutenant. Rank out Lieutenant Colonel.

Harrison, F. E. May 1863 — May 1964 Wounded Gaines Mill, retired to Invalid Corps May 1862

Hunter, A. F.— Rank in Assistant Surgeon. Rank out Assistant Surgeon.

Jackson, H. G.— Rank in Assistant Surgeon. Rank out Assistant Surgeon.

Keith, William C — Rank in Sergeant. Rank out Adjutant.

Ledbetter, D. A. September 1862 — Killed in action, Second Manassas.

Ledbetter, Daniel A.— Rank in Major. Rank out Colonel.

Lee, Thomas B.— Rank in Sergeant Major. Rank out Acting Quartermaster.

Livingston, James William — Rank in Captain. Rank out Colonel. September–November 1862 — Resigned due to poor health after Sharpsburg.

Marshall, G. W.— Rank in Ordnance Sergeant. Rank out Ordnance Sergeant.

Marshall, J. Foster — Rank in Lieutenant Colonel. Rank out Colonel. Killed in action, Second Manassas.

Marshall, John H.— Rank in Private. Rank out Quartermaster Sergeant.

Marshall, William J.— Rank in Private. Rank out Sergeant Major.

McWhorter, William D.— Rank in Private/Hospital Steward.

Mullally (Mullaly), Francis P.— Rank in Chaplain. Rank out Chaplain.

Nicholson, Andrew P. (P. A)— Rank in Private. Rank out Ordnance Sergeant.

Nicholson, E.A — Rank in Private. Rank out Ordnance Sergeant.

Norton, Joseph J.— Rank in Captain. Rank out Lieutenant Colonel.

Orr, James L.— Rank in Colonel. Rank out Colonel. Resigned to serve in Congress. Governor under President Johnson and then crossed Jordan with Hampton in '76.

Perrin, J. M. November 1862–May 1863 Killed in action, Chancellorsville

Robertson, James Townes — Rank in Junior Second Lieutenant. Rank out Lieutenant Colonel.

Sloan, B. — Rank in Adjutant. Rank out Adjutant.

Sloan, H. T. — Rank in Chaplain. Rank out Chaplain.

Sloan, Joseph Berry — Rank in Lieutenant.

Von Hadlen (VonHaden), H.E. (E.H.) — Rank in Band Musician. Rank out Band Musician.

Whistler, William M. — Rank in Assistant Surgeon. Rank out Assistant Surgeon.

COMPANY G

Charles, Joel D. — Rank in Private. Rank out First Lieutenant.

Childs, J.H. — Rank in Private. Rank out Sergeant.

Rasor (Razor), John Marshall — Rank in Private. Rank out Sergeant.

Chiles, John H. — Rank in Private. Rank out Sergeant.

Clinkscales, Frank — Rank in Private. Rank out Sergeant.

Cochran, J. Benjamin — Rank in Corporal. Rank out Corporal.

Crawford, John H. — Rank in Private. Rank out Junior Second Lieutenant.

Agnew, Alexander M. — Rank in Private. Rank out Private.

Algary, John B. — Rank in Private. Rank out Private.

Allen, Henry — Rank in Private. Rank out Private.

Anderson, William D. — Rank in Private. Rank out Private. Died of disease in the summer of 1862.

Ashley, Richard S. — Rank in Private. Rank out Private. Died of disease in the summer of 1862.

Ashley, W. Augustus — Rank in Private. Rank out Private.

Ashley, William A. (H.) — Rank in Private. Rank out Private.

Austin, William H. — Rank in Private. Rank out Private.

Beacham, Thomas J. — Rank in Private. Rank out Private. Died of disease in the summer of 1862.

Bell, P. Noble — Rank in Private. Rank out Private.

Black, George W. — Rank in Private. Rank out Private.

Bolls, Charles A. — Rank in Private. Rank out Private.

Botts, C. O. — Rank in Private. Rank out Private.

Botts, Charles A. — Rank in Private. Rank out Private.

Bowen, A. Cornelius — Rank in Private. Rank out Private.

Bowen, Bartholomew — Rank in Private. Rank out Private.

Bowen, S. Newton — Rank in Private. Rank out Private. Died of disease in the summer of 1862.

Bowie, Lewis D. — Rank in Private. Rank out Private.

Boyd, William — Rank in Private. Rank out Private.

Brock, J. D. — Rank in Private. Rank out Private.

Brock, John H. — Rank in Private. Rank out Private.

Brock, John W.— Rank in Private. Rank out Private.

Brooks, Andrew P.— Rank in Private. Rank out Private.

Brooks, James— Rank in Private. Rank out Private.

Brooks, T. Warren — Rank in Private. Rank out Private.

Brooks, Thomas W.— Rank in Private. Rank out Private.

Brothers, James W.— Rank in Private. Rank out Private.

Brothers, John W.— Rank in Private. Rank out Private.

Burton, John A.— Rank in Private. Rank out Private.

Burton, Toliver J.— Rank in Private. Rank out Private.

Callaham, Logan A.— Rank in Private. Rank out Private.

Callaham, T. Craig — Rank in Private. Rank out Private.

Callaham, Thomas E.— Rank in Private. Rank out Private.

Callihan, T.E.— Rank in Private. Rank out Private.

Calvert, Francis M.— Rank in Private. Rank out Private.

Calvert, W. James— Rank in Private. Rank out Private.

Calvert, William J.— Rank in Private. Rank out Private.

Carwile, Marshall M.— Rank in Private. Rank out Private.

Chiles, George P.— Rank in Private. Rank out Private.

Clamp, J.D.— Rank in Private. Rank out Private.

Clamp, Jacob B.— Rank in Private. Rank out Private.

Cleland, David — Rank in Private. Rank out Private.

Cockran, Samuel W.— Rank in Private. Rank out Private.

Cothran, Sam'l. W.— Rank in Private. Rank out.

Cowan, William T.— Rank in Private. Rank out Private.

Cox, Edwin — Rank in Private. Rank out Private.

Crawford, David — Rank in Private. Rank out Private.

Cochran, Samuel W.— Rank in Private. Rank out Private.

Cross, John A.— Rank in Private. Rank out Private.

Cunningham, Robert F.— Rank in Private. Rank out Private.

Dickson, John A.— Rank in Private. Rank out Sergeant.

Donnald, John — Rank in Private. Rank out Private.

Elgin, John A.— Rank in Private. Rank out Private.

Ellis, A. Rice — Rank in Private. Rank out Private.

Ellis, Amaziah R.— Rank in Private. Rank out Private.

Ellis, James Robert — Rank in Corporal. Rank out Sergeant.

Ellis, Robert M.— Rank in Private. Rank out Private.

Ellis, W. Turner — Rank in Private. Rank out Private.

Ellis, William M.— Rank in Private. Rank out Private.

Ellis, William T.— Rank in Private. Rank out Private. Died of disease in the summer of 1862.

Fields, Samuel — Rank in Private. Rank out Private.

Fisher, William A.— Rank in Private. Rank out Private.

Flinn, Marvin — Rank in Private. Rank out Private.

Flynn, Marvin — Rank in Private. Rank out Private.

Freeman, G.— Rank in Private.

Freeman, George W.— Rank in Private. Rank out Private.

Freeman, Middleton — Rank in Private. Rank out Private.

Freeman, William — Rank in Private. Rank out Private.

Fremont, G. W.— Rank in Private. Rank out Private.

Gallaway, Calvin M.— Rank in Private. Rank out Corporal.

Galloway, Calvin M.— Rank in Private. Rank out Corporal.

Galloway, J. Millen — Rank in Private. Rank out Private.

Gassaway, Benjamin F.— Rank in Private. Rank out Private.

Gordon, F. Samuel — Rank in Private. Rank out Corporal.

Gordon, John B.— Rank in Private. Rank out Private.

Gordon, Robert A.— Rank in Private. Rank out Private.

Gordon, T. Samuel — Rank in Private. Rank out Corporal.

Graham, C. Newton — Rank in Private. Rank out Private. Died of disease in the
summer of 1862.

Graham, John B.— Rank in Private. Rank out Private. Died of disease in the
summer of 1862.

Gray, Henry D.— Rank in Private. Rank out Private.

Gray, James E.— Rank in Private. Rank out Private.

Grier, J. Livingston — Rank in Private. Rank out Private.

Griffin, Larkin A.— Rank in Private. Rank out Sergeant.

Griffin, Richard A.— Rank in Private. Rank out Private.

Haddon, A. Franklin — Rank in Private. Rank out Private.

Haddon, David P.— Rank in Private. Rank out Private.

Haddon, Robert W.— Rank in Corporal. Rank out Private.

Haddon, W. Lafayette — Rank in Private. Rank out Private.

Hamphill, J.L.— Rank in Private. Rank out Private.

Harkness, William M.— Rank in Private. Rank out Private.

Hawthorn, I.M.— Rank in Private. Rank out Private.

Hawthorne, D.M.— Rank in Private. Rank out Private.

Hawthorne, Thomas M.— Rank in Private. Rank out Private.

Hemphill, John L.— Rank in Private. Rank out Private.

Hemphill, Robert R.— Rank in Private. Rank out Sergeant Major.

Higgins, William W.— Rank in First Lieutenant. Rank out First Lieutenant.

Hinton, J. Richard — Rank in Private. Rank out Private.

Hinton, James R.— Rank in Private. Rank out Private.

Humphries, Elias J.— Rank in Private. Rank out Private.

Jennings, William A.— Rank in Private. Rank out Private.

Johnson, A. Cornelius— Rank in Private. Rank out Corporal.

Jones, J. Moon — Rank in Private. Rank out Private. Died of disease in the summer of 1862.

Killingsworth, J. Marcus— Rank in Private. Rank out Private.

Killingsworth, James M.— Rank in Private. Rank out Private.

Killingsworth, M.— Rank in Private. Rank out Private.

Koon, Andrew S.— Rank in Private. Rank out Private.

Langston, Elias G.— Rank in Private. Rank out Private.

Langston, Lemuel M.— Rank in Private. Rank out Private.

Latimer, B. Milton — Rank in Second Lieutenant. Rank out Second Lieutenant.

Latimer, James F.— Rank in Private. Rank out Private.

Latimer, James S.— Rank in Private. Rank out Private.

Latimer, William T.— Rank in Private. Rank out Private.

Lindsay, A. Pointsett — Rank in Private. Rank out Private.

Lindsay, Winfield W.— Rank in Private. Rank out Sergeant.

Lister, J. B.— Rank in Private. Rank out Private.

Long, Gabriel W.— Rank in Private. Rank out Sergeant.

Low (Law), Thomas G.— Rank in Private. Rank out Private. Died of disease in the summer of 1862.

Madden, Luther C.— Rank in Private. Rank out Private.

Maddon, Luther C.— Rank in Private. Rank out Private.

Martin, James G.— Rank in Private. Rank out Private.

Mattison, J. Marion — Rank in Private. Rank out Private.

Mattison, James M.— Rank in Private. Rank out Private.

Mattison, James William — Rank in Private. Rank out Corporal.

Mattison, U. J.— Rank in Private. Rank out Private.

McAdams, James R.— Rank in Private. Rank out Private. Died of disease in the summer of 1862.

McConnel, William T.— Rank in Private. Rank out Private.

McDell, W. H.— Rank in Private. Rank out Private.

McDill, David T.— Rank in Private. Rank out Private.

McDill, W. Henry — Rank in Private. Rank out Private.

McGee, Abner H. J.— Rank in Private. Rank out Private.

McGee, Abner H.— Rank in First Sergeant. Rank out Sergeant Major.

McGee, John Lewis— Rank in Private. Rank out Private.

McGill, David T.— Rank in Private. Rank out Private.

McKee, Frank M.— Rank in Private. Rank out Private. Died of disease in the summer of 1862.

McWhorter, John Thomas— Rank in Private. Rank out Private. Died of disease in the summer of 1862.

Means, T. Benjamin — Rank in Sergeant. Rank out Second Lieutenant.

Means, Thomas B.— Rank in Sergeant. Rank out Second Lieutenant.

Milford, Clayton B.— Rank in Private. Rank out Private.

Milford, David M.— Rank in Private. Rank out Private.

Milford, George W.— Rank in Private. Rank out Private.

Miller, George McDuffie — Rank in Captain. Rank out Colonel.

Millford, Clayton B.— Rank in Private. Rank out Private.

Millford, David M.— Rank in Private. Rank out Private.

Millford, George W.— Rank in Private. Rank out Private.

Moffatt, Isaiah — Rank in Private. Rank out Private.

Monday, W. R.— Rank in Private. Rank out.

Morrison, William — Rank in Private. Rank out Private.

Morrison, William P.— Rank in Private. Rank out Private.

Morrow, W. Ripley — Rank in Private. Rank out Private.

Mulinix, John E.— Rank in Private. Rank out Private.

Mullinix, John E.— Rank in Private. Rank out Private.

Munday, William R.—Rank in Private. Rank out Private .
Mundy, William R.—Rank in Private. Rank out Private.
Patton, Edward L.—Rank in Private. Rank out Private.
Pratt, James—Rank in Junior Second Lieutenant. Rank out Captain.
Pratt, Joseph J. B.—Rank in Private. Rank out Private.
Pratt, S. Langdon—Rank in Sergeant. Rank out Sergeant. Died of disease in the
    summer of 1862.
Pratt, T. Rufus—Rank in Private. Rank out First Sergeant.
Prewitt, John M.—Rank in Private. Rank out Private.
Pruit, Enoch W.—Rank in Private. Rank out Private.
Pruitt, John M.—Rank in Private. Rank out Private.
Pruit, John Marion—Rank in Private. Rank out Private.
Purdy, Samuel A.—Rank in Private. Rank out Private.
Reid, Samuel O.—Rank in Private. Rank out Private.
Richardson, Samuel M.—Rank in Private. Rank out Private.
Richardson, Samuel R.—Rank in Private. Rank out Private.
Richey, George B.—Rank in Private. Rank out Private.
Robertson, Abner H.—Rank in Private. Rank out Private.
Robertson, Lucien K.—Rank in Private. Rank out Private.
Robertson, R. A.—Rank in Private. Rank out Private.
Robertson, Wesley—Rank in Corporal. Rank out Private.
Robinson, Jacob—Rank in Private. Rank out Private.
Robinson, L.K.—Rank in Private. Rank out Private.
Robison, Jacob—Rank in Private. Rank out Private.
Seawright, William—Rank in Private. Rank out Private.
Shannon, F.—Rank in Private. Rank out Private.
Shannon, Terry—Rank in Private. Rank out Private.
Sharp, Erskine A. (H.)—Rank in Private. Rank out Sergeant.
Sharp, William H.—Rank in Private. Rank out Private.
Shirley (Shily), William N. (M.)—Rank in Private. Rank out Private. Died of
    disease in the summer of 1862.
Simpson, William H.—Rank in Private. Rank out Private.
Simson, William H.—Rank in Private. Rank out Private.
Singeltary, William H.—Rank in Private. Rank out Private.
Singleton, Armestead R.—Rank in Private. Rank out Private.
Singleton, Henry M.—Rank in Private. Rank out Private.
Smith, Moses, James R.—Rank in Private. Rank out Corporal. Died of disease
    in the summer of 1862.
Slaton, William W.—Rank in Private. Rank out Private.
Smith, James M.—Rank in Private. Rank out Private.
Smith, Joseph—Rank in Private. Rank out Private.
Strickland, John B.—Rank in Private. Rank out Private.
Swansey, James R.—Rank in Private. Rank out Corporal. Died of disease in the
    summer of 1862.
Thomson, John W.—Rank in Private. Rank out Corporal.
Tribble, William M.—Rank in Private. Rank out Private.

Vandever (Vandiver), William S.— Rank in Private. Rank out Private.
White, Robert J.— Rank in Private. Rank out Sergeant.
Williams, John F.— Rank in Private. Rank out Private.
Willson, James S.— Rank in Private. Rank out Private.
Young, James A. B.— Rank in Private. Rank out Private.
Young, Luther J.— Rank in Private. Rank out.Private.
Young, Samuel R.— Rank in Private. Rank out Private.
Zeigler, M. Govard (Gavin)— Rank in Sergeant. Rank out Sergeant.

The South Carolina 6th Cavalry Regiment

FIELD STAFF AND BAND

Aiken, H. K.— Rank in Colonel. Rank out Colonel.
Barnett, B. F.— Rank in Musician. Rank out Musician.
Glanton, William — Rank in Musician. Rank out Musician.
Jandon (Jaudon), Paul B.— Rank in Private. Rank out Musician.
Jaudon, P. B — Rank in Private. Rank out Musician.
Jones, Silas N.— Rank in Private. Rank out Musician.
King, S. J.— Rank in Private. Rank out Musician.
McCarty, W. C.— Rank in Private. Rank out Musician.
Schipman, B. M.— Rank in Private. Rank out Sergeant Major.

COMPANY G

Addison, William A.— Rank in Private. Rank out Private.
Alewine, M.— Rank in Private. Rank out Private.
Anderson, James P.— Rank in Private. Rank out Private.
Armstrong, A. T.— Rank in Private. Rank out Private.
Asbell, James E.— Rank in Private. Rank out Private.
Baits, A. J.— Rank in Private. Rank out Private.
Baits, J. A — Rank in Private. Rank out Private.
Barmore, H. R.— Rank in Private. Rank out Private.
Barmore, W. E.— Rank in Private. Rank out Private.
Barnes, James F.— Rank in Private. Rank out Private.
Baskins, Robert — Rank in Private. Rank out Private.
Bates, A. J.— Rank in Private. Rank out Private.
Bates, J. A.— Rank in Private. Rank out Private.
Beckwith, L. R.— Rank in First Sergeant. Rank out First Sergeant.
Betha, E.— Rank in Private. Rank out Private.
Bethea, James A.— Rank in Private. Rank out Private.
Blackman, G. W.— Rank in Private. Rank out Private.
Blackman, R.— Rank in Private. Rank out Private.
Boatwright, Benjamin — Rank in Private. Rank out Private.
Boatwright, Faust — Rank in Private. Rank out Private.

Bohannan, D. G.— Rank in Private. Rank out Private.
Bohannon, D. J.— Rank in Private. Rank out.
Bowen, W. H.— Rank in Private. Rank out Private.
Bowen, William M.— Rank in Private. Rank out Private.
Branyan, T. M.— Rank in Private. Rank out Private.
Brown, James M.— Rank in Private. Rank out Private.
Burton, John D.— Rank in Private. Rank out Private.
Burton, P. S.— Rank in Corporal. Rank out Private.
Cantrell, J. M.— Rank in Private. Rank out Private.
Cantrell, W. S.— Rank in Private. Rank out Private.
Chambers, John R.— Rank in Private. Rank out Private.
Chamlee, R. T.— Rank in Sergeant. Rank out Private.
Clinkscales, E. K.— Rank in Lieutenant.
Clinkscales, E. R.— Rank in First Lieutenant. Rank out Captain.
Clinkscales, J. R.— Rank in Sergeant. Rank out Private.
Cobb, C. A.— Rank in Private. Rank out Private.
Conner, G. W.— Rank in Private. Rank out Private.
Corcoran, I. H.— Rank in Private. Rank out Private.
Corcoran, James F.— Rank in Private. Rank out Private.
Covington, J. W.— Rank in Private. Rank out Private.
Covington, John — Rank in Private. Rank out Private.
Dansby, J. W.— Rank in Private. Rank out Private.
Dansley, Isaac W.— Rank in Private.
Drake, J. N.— Rank in Private. Rank out Private.
Duncan, John C.— Rank in Private. Rank out Private.
Eakins, G. E.— Rank in Private. Rank out Private.
Eakins, G. S.— Rank in Private. Rank out Private.
Earnest, T. J.— Rank in Private. Rank out Private.
Earnest, W. J.— Rank in Private. Rank out Private.
Elgan, Jacob — Rank in Private. Rank out Private.
Elgan, W. J.— Rank in Private. Rank out Private.
Elgin, D. J.— Rank in Private. Rank out Private.
Elgin, Jacob — Rank in Private. Rank out Private.
Elgin, Joab — Rank in Private. Rank out Private.
Elgin, W. J.— Rank in Private. Rank out Private.
Ernest, T. J.— Rank in Private. Rank out Private.
Ernest, W. J.— Rank in Private. Rank out Private.
Gable, J. M.— Rank in Private. Rank out Private.
Gabrel, J. M.— Rank in Private. Rank out Private.
Garratt, J.— Rank in Private. Rank out Private.
Garrett, John — Rank in Private. Rank out Private.
Gentry, W. G.— Rank in Private. Rank out Private.
Gentry, W. J.— Rank in Private. Rank out Private.
Gillstrap, A. G.— Rank in Private. Rank out Private.
Gillstrap, Ephraim — Rank in Private. Rank out Private.
Gillstrap, L. J.— Rank in Private. Rank out Private.

Gilmer, C. B.— Rank in Private. Rank out Sergeant.

Glenn, A. H.— Rank in Corporal. Rank out Private.

Glenn, H. A.

Hackett, Thomas— Rank in Private. Rank out Private.

Hall, Fenton — Rank in Private. Rank out Private.

Hall, J. M.— Rank in Private. Rank out Private.

Hall, L. B.— Rank in Private. Rank out Private.

Hall, S. A — Rank in Private. Rank out Private.

Hall, W. N.— Rank in Corporal. Rank out Sergeant (nephew to Fenton Hall).

Harris, Andrew — Rank in Private. Rank out Private.

Harris, J. W.— Rank in Private. Rank out Private.

Harris, W. H.— Rank in Private. Rank out Private.

Henerey, John T.— Rank in Private. Rank out Ordnance Sergeant.

Henry, J. T.— Rank in Private. Rank out Private.

Hester, John H.— Rank in Private. Rank out Private.

Hestor, John H.— Rank in Private. Rank out Private.

Hinckle, E.— Rank in Private. Rank out Private.

Hinkle, Elijah — Rank in Private. Rank out Private.

Holingsworth, F. P.— Rank in Private. Rank out Private.

Hollingsworth, F. P.— Rank in Private. Rank out Private.

Howard, G. M.— Rank in Private. Rank out Corporal.

Howard, John D.— Rank in Private. Rank out Private.

Howard, John J.— Rank in Private. Rank out Private.

Howard, Nathan — Rank in Private. Rank out Private.

Howlet, F. B.— Rank in Private. Rank out Private.

Hughes, B. F.— Rank in Private. Rank out Corporal.

Hughes, F. B.— Rank in Private. Rank out Corporal.

Hunnicutt, John B.— Rank in Private. Rank out Private.

Hutchinson, S. A.— Rank in Private. Rank out Private.

Kay, A. J.— Rank in Private. Rank out Private.

Kemp, W. B.— Rank in Private. Rank out Private.

Kennerly, John — Rank in Junior Second Lieutenant. Rank out Second Lieutenant.

Knauff, H. J.— Rank in Private. Rank out Private.

Kneuff, H. J.— Rank in Private. Rank out Private.

Langley, J. A.— Rank in Private. Rank out Private.

Langley, Jacob — Rank in Private. Rank out Corporal.

Martin, John — Rank in Private. Rank out Private.

Martin, R. H.— Rank in Private. Rank out Private.

Matthews, Owen — Rank in Private. Rank out Private.

Matthews, William — Rank in Private. Rank out Private.

Matthis, William — Rank in Private. Rank out Private.

Mattison, John R.— Rank in Private. Rank out Private.

McCartha, J. C.— Rank in Private. Rank out Private.

McClellan, D. R.— Rank in Private. Rank out Private.

McClellan, W. C.— Rank in Private. Rank out Private.

McClelland, D. R.— Rank in Private. Rank out Private.
McClelland, W. C.— Rank in Private. Rank out Private.
McDill, W. H.— Rank in Private. Rank out Private.
McElwee, John H.— Rank in Private. Rank out Private.
McJunkin, D. A.— Rank in Private. Rank out Private.
McJunkin, D. J.— Rank in Private. Rank out Private.
McKee, W. L.— Rank in Private. Rank out Private.
McLin, John — Rank in Private. Rank out Private.
MeManas, J. Parker — Rank in Private. Rank out Private.
Merriam, C. P.— Rank in Private. Rank out Private.
Merrian, C. P.— Rank in Private. Rank out Private.
Messer, John M.— Rank in Private. Rank out Private.
MeSteele, G. E.— Rank in Sergeant. Rank out Sergeant.
Meyers, William — Rank in Private. Rank out Private.
Milford, S. V.— Rank in Private. Rank out Private.
Miller, L. P.— Rank in Private. Rank out Lieutenant Colonel.
Millford, S. V.— Rank in Private. Rank out Private.
Milton, S. B.— Rank in Private. Rank out Private.
Miot, John R.— Rank in Captain. Rank out Captain.
Moates, George — Rank in Corporal. Rank out Private.
Moates, Jesse — Rank in Private. Rank out Private.
Montgomery, J. A.— Rank in Private. Rank out Private.
Montgomery, S. L.— Rank in Private. Rank out Private.
Motes, George — Rank in Corporal. Rank out Private.
Motes, Jesse — Rank in Private. Rank out Private.
Mungo, C. P.— Rank in Sergeant. Rank out Private.
Myers, D. R.— Rank in Private. Rank out Private.
Myers, David — Rank in Private. Rank out Private.
Myres, David — Rank in Private. Rank out Private.
Napper, J. M.— Rank in Private. Rank out Private.
Napper, James— Rank in Private. Rank out Private.
Nelken, Samuel — Rank in Private. Rank out Private.
Nelkin, S.— Rank in Private.
Nelson, M. P.— Rank in Private. Rank out Private.
Nelson, R. M.— Rank in Private. Rank out Private.
Nelson, Richard M.— Rank in Private.
Orchard, F. B.— Rank in Corporal. Rank out Private.
Owens, H. Young — Rank in Private. Rank out Private.
Owens, Richard — Rank in Private. Rank out Private.
Owens, Y. H.— Rank in Private. Rank out Private.
Phillips, R.R.— Rank in Private. Rank out Private.
Phillips, W.R — Rank in Private. Rank out Corporal.
Pressley, B.C.— Rank in Sergeant. Rank out Private.
Prichard, A.C.— Rank in Private. Rank out Private.
Putman, A.P.— Rank in Private. Rank out Private.
Rampey, D.G.— Rank in Private. Rank out Sergeant.

Rampey, S. Gaines— Rank in Private.
Rampey, S.G.— Rank in Private. Rank out Private.
Rampy, D.G.— Rank in Private. Rank out Sergeant.
Rampy, S.G.— Rank in Private. Rank out Private.
Randall, Philip — Rank in Private. Rank out Private.
Rodgers, E.A.— Rank in Private. Rank out Private.
Rogers, E.A.— Rank in Private.
Rogers, Ephraim — Rank in Private. Rank out Private.
Romp, George — Rank in Private. Rank out Private.
Rumph, G.W.— Rank in Private. Rank out Private.
Rumph, George — Rank in Private. Rank out Private.
Saxon, J.A.— Rank in Private. Rank out Private.
Saxon, J.S.— Rank in Private. Rank out Private.
Scott, J.— Rank in Private. Rank out Private.
Scott, John — Rank in Private. Rank out Private.
Sharpe, A. W.— Rank in Private. Rank out Private.
Sharpe, W.— Rank in Private. Rank out Private.
Shaw, A. J.— Rank in Private. Rank out Private.
Shaw, Samuel — Rank in Private. Rank out Private.
Shockley, A. F.— Rank in Private. Rank out Private.
Singleton, Miles— Rank in Private. Rank out Private.
Sings, T. T.— Rank in Private. Rank out Corporal.
Snipes, Elisha — Rank in Private. Rank out Private.
Sowell, J. E.— Rank in Private. Rank out Private.
Sowell, L.— Rank in Private. Rank out Private.
Spearmans, D. D.— Rank in Private. Rank out Private.
Steele, G.E.M.— Rank in Sergeant. Rank out Sergeant.
Stone, B.F.— Rank in Private. Rank out Private.
Strickland, A.— Rank in Private. Rank out Private.
Strickland, D.O.— Rank in Private. Rank out Private.
Strickland, M.L.— Rank in Private. Rank out Private.
Strickland, W.L.— Rank in Private. Rank out Private.
Taggart, Jr., James— Rank in Second Lieutenant. Rank out First Lieutenant.
Teddards, Wiley.
Tucker, R.A.— Rank in Private. Rank out Private.
Tucker, Robert — Rank in Private. Rank out Private.
Turner, J.N.W.— Rank in Private. Rank out Private.
Welch, J.F.— Rank in Private. Rank out Private.
Welsh, John F.— Rank in Private. Rank out Private.
Whitaker, E.L.— Rank in Private. Rank out Private.
Williams, Isaac — Rank in Private. Rank out Private.
Williams, J.H.— Rank in Private. Rank out Private.
Williams, J.W.— Rank in Private. Rank out Private.
Williams, N.G.— Rank in Private. Rank out Private.
Williams, N.J.— Rank in Private. Rank out Private.
Williams, Nathaniel — Rank in Private. Rank out Private.

7th South Carolina Infantry Regiment

FIELD STAFF AND BAND

Colonels

David Wyatt Aiken — Born on March 17, 1828. Planter and teacher before the war. After the war a newspaperman and congressman. Elected at reorganization on May 13, 1862. Seriously wounded and captured at Antietam on September 17, 1862. Paroled on November 8, 1862. Resigned on July 14, 1864. Died on April 6, 1887.

Thomas Glascock Bacon — Born on June 24, 1812. Clerk of the court at the time of the 1860 census. Elected at organization on April 15, 1861. Resigned on May 4, 1862, failing health. Died on September 25, 1876.

James H. Mitchell — Born on January 7, 1835. Farmer at the time of the 1860 census. Promoted to command regiment on May 6, 1864, but records do not indicate he was promoted from captain. Wounded at Cedar Creek on October 19, 1864. Surrendered at Augusta on May 19, 1865. Died on August 31, 1893.

Lieutenant Colonels

Elbert Bland — Born on April 29, 1823. Physician. Elected at re–organization on May 14, 1862. Wounded seriously in right leg at Savage Station on June 29, 1862. Wounded slightly at Fredericksburg on December 13, 1862. Wounded slightly in thigh at Gettysburg on July 2, 1863. Killed at Chickamauga on September 20, 1863.

Robert Anderson Fair — Born on December 12, 1820. Lawyer. Elected at organization on April 15, 1861. Resigned at reorganization on May 14, 1862. Died on April 11, 1899.

Elijah Jeremiah Goggans— Born on September 30, 1834. Wounded slightly in face at Savage Station on June 29, 1862. Assumed command of regiment at Chickamauga on September 20, 1863. Promoted on January 12, 1865, backdated to September 20, 1863. Wounded in right arm at the Wilderness on May 6, 1864. In hospital or on furlough until January 6, 1865 when ordered to rejoin his command, but never did.

Thomas Allison Hudgens— Born on June 19, 1831. Physician. Wounded slightly at Fredericksburg on December 13, 1862. Wounded in the right thigh at the Wilderness on May 6, 1864. Takes command of regiment at Cedar Creek on October 19, 1864. Promoted at consolidation on April 9, 1865.

Emmett Seibels— Born on October 3, 1821. Lawyer. Promoted May 9, 1862. Resigned at reorganization on May 14, 1862. Died on December 19, 1899.

Majors

William Caspers White — Born on November 17, 1821. Overseer. Elected at re–organization on May 14, 1862. Killed at Antietam on September 17, 1862.

John Stuart Hard—Born on December 2, 1842. Promoted on September 18, 1862. Killed at Chickamauga on September 20, 1863.

Emmett Seibels—Elected at organization on April 15, 1861. Promoted to lieutenant colonel on May 9, 1862.

Adjutants

David Wyatt Aiken—Elected at organization April 15, 1861. Elected colonel at reorganization on May 13, 1862.

John Richard Carwile—Detailed on September 13, 1862. Appointed aide-de-camp on brigade staff on November 17, 1864.

Thomas Milton Chilton—Born about 1840. Appointed at reorganization on May 14, 1862. Wounded slightly in the face at Maryland Heights on September 13, 1862. Killed at Antietam on September 17, 1862.

Amon C. Stallworth—Born about 1839. Overseer. Promoted on October 17, 1862.

Quartermasters

Benjamin Franklin Lovelace—Born about 1834. Teacher. Elected at organization on April 15, 1862. Promoted to brigade quartermaster on November 18, 1862.

James A. Townsend—Born about 1837. Wounded in left arm at Maryland Heights on September 13, 1862. Acting quartermaster December 1862–April 9, 1865 when promoted to captain of Company B.

Commissary Sergeants

John Edmund Bacon—Retired August 2, 1862.

Frederick L. Smith—Manufacturer. Detached to assist in commissary department in August 1861. Promoted on May 15, 1862. Resigned February 28, 1863.

Surgeons

Allen Stokes Dozier—Born on November 9, 1833. Physician. Promoted on April 30, 1862. Resigned on June 1862.

O.R. Horton—Promoted on April 13, 1863, served through unknown date.

Assistant Surgeons

Richard Coleman Carlisle—Born on December 5, 1835. Physician. Promoted on June 14, 1862. Resigned on June 6, 1864. Died on August 21, 1806.

Allen Stokes Dozier—Elected at organization April 15, 1861. Promoted to surgeon on April 30, 1862.

J.R. Speahe—promoted on February 20, 1864. Paroled at surrender on May 2, 1865.

Chaplains

John Mason Carlisle — Born on October 29, 1826. Methodist minister. Elected May 15, 1861. Resigned December 1861. Served again from sometime in 1863 until June 6, 1864. Died on June 7, 1805.

COMPANY D

Officers

Allen, T. Warren — Captain
Hester, Samuel J.— Captain
Williams, J. C.— Captain
Carlisle, James C.—1st Lieutenant
Cunningham, James R.—1st Lieutenant
Owen, John T.—1st Lieutenant
Parkman, William —1st Lieutenant
Power, Ephraim F.— 1st Lieutenant
Allen, John B.— 2nd Lieutenant
Carlisle, R. H.— 2nd Lieutenant
McDuffie, 2nd Lt.
Prince, Hugh M.— 2nd Lieutenant
Reaves, J. W.— 2nd Lieutenant
Davis, Banister A.— Bvt 2nd Lieutenant
Hester, John H.— 3rd Lieutenant

Non Commissioned Officers

Dannelly, John F.—1st Sergeant
Kennedy, J. Thompson —1st Sergeant
Youngblood, B. L.—1st Sergeant
Boyd, Daniel — Sergeant
Clark, Alfred D.— Sergeant
Gibert, James S.— Sergeant
Jones, W. B.— Sergeant
McCurry, William L.— Sergeant
Bames, A. Jefferson — Corporal
Bowen, J. T.— Corporal
Bowen, Leander M.— Corporal
Broadwater, N. L.— Corporal
Calhoun, W. N.— Corporal
Coleman, D. R.— Corporal
Craven, W. H.— Corporal
Freeman, Henry R.— Corporal
Griffith, A. B.— Corporal
Haddon, S. Pingen — Corporal
Hill, James A.— Corporal

Huckabee, J. P.— Corporal
Kennedy, J. C.— Corporal
Mixon, W. T.— Corporal
Norwood, O. A.— Corporal
Rambo, J. C.— Corporal
Watts, Anderson — Corporal

Privates

Adams, H.
Alewine, James H.
Alford, Walter
Amacker, E.
Baskin, John T.
Bass, John J.
Bell, James Henry
Bell, R. F.
Black, James P.
Black, William P.
Bowen, William
Boyd, Andrew
Boyd, R. Pressley
Broadwater, S.
Brooks, John M.
Brooks, Silas H.
Brown, F. M.
Brown, S. M.
Brown, T. A.
Bumett, H.
Burriss, W. W.
Burton, R. H.
Bussey, G. W.
Caldwell, J. E.
Campbell, Benjamin M
Campbell, J. T.
Campbell, W. A.
Carter, J. C.
Clinkscales, W. Laurence
Coffin, J. M.
Coombe, John
Cowen, Hiram F.
Crumley, J. C.
Cunningham, John
Dean, A. R.
Dean, S. P.
Dodgen, H. C.
Dom, H.

Dom, W.
Duckworth, H. J.
Duffle, Jesse
Duncan, David
Dunlap, William
Edge, J. H.
Edwards, Epam
Fleming, W. E.
Granger, William
Grant, G. W. D.
Griffith, P. H.
Guffin, J. T.
Hall, Asbury
Hampton, W. H.
Harkness, William B.
Harling, P.
Hodges, John L.
Inabinet, E.
Jay, John
Johnson, George W.
Johnson, T. J.
Kennedy, L. D.
Key, William A.
Latimer, William A.
Lochridge, William L.
Long, J. M.
Manous, William
Mathis, G. W.
Mauldin, T. H.
McCombe, J. F.
McCurry, N. C.
McDaniel, E. C.
McGehee, M.
Morrow, W. R.
Newby, John N.
Oliver, P. Erastus
Owzts, D.
Patrick, N.

Power, J. W.
Pressly, R. Alexander
Quarles, W. S.
Reese, L. D.
Richie, Warren
Rushton Jr., William M.
Russell, William H.
Sanders, John W.
Scott, James E.
Scott, Joel T.
Shaw, James E.
Shaw, John A.
Shermer, E. H.
Shoemaker, Albert M.
Shoemaker, John W.
Simpson, J. E.

Smith, E. M.
Smith, W. H.
Smith, W. S.
Stevens, J.
Stevenson, James E
Swilling, J. Z. H.
Taylor, E. M. B.
Timmerman, W. B.
Townsend, F. A.
Turner, Thomas
West, D. P.
Whitcombe, James
Williams, Benjamin W.
Williams, Turner A.
Witt, P. B.
Wright, W. H.

19th South Carolina Infantry Regiment

FIELD STAFF AND BAND

R. G. Lamar — Rank in Regimental Quartermaster. Rank out Regimental Quartermaster.

Colonels

Lythgoe, Augustus J.
Pressley, J. F.

Moragne, Wm. C.

Lieutenant Colonels

Jones, Abraham

Shaw, Thomas P.

Majors

Jones, Abraham
Crowder, John A.
Watson, Tillman

White, J. L.
Ferrell, J. O.

Staff

Beck, W. C.
Bryan (ACS), B. C.
Eskew, G. W.
Gibbs, John H. (Assistant Surgeon)
Hawkins, William H. (Surgeon)
Jones, J. A. (AQM)
Lamar, R. G. (QM)

Lynch, J. N. M. (Surgeon)
Parker, Wm. H. (ADJ)
Pate, B. T.
Rainwater, G.H.
Simpson, Washington
Sullivan, J. B. (AQM)

Company G

Alewine, John Calvin — Rank in Private. Rank out Private.
Arnold, D. M.— Rank in Private. Rank out Corporal.
Arnold, M. D.— Rank in Private. Rank out Corporal.
Arnold, Preston — Rank in Private. Rank out Private.
Arnold, William P.— Rank in Private. Rank out Private.
Baker, H. Oscar — Rank in Private. Rank out Sergeant.
Baker, Theodore — Rank in Private. Rank out Private.
Barnes, Christian V.— Rank in Private. Rank out Hospital Steward.
Barns, C. V.— Rank in Private. Rank out Hospital Steward.
Baskin, W. S.— Rank in Second Lieutenant. Rank out Second Lieutenant.
Bass, Alexander — Rank in Private. Rank out Private.
Bass, William — Rank in Private. Rank out Private.
Bell, Massalon — Rank in Private. R.ank out Private.
Bell, P.M.— Rank in Private. Rank out Private.
Bell, P.N.— Rank in Private. Rank out Private.
Ben, Ebenezer H.— Rank in Private. Rank out Private.
Bowen, James— Rank in Private. Rark out Corporal.
Bowen, John Wesley — Rank in Private. Rank out Private.
Bowen, Wesley — Rank in Private. Rank out Private.
Bowman, Alonzo Z.— Rank in Private. Rank out Private.
Boyd, J. Thomas— Rank in Private. Rank out Private.
Brooks, Jason T.— Rank in Private. Rank out Private.
Burkhead, J. Dew — Rank in Private. Rank out Private.
Burton, Alv.— Rank in Private. Rank out Private.
Campbell, J.J.— Rank in Third Lieutenant. Rank out Brevet Second Lieutenant.
Campbell, W.F.— Rank in Private. Rank out Private.
Carlile, J. Marion — Rank in Corporal. Rank out Second Lieutenant.
Carlisle, J. Marion — Rank in Corporal. Rank out Second Lieutenant.
Charping, S.Wilson — Rank in Private. Rank out Private.
Chatham, Robert N.— Rank in Corporal. Rank out Captain.
Cheatham, J.W.— Rank in Private. Rank out Private.
Cheatham, R.N.— Rank in Corporal. Rank out Captain.
Cheatham, W.J.— Rank in Private. Rank out Private.
Clinkscales, F. William — Rank in Private. Rank out Private.
Clinkscales, William F.— Rank in Private. Rank out Private.
Clinkscales, William H.— Rank in Private. Rank out Sergeant.
Cochran, W. H.— Rank in Corporal. Rank out Corporal.
Conner, B.— Rank in Private. Rank out Private.
Conner, M. R.— Rank in Private. Rank out Private.
Conner, Martin B.— Rank in Private. Rank out Private.
Connor, Martin B.— Rank in Private. Rank out Private.
Cosby, J. W.— Rank in Private. Rank out Corporal.
Cozby, John W.— Rank in Private. Rank out Corporal.
Crawford, John W.— Rank in Private. Rank out Private.

Cunningham, J.J.— Rank in Sergeant. Rank out Quartermaster Sergeant.
Cunningham, Joseph H.— Rank in Captain. Rank out Captain.
Daniel, G.W.— Rank in Private. Rank out Private.
Davis, E.L.— Rank in Private. Rank out Private.
Douglass, G.A.— Rank in Private. Rank out Private.
Drennan, Jolm G. C.— Rank in Private. Rank out Private.
Freeman, J. T.— Rank in Private. Rank out Private.
Gantt, Richard G.— Rank in Private. Rank out Private.
Gassaway, William — Rank in Private. Rank out Private.
Gray, James E.— Rank in Private. Rank out Private.
Hall, A.M.— Rank in Private. Rank out Private.
Hall, Hezekiah — Rank in Private. Rank out Private.
Hall, John W.— Rank in Private. Rank out Private.
Hall, Lewis S.— Rank in Private. Rank out Private.
Hall, M.— Rank in Private. Rank out Private.
Huckabee, Jouette M.— Rank in Private. Rank out First Sergeant.
Hughes, John — Rank in Private. Rank out Private.
Hughs, John — Rank in Private. Rank out Private.
Hunter, Samuel — Rank in Sergeant. Rank out Sergeant.
Hutchens, Abner L.— Rank in Private. Rank out Private.
Hutchings, William S.— Rank in Private. Rank out Private.
Janes, J.L.— Rank in Private. Rank out Private.
Jenkins, Francis— Rank in Private. Rank out Private.
Jolmson, John H.— Rank in Private. Rank out Private.
Jones, James S.— Rank in Private. Rank out Private.
Jordan, Seth A.— Rank in Sergeant. Rank out Sergeant.
Jordon, Seth A.— Rank in Sergeant. Rank out Sergeant.
Kennedy, Isaac C.— Rank in Private. Rank out Private.
Kennedy, J.J.— Rank in Private. Rank out Private.
Kennedy, L. Dow — Rank in Private. Rank out Corporal.
Latimer, James T.— Rank in Private. Rank out Private.
Latimer, Joseph T.— Rank in Private. Rank out Private.
Latimer, William A.— Rank in Private. Rank out Private.
Lee, Lawrence D.— Rank in Private. Rank out Corporal.
Lockhart, J. Yancy — Rank in Private. Rank out Private.
Mann, R. R.— Rank in Private. Rank out Private.
Martin, J. M.— Rank in Private. Rank out Private.
McAdams, Samuel T.— Rank in Private. Rank out Private.
McAlister, J. A.— Rank in Private. Rank out Corporal.
McAllister, Jesse A.— Rank in Private. Rank out Corporal.
McCann,Seaborn S.— Rank in Private. Rank out Private.
McCurry, S. S.— Rank in Private. Rank out Private.
McDonald, John M.— Rank in Private. Rank out Brevet Second Lieutenant.
McKee, A. Jasper — Rank in Private. Rank out Private.
McKey, A. J.— Rank in Private. Rank out Private.
McMahen, A. F.— Rank in Private. Rank out Private.

McMahen, F. A.— Rank in Private. Rank out Private.

McMahen, Obadiah — Rank in Private. Rank out Private.

McMahen, William L.— Rank in Private. Rank out Private.

McMahon, F. A.— Rank in Private. Rank out Private.

Means, John H.— Rank in Private. Rank out Private.

Moore, Thomas A.— Rank in Private. Rank out Private.

Mullikin, James M.— Rank in Sergeant. Rank out First Lieutenant.

Noble, Edward — Rank in Private. Rank out First Lieutenant.

Oliver, C. Wistor — Rank in Private. Rank out Private.

Owens, Patrick — Rank in Private. Rank out Private.

Parker, William H.— Rank in First Sergeant. Rank out Adjutant.

Phillips, William J.— Rank in Private. Rank out Private.

Prince, Hugh M.— Rank in Private. Rank out Private.

Prince, Washington L.— Rank in Corporal. Rank out Sergeant.

Recel, Jacob — Rank in Private. Rank out Private.

Saunders, A.— Rank in Private. Rank out Private.

Saxon, William P.— Rank in Private. Rank out Private.

Schrader, John V.— Rank in Private. Rank out Private.

Simpson, J. T.— Rank in Private. Rank out Private.

Simpson, Jason L.— Rank in Private. Rank out Private.

Smith, W.A.— Rank in Private. Rank out Private.

Smith, W.J.— Rank in Private. Rank out.

Sprewell (Spruel), James W.— Rank in Private. Rank out Private.

Stark, S.J.A.— Rank in Private. Rank out Private.

Stokes, Thomas H.— Rank in Private. Rank out Private.

Talbott (Tolbert), James F.— Rank in Private. Rank out Private.

Taylor, E.B.— Rank in Private. Rank out Private.

Townsend, W. Thomas— Rank in Private. Rank out Private.

Townsend, W.D.— Rank in Private. Rank out Private.

Townsend, W.J.— Rank in Private. Rank out Private.

Tucker, J.H.— Rank in Private. Rank out Private.

Wickliffe, William — Rank in Private. Rank out Third Lieutenant.

Williams, Robert.— Rank in Private. Rank out Private.

Wilson, Hugh J.— Rank in Private. Rank out Sergeant.

Wilson, Robert W. (W. R)— Rank in Private. Rank out Private.

Young, Joseph P.— Rank in Private. Rank out Private.

Notes

Prologue

1. Certificate of Death for Mary Jane Boyd Hall; June 30, 1923.
2. Lowry Ware, *Abbeville District, South Carolina Newspaper Notices of Land Cases and Sales, 1836–1872* (London: SCM, 1999), 27.
3. Crowther Family History file at Pope County, Arkansas, Public Library.
4. United States Census, 1860, Abbeville County, South Carolina.
5. Wikipedia: http://en.wikipedia.org/wiki/Abbeville,_South_Carolina.
6. *Official Records* Series 1, vol, 1, Chapter 1, 59–60.

1861

1. John Rigdon, *Historical Sketch and Roster, SC 7th Infantry Regiment,* 5th ed. (Clearwater, SC: Eastern Digital Resources, 2008), 20.
2. Robert S. Seigler, *South Carolina's Military Organizations During the War Between The States: The Midlands* (Charleston, SC: History, 2008), 156
3. Compiled Service Records, Company D, 7th South Carolina Infantry, raw data, National Archives, Washington, DC.
4. William C. Davis, *Battle at Bull Run: A History of the First Major Campaign of the Civil War. Louisiana* (Baton Rouge: Louisiana State University Press, 1981), 26.
5. "Battle of Big Bethel," Civil War Encyclopedia, Blue and Gray Trail, 5 May 2006. Web. 23 August 2009. <http://www.blueandgraytrail.com/event/Battle_of_Big_Bethel>.

6. "From Our Special Correspondent." *Mobile Advertiser & Register* [Mobile, AL], 13 June 1861, 2.
7. Davis, 108.
8. Davis, 109.
9. Davis, 110–111.
10. "Medical Care, Battle Wounds, and Disease." Civil War Medicine, Civil War Home, 10 February 2002. Web. 23 August 2009. <http://www.civilwarhome.com/civilwarmedicine.htm>.

1862

1. Compiled Service Records for John Thomas Boyd; 19th South Carolina Infantry.
2. Seigler, 243.
3. Compiled Service Records for John Thomas Boyd; 19th South Carolina Infantry.
4. Compiled Service Records for William Boyd; 2nd South Carolina Rifles Regiment.
5. Edward Cunningham, *Shiloh and the Western Campaign of 1862* (Mason City: Savas Beatie, 2007), 275–277.
6. John Rigdon, *Historical Sketch & Roster, SC 1st Infantry Regiment Rifles,* 7th ed. (Clearwater, SC: Eastern Digital Resources, 2008).
7. D. Augustus Dickert, *History of Kershaw's Brigade: With Complete Roll of Companies, Biographical Sketches, Incidents, Anecdotes, Etc.* (New York: General, 2010), 102.
8. Compiled Service Records for William Boyd; 2nd South Carolina Rifles Regiment.
9. Randolph W. Kirkland, Jr., *Broken Fortunes South Carolina Soldiers,*

Sailors and Citizens Who Died in the Service of Their Country and State in the War for Southern Independence, 1861–1865 (Chapel Hill: University of North Carolina Press, 1997).

10. Rigdon, *SC 7th Infantry Regiment*, 107.

11. Stephen W. Sears, *Landscape Turned Red: The Battle of Antietam* (New York: Mariner, 2003), 90.

12. Sears, 95.

13. Mark Snell, "The Maryland Campaign Diary of Captain Henry Lord Page King: Maryland Campaign of 1862 and Its Aftermath," *Civil War Regiments: A Journal of the American Civil War* vol. 6, no. 2 (1999): 32.

14. Snell, 32–33.

15. Sears, 124.

16. John M. Priest, *Antietam: The Soldiers' Battle* (New York: Oxford University Press, 1993), 103–104, 120–121.

17. Priest, 122.

18. Priest, 122.

19. Priest, 123–124.

20. Claudius Hornby Pritchard, *Colonel D. Wyatt Aiken, 1828–1887: South Carolina's Militant Agrarian* (Hampden-Sydney, VA: privately printed, 1970), 1–5.

21. Pritchard, 9.

22. Pritchard, 5.

23. D. Wyatt. Aiken, *Autobiography of Colonel D. Wyatt Aiken*, manuscript written in April 1864 on the back of Confederate Army "Leave of Absence" blanks while he was Commandant of Troops and Defenses at Macon, Georgia.

24. Pritchard, 10.

25. Pritchard, 15.

26. Pritchard, 20.

27. Compiled Service Records for James Hyley Alewine; 7th South Carolina Infantry.

28. Francis Augustin O'Reilly, *The Fredericksburg Campaign: Winter War on the Rappahannock* (Baton Rouge: Louisiana State University Press, 2006), 36–37.

29. John Rigdon, *Historical Sketch & Roster, SC 6th Cavalry Regiment*, 7th ed. (Clearwater, SC: Eastern Digital Resources, 2008), 12.

30. Robert S. Seigler, *South Carolina's Military Organizations During the War Between The States: Statewide Units, Militia and Reserves* (Charleston, SC: History, 2008), 105.

31. Seigler, *Statewide Units, Militia and Reserves*, 109.

32. Rigdon, *SC 7th Infantry Regiment*, 15.

33. O'Reilly, 348–349.

34. O'Reilly, 349.

35. Gary W. Gallagher, ed., *The Fredericksburg Campaign: Decision on the Rappahannock* (Chapel Hill: University of North Carolina Press, 2008), 66.

1863

1. Compiled Service Records for John Thomas Boyd; 19th South Carolina Infantry.

2. "January, 1900," *Confederate Veteran Magazine* (1931), rpt. National Historical Society (1980): 87.

3. "January, 1920," *Confederate Veteran Magazine* (1931), rpt. National Historical Society (1980): 128.

4. Lee Spruill and Matt Spruill, "Narrative of Arthur M. Manigault," in *Winter Lightning: A Guide to the Battle of Stones River* (Memphis: University of Tennessee Press, 2007), 89–91.

5. Spruill, 89–91.

6. *Abbeville Press* [Abbeville, SC] 30 January 1863.

7. Compiled Service Records for John Thomas Boyd; 19th South Carolina Infantry.

8. "1st SC State Troops, Company I-1863," SC Rebels, Bill Brasington. Web. 27 August 2009. <http://www.geocities.com/screbels_1864/ST0163CoI.html>.

9. Rigdon, *SC 6th Cavalry Regiment*, 119.

10. Compiled Service Records for

Davis Hall; 24th South Carolina Infantry.

11. Seigler, *Statewide Units, Militia and Reserves*, 109.

12. John Rigdon, *Historical Sketch & Roster, SC 19th Infantry Regiment*, 7th ed. (Clearwater, SC: Eastern Digital Resources, 2009), 138.

13. Dickert, 282.

14. Dickert, 79.

15. Gerald D. Brown, *A Genealogy of a Hall Family* (Scranton, SC: Gerald D. Brown, 1988), 72.

16. Seigler, *Midlands*, 244.

17. "July, 1895," *Confederate Veteran Magazine* (1895), rpt. National Historical Society (1980): 213.

18. John Abney Chapman, *History of Edgefield County: From the Earliest Settlements to 1897 : Biographical and Anecdotal, With Sketches of the Seminole War, Nullification, Secession, ... From Edgefield in the War of Secession 1897* (New York: Cornell University Library, 2009), 456.

19. Seigler, *Statewide Units, Militia and Reserves*, 111.

20. H. David Stone, Jr., *Vital Rails: The Charleston & Savannah Railroad and the Civil War in Coastal South Carolina* (Columbia: University of South Carolina Press, 2008), 145,146.

21. Stone, 147.

22. Stone, 147.

23. Clement Anselm Evans, "Additional Sketches Illustrating The Services of Officers, Privates and Patriotic Citizens of Louisiana." In *Confederate Military History, vol. 10: A Library of Confederate States History* (New York: General, 2010), 323–324.

24. Josiah Gorgas, "Biographical Directory Family and Friends of Josiah Gorgas." In *The Journals of Josiah Gorgas, 1857–1878* (Tuscaloosa: University Alabama Press, 1995), 256.

25. Compiled Service Records; Company D, 7th South Carolina Infantry, raw data, National Archives, Washington, DC.

26. Harry W. Pfanz, *Gettysburg: The Second Day* (Chapel Hill: University of North Carolina Press, 1998), 253–256.

27. Pfanz, 278–282.

28. Pritchard, 42.

29. Compiled Service Records for Daniel Boyd; 7th South Carolina Infantry.

1864

1. Compiled Service Records for Andrew Boyd; 7th South Carolina Infantry.

2. Clement A. Evans, *Confederate Military History*, vol. 5 (Atlanta, GA: Confederate Publishing Company, 1899), 412.

3. Dickert, 344–352.

4. Dickert, 344–352.

5. Dickert, 344–352.

6. Dickert, 344–352.

7. Dickert, 344–352.

8. Dickert, 344–352.

9. Dickert, 359–360.

10. Dickert, 359–360.

11. Compiled Service Records for Andrew Boyd; 7th South Carolina Infantry.

12. "Civil War Hospitals in Lynchburg: Old City Cemetery, Lynchburg, Virginia." Old City Cemetery of Lynchburg, Virginia. Web. 23 October 2009. <http://www.gravegarden.org/hospitals.htm>.

13. Old City Cemetery Burial Records, May 31, 1864

14. "Diuguid Undertakers: Old City Cemetery, Lynchburg, Virginia." Old City Cemetery of Lynchburg, Virginia. Web. 23 October 2009. <http://www.gravegarden.org/diuguid.htm>.

15. CWSAC Battle Summaries. National Park Service. Web. 23 August 2009. <http://www.nps.gov/history/hps/abpp/battles/va070.htm>.

16. "Gen. James Connor," *New York Times*, 27 June 1883.

1865

1. "January, 1931," *Confederate Veteran Magazine* (1931), rpt. National Historical Society (1980): 20–24.
2. "January, 1931."
3. "January, 1931."
4. "January, 1931."
5. "January, 1931."
6. "January, 1931."
7. Clint Johnson, *Pursuit: The Chase, Capture, Persecution, and Surprising Release of Confederate President Jefferson Davis* (New York: Citadel, 2008).
8. "January, 1931."

Epilogue

1. Ware, 186.
2. *History of Pope County, Arkansas* (n.p.: Pope County Historical Association, 1979).

Bibliography

Abbeville Press [Abbeville, SC] 30 January 1863.

Aiken, D. Wyatt. *Autobiography of Colonel D. Wyatt Aiken.* Manuscript written in April 1864 on the back of Confederate Army "Leave of Absence" blanks while he was Commandant of Troops and Defenses at Macon, Georgia.

"Battle of Big Bethel." Civil War Encyclopedia. Blue and Gray Trail, 5 May 2006. Web. 23 August 2009. <http://www.blueandgraytrail.com/event/Battle_of_Big_Bethel>.

Brasington, Bill. "1st SC State Troops, Company I-1863<in> SC Rebels. Web. 27 August 2009. <http://www.geocities.com/screbels_1864/ST0163CoI.html>.

Brown, Gerald D. *A Genealogy of a Hall Family.* Scranton, SC: Gerald D. Brown, 1988.

Chapman, John Abney. *History of Edgefield County: From the Earliest Settlements to 1897: Biographical and Anecdotal, With Sketches of the Seminole War, Nullification, Secession, ... From Edgefield in the War of Secession 1897.* Easley, SC: Southern Historical, 1976.

"Civil War Hospitals in Lynchburg: Old City Cemetery, Lynchburg, Virginia." Old City Cemetery of Lynchburg, Virginia. Web. 23 October 2009. <http://www.grave-garden.org/hospitals.htm>.

Crowther Family History file at Pope County, Arkansas, Public Library.

Cunningham, Edward. *Shiloh and the Western Campaign of 1862.* Mason City , IA: Savas Beatie, 2007.

CWSAC Battle Summaries. National Park Service. Web. 23 August 2009. <http://www.nps.gov/history/hps/abpp/battles/va070.htm>.

Davis, William C. *Battle at Bull Run: A History of the First Major Campaign of the Civil War.* Baton Rouge: Louisiana State University Press, 1981.

Dickert, D. Augustus. *History of Kershaw's Brigade: With Complete Roll of Companies, Biographical Sketches, Incidents, Anecdotes, Etc.* New York: General, 2010.

"Diuguid Undertakers: Old City Cemetery, Lynchburg, Virginia." Old City Cemetery of Lynchburg, Virginia. Web. 23 October 2009. <http://www.gravegarden.org/diuguid.htm>.

Evans, Clement Anselm. "Additional Sketches Illustrating The Services of Officers, Privates and Patriotic Citizens of Louisiana." In *Confederate Military History, vol. 10: A Library of Confederate States History.* New York: General, 2010.

"From Our Special Correspondent." *Mobile Advertiser & Register* [Mobile, AL] 13 June 1861.

Gallagher, Gary W., ed. *The Fredericksburg Campaign: Decision on the Rappahannock.* Chapel Hill: University of North Carolina Press, 2008.

"Gen. James Connor." *New York Times,* 27 June 1883.

Gorgas, Josiah. "Biographical Directory Family and Friends of Josiah Gorgas." In *The Journals of Josiah Gorgas, 1857–1878.* Tuscaloosa: University of Alabama Press, 1995.

History of Pope County, Arkansas. N.p.: Pope County Historical Association, 1979.

"January, 1900." *Confederate Veteran Magazine* (1931), rpt. National Historical Society, 1980.

"January, 1920." *Confederate Veteran Magazine* (1931), rpt. National Historical Society, 1980.

"January, 1931." *Confederate Veteran Magazine* (1931), rpt. National Historical Society, 1980.

Johnson, Clint. *Pursuit: The Chase, Capture, Persecution, and Surprising Release of Confederate President Jefferson Davis.* New York: Citadel, 2008.

"July, 1895." *Confederate Veteran Magazine* (1895), rpt. National Historical Society, 1980.

Kirkland, Randolph W., Jr. *Broken Fortunes South Carolina Soldiers, Sailors and Citizens Who Died in the Service of Their Country and State in the War for Southern Independence, 1861–1865.* Chapel Hill: University of North Carolina Press, 1997.

"Medical Care, Battle Wounds, and Disease." Civil War Medicine. Civil War Home, 10 February 2002. Web. 23 August 2009. <http://www.civilwarhome.com/civilwarmedicine.htm>.

O'Reilly, Francis Augustin. *The Fredericksburg Campaign: Winter War on the Rappahannock.* Baton Rouge: Louisiana State University Press, 2006.

Pfanz, Harry W. *Gettysburg: The Second Day.* Chapel Hill: University of North Carolina Press, 1998.

Priest, John M. *Antietam: The Soldiers' Battle.* New York: Oxford University Press, 1993.

Pritchard, Claudius Hornby. *Colonel D. Wyatt Aiken, 1828–1887: South Carolina's Militant Agrarian.* Hampden-Sydney, VA: privately printed, 1970.

Rigdon, John. *Historical Sketch & Roster, SC 1st Infantry Regiment Rifles,* 7th ed. Clearwater, SC: Eastern Digital Resources, 2008.

_____. *Historical Sketch & Roster, SC 6th Cavalry Regiment,* 7th ed. Clearwater, SC: Eastern Digital Resources, 2008.

_____. *Historical Sketch & Roster, SC 7th Infantry Regiment,* 5th ed. Clearwater, SC: Eastern Digital Resources, 2008.

_____. *Historical Sketch & Roster, SC 19th Infantry Regiment,* 7th ed. Clearwater, SC: Eastern Digital Resources, 2009.

Sears, Stephen W. *Landscape Turned Red: The Battle of Antietam.* New York: Mariner, 2003.

Seigler, Robert S. *South Carolina's Military Organizations During the War Between The States: The Midlands.* Charleston, SC: History, 2008.

_____. *South Carolina's Military Organizations During the War Between The States: Statewide Units, Militia and Reserves.* Charleston, SC: History, 2008.

Snell, Mark. "The Maryland Campaign Diary of Captain Herny Lord Page King: Maryland Campaign of 1862 and Its Aftermath." *Civil War Regiments: A Journal of the American Civil War* vol. 6, no. 2 (1999).

Spruill, Lee, and Matt Spruill. "Narrative of Arthur M. Manigault." In *Winter Lightning: A Guide to the Battle of Stones River.* Memphis: University of Tennessee Press, 2007.

Stone, H. David, Jr. *Vital Rails: The Charleston & Savannah Railroad and the Civil War in Coastal South Carolina.* Columbia: University of South Carolina Press, 2008.

Ware, Lowry. *Abbeville District, South Carolina Newspaper Notices of Land Cases and Sales, 1836–1872.* London: SCM, 1999.

Index